INTERVIEWING, INTERROGATION

&

COMMUNICATION for LAW ENFORCEMENT

(3rd ed.)

$$(\exists x)P(x) \neq (\forall x)P(x)$$

$$P \Rightarrow Q \neq Q \Rightarrow P$$

$$\sim (A \cap B \cap C) \neq \sim A \cap \sim B \cap \sim C$$

Davis, Leslie, Davis

INTERVIEWING, INTERROGATION & COMMUNICATION for LAW ENFORCEMENT

(3rd ed.)

$(\exists x)P(x) \neq (\forall x)P(x)$

$P \Rightarrow Q \neq Q \Rightarrow P$

$\sim(A \cap B \cap C) \neq \sim A \cap \sim B \cap \sim C$

Wayne L. Davis, Ph.D.

Paul J. Leslie, Ed.D.

Ashley B. Davis

Copyright © 2014 by Davis, Leslie, Davis.

Library of Congress Control Number:		2014916548
ISBN:	Softcover	978-1-4990-6587-9
	eBook	978-1-4990-6588-6

All rights reserved. No part of this book may be reproduced or transmitted in any form or by any means, electronic or mechanical, including photocopying, recording, or by any information storage and retrieval system, without permission in writing from the copyright owner.

Any people depicted in stock imagery provided by Thinkstock are models, and such images are being used for illustrative purposes only.
Certain stock imagery © Thinkstock.

Print information available on the last page.

Rev. date: 06/05/2017

Xlibris
1-888-795-4274
www.Xlibris.com
552545

PREFACE

This book provides an overview of effectively collecting, understanding, and presenting information. First, this book examines various situations via math, grammar, and logic. It is important for officers to apply math and English to the law so that they may be able to effectively articulate their actions in court. For example, laws and police actions can be evaluated via truth tables and Venn Diagrams. Second, this book discusses interrogation techniques and body language. Manipulating a suspect and collecting the right information in a legal and effective manner is a part of police work. Third, this book presents a deposition. The defense lawyer may ask certain questions in order to discredit the officer or to undermine the officer's report. Police officers should ask themselves the purpose of each question that is being asked during a deposition. Fourth, this book presents some resume information and typical job interview questions for potential police officers. Knowing what kinds of questions will be asked during an interview and effectively communicating to potential employers is essential. Fifth, this book discusses code information and handwriting comparisons. Code information may be important in a prison environment and handwriting comparisons allows for a totality of circumstance exercise. Sixth, this book discusses assumptions and limitation associated with information. Magic is a useful tool to demonstrate how flawed assumptions may lead to inaccurate conclusions. Seventh, this book provides a table that can be used to generate impromptu speeches. Various words can be randomly selected and the reader can use the words to create a short story. Eighth, this book discusses how to handle situations that deal with special situations and individuals who have disabilities. Finally, this book discusses various search techniques for evidence collection.

AUTHORS

Wayne L. Davis, Ph.D.

Wayne L. Davis holds a Bachelor of Science in Electrical Engineering from the University of Michigan-Dearborn, a Master of Science in Business Administration from Madonna University, and a Ph.D. in Criminal Justice from Capella University. In addition, Dr. Davis has earned a helicopter pilot license, an advanced open water scuba diver certification, a technician plus amateur radio license (N8ZFG), and a basic emergency medical technician certificate from the State of Michigan.

Dr. Davis has graduated from city, state, and federal law enforcement academies: Schoolcraft College in Livonia, Michigan, the Indiana Law Enforcement Law Academy, and the Federal Law Enforcement Training Center. He has over 20 years of law enforcement experience with city, state, and federal law enforcement agencies. Dr. Davis has earned the U.S. Customs & Border Protection Commissioner's Award, the U.S. Customs & Border Protection Scholastic Award, the highest test score when officers in his Indiana State Police graduating class were assessed, and appointment to a field-training officer by the Indiana State Police.

While he worked as a product design engineer at Ford Motor Company, Dr. Davis introduced the electronic engine control module into the pleasure boat industry. This included writing a product specification manual and performing test-to-failure statistical research. As a result, Dr. Davis was nominated for the Ford Motor Company Electronics Division Worldwide Leadership Excellence Award. Subsequently, this led to his research paper called, *A Study of Factors Affecting a Supply Decision by the Ford Motor Company International Division for Original Equipment*.

In addition, Dr. Davis has conducted two academic research studies called, *A Correlational Study of Childhood Religiosity, Childhood Sport Participation, and Sport-Learned Aggression among African American Female Athletes* and *The Effect of Application*

Based Training on the Emotional Intelligence of Criminal Justice Students. Dr. Davis has also published several textbooks, which include a) *Report Writing for Police Officers,* b) *Police-Community Relations: Different Lenses & Perceptions of Truth,* c) *Critical Thinking: Totality of Circumstances,* and d) *Terrorism, Homeland Security, and Risk Assessment via Research Proposal.*

Recently, Dr. Davis has created table top police scenes for which he has filed a patent. In addition, he has served as the Academic Coordinator for the Criminal Justice and Human Services Programs at Aiken Technical College in Aiken, SC. With the support of local law enforcement agencies, Dr. Davis has created an application-based criminal justice program that meets the needs of the local community.

Paul J. Leslie, Ed.D.

Paul J. Leslie holds a Bachelor of Arts in History from Armstrong Atlantic University in Savannah, Georgia and a Doctorate in Counseling Psychology from Argosy University in Sarasota, Florida.

Currently, he serves as Academic Coordinator of Psychology at Aiken Technical College where he is also an advisor in the Human Services degree program and teaches courses in abnormal psychopathology, substance abuse counseling, and interviewing techniques.

Dr. Leslie is a Licensed Counselor and a Human Services - Board Certified Practitioner. He has a private practice in counseling, coaching and clinical hypnotherapy in Aiken, South Carolina. Dr. Leslie is the co-author of *Critical Thinking: Totality of Circumstances, The Effect of Application Based Training on the Emotional Intelligence of Criminal Justice Students*, and *Get Out of Your Seat: An Average Passenger's Guide to Overcoming Airline Terror.*

Ashley B. Davis

Ashley B. Davis is currently pursuing a bachelor's degree in French and Japanese at Michigan State University. Currently she works for the Natural Sciences Department at Michigan State University, she is the undergraduate representative for the Romance and Classical Studies Department for French majors, she is the webmaster for the French Club, and she is a member of the Anime and Japan Clubs at Michigan State University. In the future she wishes to become an interpreter.

Wayne L. Davis   Paul J. Leslie   Ashley B. Davis

Table of Contents

List of Tables vi
List of Figures viii

Chapter 1.   Constitutional & Criminal Law 1
Chapter 2.   Reasonsing & Flowcharting 41
Chapter 3.   Truth Tables 52
Chapter 4.   Meanings Of Truth 78
Chapter 5.   Communication Theory 126
Chapter 6.   Police Officer Communications 165
Chapter 7.   Interviewing, Questions, And Their Uses 202
Chapter 8.   Body Language 220
Chapter 9.   Interrogation 272
Chapter 10. Building An Effective Resume 326
Chapter 11. Code Communication 339
Chapter 12. Job Interview & Oral Presentations 371
Chapter 13. Science & Truth 401
Chapter 14. Assessing Information 413
Chapter 15. Media 425
Chapter 16. Police & Technology 430
Chapter 17. Individuals With Disabilities 436
Chapter 18. Special Situations 456
Appendix A. Crime Scene Search Patterns 501
Appendix B. Crime Scene Investigations 512

List of Tables

Table 1. Interpretation of Figure 2 Venn Diagram......................73
Table 2. Different Lenses of Truth..84
Table 3. Interpretation of Sport Statement 101
Table 4. Interpretation of Weather Statement...........................101
Table 5. Interpretation of Witness Statement 102
Table 6. Interpretation of Conditional Statement 105
Table 7. Interpretation of Law 106
Table 8. Various Theories and their Limitations.......................109
Table 9. Police Reports and their Purpose................................171
Table 10. Difference between Interview and Interrogation.........196
Table 11. Qualities of Good Interviewers and Interrogators 196
Table 12. Body Language and Body Movements 222
Table 13. Body Language and Emotions.....................................223
Table 14. Body Language..224
Table 15. Content of Words 225
Table 16. Interpreting a Suspect's Response 227
Table 17. Verbal Abstract Techniques 234
Table 18. Human Behavior..250
Table 19. Signs of Truthfulness...274
Table 20. Signs of Deception...274
Table 21. Techniques for Interrogation Questions 275
Table 22. Handling less than Complete/Truthful Responses.......276
Table 23. Pre-interrogation Checklist...277
Table 24. Examples of Improper Threats and/or Promises 279
Table 25. Factors that May Impact the Credibility of a
          Suspect's Statement 279
Table 26. Pros and Cons of the Reverse Chronological and
          Functional Resumes..328
Table 27. Magic Definitions 340
Table 28. Misdirection...340
Table 29. Baseball Secret Codes 342
Table 30. Different Types of Evidence to Support a Speech.......380
Table 31. Words for Impromptu Story Telling 392
Table 32. Handwriting Characteristics 404
Table 33. Clues to Assess Handwriting. 409
Table 34. Handwriting Comparison Guidelines 410

Table 35. Summary of Songs Lyrics Variables............................420
Table 36. Types of Hostage-taker..456
Table 37. Signs of Hostage-taker Negotiations..........................459
Table 38. Crime Scene Search Patterns.......................................501
Table 39. Basic Crime Scene Supplies...514
Table 40. Ways to Identify Fakes, Forgeries, and Counterfeits....518

List of Figures

Figure 1.	Totality of circumstances.	71
Figure 2.	Venn diagram.	72
Figure 3.	DUI Venn diagram.	74
Figure 4.	Types of ethical systems.	92
Figure 5.	Acceptable chance of wrongful conviction	99
Figure 6.	Interpretation of conditional statement.	105
Figure 7.	Balance theory - totality of circumstances.	135
Figure 8.	Field Interview position.	197
Figure 9.	Personal space	323
Figure 10.	Interrogation proximity	323
Figure 11.	Interrogation room	324
Figure 12.	Magic box.	339
Figure 13.	Football secret codes for offense.	343
Figure 14.	Key for marked card deck.	344
Figure 15.	Morse code keyer.	358
Figure 16.	Polygraph test output	401
Figure 17.	Electronic voice output	403
Figure 18.	Handwriting analysis	404
Figure 19.	Crime scene search patterns.	505

CHAPTER 1. CONSTITUTIONAL & CRIMINAL LAW

Below is a summary of select Constitutional laws (del Carmen, 2014).

Confidence Level

- No information (not sufficient in any legal proceedings) — **LOWEST**
- Hunch (not sufficient in any legal proceedings)
- Reasonable doubt (acquit suspect)
- Suspicion (starts criminal investigation)
- Reasonable suspicion (criminal - stop & frisk by police)
- Preponderance of the evidence
- (needed to win civil case)*
- Probable Cause (warrant; arrest & seizure; indictment)*
- Clear & convincing evidence (overturn warrant in court)
- Guilty beyond a reasonable doubt (convict suspect) — **HIGHEST**
- Absolute certainty (not required)

* equal levels

5th Amendment

5th Amendment – No person shall be compelled in any criminal case to be a witness against himself & he shall not be deprived of life, liberty, or property, without due process of law.

Miranda Warning

Miranda v. Arizona (1966): law enforcement officers must give suspects the following warnings whenever there is a custodial interrogation: (1) You have the right to remain silent; (2) Anything you say can be used against you in a court of law; (3) You have the right to the presence of an attorney; (4) If you cannot afford a lawyer, one will be appointed to you prior to questioning; and (5) You may terminate the interview at any time. A person subjected to custodial interrogation must be given the Miranda warnings regardless of the nature or severity of the offense. Exception: The roadside questioning of a motorist detained pursuant to a routine traffic stop does to constitute a custodial interrogation, so there is no need to give Miranda warnings.

Miranda Warning

- When suspect is in custody (not free to leave)
- Before being interrogated
- Does not apply to unsolicited statements

Right to Remain Silent

Once the suspect has invoked the right to remain silent, the suspect cannot be questioned again for the same offense unless he or she initiates further communication, exchanges, or conversations with police.

Communication for Police Officers

- Goal is to determine truth
- Officer must be culturally adroit
- Officer must be self-controlled and confident
- Requires 2-way communication
- Encourage conversation
- Eliminate physical barriers
- Ask simple questions one at a time
- Listen and Observe

Emotional Barriers to Communication

- Attitudes and prejudices
- Fear
- Anger or hostility
- Self-preservation

Interview v. Interrogation

- Interviewing = questioning person who may know something about a crime but is not believed to be a suspect
- Interrogating = questioning person who is suspected of being directly or indirectly involved in a crime

Confession vs. Admission

- **Confession** = information supporting the elements of a crime given by a person involved in committing the crime; suspect says he committed the act
- **Admission** means the suspect admits to something related to an act but does not claim that he committed the act; contains some information concerning the elements of a crime but falls short of a full confession
- **Adoptive admission** = person does not deny allegations made against him or her when given the opportunity

Confession

- May be obtained orally or in writing
- Needs to be corroborated by other evidence
- Permission from parent/guardian needs to be obtained before questioning a youth

3 Tests for Miranda

Three questions are posed to determine if the Miranda warning was given properly

1. Was the Miranda warning given by police?
2. If given, was there a waiver?
3. If there was a waiver, was it given intelligently and voluntarily?

Miranda

- Confessions are invalid if the police use coercion or brutality
- Confessions are invalid if deception is used as a means of psychological pressure
- Confessions are invalid if suspect does not have complete freedom of mind

Right to Counsel

- Right to counsel falls under 6th Amendment
- Suspect is entitled to a lawyer during interrogation so that the right against self-incrimination is protected.
- Even if Miranda warnings are properly given, the evidence is not admissible if the right to counsel under the 6th Amendment is violated.

Waiver

- **Intelligently** – suspect knows what she is doing and is sufficiently competent to waive right
- **Voluntarily** – not the result of any threat, force, coercion; waiver is made of own free will. Court ruled that statements are not admissible in court if coercion is exerted by the **police** and not by someone else (e.g., God).
- Signed waiver not required

Prolonged Interruption

The Court hinted that if the police read a suspect the Miranda warning and then take a **prolonged** break, then the Miranda warning should be read again to the suspect before re-questioning the suspect

How long is prolonged?
Although the time has not been clearly established by the Court, several hours may be considered prolonged.

Situations in which Miranda warnings are not needed

- When officers do not ask any questions
- During general on-the-scene questioning
- When the statement is volunteered
- When asking the suspect routine identification questions
- When questioning witnesses who are not suspects
- In stop & frisk cases
- During lineups, show-ups, or photographic identifications (because evidence is physical in nature and does not constitute testimonial self-incrimination)
- When the statement is made to a private person
- When the suspect testifies before the grand jury (such interrogation does not present the same opportunities for abuse as custodial interrogation by police)
- When there is a threat to public safety (immediate danger to public, such as when a gun has been thrown away by a suspect)
- When an undercover officer poses as an inmate and asks questions (not a police-dominated atmosphere)

Totality of Circumstances

- Reviewing courts must look at the totality of circumstances
- Each factor in and of itself may not indicate a crime
- Together the factors may indicate a crime
- Officers allowed to draw upon personal experience and specialized training
- Probable cause and reasonable suspicion are fluid and cannot be defined with precision

Exclusionary Rule

- Any evidence obtained by the government in violation of the 4th Amendment guarantee against unreasonable search & seizure is not admissible in a criminal prosecution to prove guilt
- Court states that the rule is a judicially created remedy to safeguard 4th Amendment rights.
- Therefore, not every violation (e.g., 5th and 6th Amendment violations) comes under the exclusionary rule
- Evidence collected from other Constitutional violations is also excludable, but under other rules
- For example, the self-incrimination clause (5th Amendment) contains its own exclusionary rule

Probable Cause (PC) After-the-Fact

- PC must exist at time of police action
- PC determined after-the-fact does not make the act legal (evidence found in such cases will not be allowed in court)
- What is not included in an affidavit cannot be later used to establish PC

Suspicion

- Suspicion alone is never sufficient for an arrest
- Mere suspicion may develop into PC
- Once PC is developed, any evidence may be used in court
- Courts recognize that affidavits are often prepared hastily and in the midst of criminal investigations so they are to be interpreted with common sense over technical manners

Probable Cause

- PC = enough factual information to make the average reasonable person with same training and experience to believe that the person has committed a crime
- Practical definition = 51% confident
- Must use totality of the circumstances

Factors Used to Establish Probable Cause

- Police officer training
- Education
- Culture
- Unique life experiences
- Knowledge of community
- Prior criminal record of suspect
- Suspect flees when officer arrives
- Highly suspicious conduct by the suspect
- Admission or confession by suspect
- Presence of incriminating evidence
- Unusual hour
- Resemblance of suspect to perpetrator
- Failure to answer questions satisfactorily

Consensual Encounter with Police Car

- Police may pull along someone and ask questions
- Do not block person's car so the person cannot leave
- Person must be free to leave
- Police may shine spot light in car
- Court has stated that person in car has no legal authority to submit to police when illuminated by white light
- Once red and blue lights are illuminated, the person is required to submit to police; officer is using legal authority to detain person

Detention

- Temporary stopping of a person by exerting authority
- Person is not free to leave
- Less than arrest but more than consensual encounter
- Need reasonable suspicion (RS)
- Hunch < Reasonable Suspicion < Probable Cause < Beyond Reasonable Doubt

Detention May Exist If

- Person is restrained
- Officer gives specific order that the person feels obligated to obey
- Actions or questions that indicate the person is the suspect of a crime

Arrest

- Taking a person into custody in manner authorized by law
- Physically restraining or touching the person
- Handcuffing
- Person is required to submit to authority
- May use reasonable force to overcome resistance
- Need PC

Investigation

- Once police officer stops a suspect, officer may investigate the situation
- May question suspect about his identification and conduct, may contact others to verify story and identification, can check for outstanding warrants, can check nearby buildings to determine if crime occurred, can bring witness to suspect for show-up

Articulation

- Must be able to articulate facts in report and in court
- For reasonable suspicion to be valid, there is a 2 prong test
  - Criminal activity may be taking place
  - The person detained is somehow connected to possible criminal activity

4th Amendment

- Right of individuals to be secure in their persons, houses, papers and effects against unreasonable searches and seizures and no warrant shall be issued but upon PC, supported by Oath or affirmation, that particularly describes the place to be searched, and the persons or things to be seized.
- For an arrest, it must be determined if a seizure has occurred
- If no seizure, then 4th Amendment does not apply
- If seizure, then must determine what kind of seizure
- Not all contact with the police is considered a seizure under the 4th Amendment
- Whether a seizure exists depends upon the level of intrusiveness

Examples Not Considered Seizures

- Police asking questions of people on street to gather general information
- Police asking driver to get out of car after a stop
- Police boarding bus and asking questions that a person is free to refuse to answer
- Police riding alongside a person to see where he is going
- Police asking witnesses questions about a crime

Arrest & Seizures

- Every arrest is a seizure, but not every seizure is an arrest
- There are different types of seizures
- Arrest is one type of seizure
- Arrest requires an intentional acquisition of physical control and only applies when there is governmental termination of freedom of movement through means intentionally applied

Seizure Test

- Court ruled a seizure has occurred if a reasonable person, considering the totality of the circumstances, would conclude that the police had in some way restrained a person's liberty so that he or she was not free to leave
- Court ruled that there is no single, clear, hand-and-fast rule that is applicable to all investigatory pursuits

Seizure

- When a reasonable person, taking into account all of the circumstances surrounding the encounter, perceives that the police have communicated that he was not at liberty to ignore the police and go about his business

Reasonable Person

- Who decides the definition of a reasonable person?
- Jury or judge who tries the case
- Standard is subjective and may vary

Court Ruled Factors that Involve Seizure

- Threatening presence of police
- Display of weapon by police
- Some physical touching by police
- Use of language or tone of voice indicating that compliance with the officer's request might be compelled

Arrest

- The taking of a person into custody against the person's will for the purpose of criminal prosecution or interrogation
- Occurs only when there is a governmental termination of freedom of movement through means intentionally applied
- Arrest deprives a person of liberty by legal authority
- Mere words alone do not normally constitute an arrest
- There must be some kind of restraint
- It does not matter whether the specific act is termed arrest, stop, or detention under state law
- Totality of circumstances is the standard
- Test of reasonableness = reasonable person
- Not free to leave

Forced Detention & Arrest

- It does not matter what state law calls it, if person is taken into custody against his will for the purpose of criminal prosecution or interrogation, then it is an arrest under the 4th Amendment

Length of Detention & Arrest

How long can a suspect be detained and how intrusive must the investigation be before a stop becomes an arrest, which requires PC?

It depends upon the reasonableness of the detention and the level of intrusion.

The detention must not be longer than that required by the circumstances, and it must take place by the least intrusive means to verify or dispel the officer's suspicions

In Sum – Seizure

- A person has been seized if, under the totality of the circumstances, a reasonable person would not have felt free to leave. This applies to seizures of persons in general, such as stop & frisk, not just in arrest cases.

Mere Words

- Mere words alone do not constitute an arrest
- Saying "You are under arrest" is not sufficient
- An actual or constructive seizure must be present for an arrest to take place

Disposition of Prisoners After Arrest

- After a person is arrested, does the person have a Constitutional right to make a phone call?
- The Supreme Court has not addressed this issue.
- It is safe to say that there is no constitutional right to a phone call. However, state law may allow phone call. When the call is actually allowed varies by jurisdiction. However, an arrestee is constitutionally entitled to call an attorney prior to questioning.

Booking

- Involves making an entry in the police arrest book indicating the suspect's name, time of arrest, and offense charged.
- Suspect may be fingerprinted or photographed for serious offenses.
- If minor offense, suspect may be released on stationhouse bail, which involves posting cash and promising to appear in court for a hearing at a specific date
- If offense is serious, arrestee will be held in a temporary holding facility (jail) until bail, as set by the magistrate, is posted.
- In the process of booking, an inventory of the arrestee's personal property may be conducted without a warrant.
- However, such as inventory cannot be used as a fishing expedition to find evidence.
- For example, if a non-evidentiary letter is found in a purse, the letter will be inventoried but may not be read by police.

Establishing PC

- Officer may use any trustworthy information to establish PC, even it the evidence is not admissible in court (e.g., hearsay & prior criminal record)
- Evidence may include tips from citizens, police radio bulletins, reports from victims, anonymous tips, tips from informants, etc.
- Judge may consider any evidence, regardless of the source
- PC based on totality of circumstances
- More information means better PC
- Officer's own knowledge of particular facts and circumstances
- Information given by a reliable 3rd person
- Information + corroboration
- PC is not based on hard certainty but it is based on probabilities and confidence levels

PC & No Warrant

- If officer acts with no warrant, then officer will have to establish PC by oral testimony in court during trial
- In some jurisdictions, judge may require oral testimony in addition to written affidavit

Motor Vehicles

- Can police arrest passengers if they have PC to arrest driver?
- Yes, if occupants have knowledge of and exercise control over crime (e.g., drugs)
- A motor vehicle is a relatively small area and not a public environment
- Guilt by association is not a good defense
- Police must decide if crime committed solely or jointly – may be decided case-by-case in court

Erroneously Admitted Evidence

- Erroneously admitted evidence during trial will be overturned in appeal unless prosecutor can show error was harmless

Purpose of the Exclusionary Rule

- To deter police misconduct
- Assumption: If illegally obtained evidence is not allowed in court, then police misconduct will be minimized
- Applies to state and federal cases

Due Process

- Evidence obtained in violation of the constitutional right to due process is inadmissible under the 5th and 14th Amendments.
- Due process violations can lead to civil liability under federal law

Invoking Exclusionary Rule

- May be invoked at about any stage of the criminal justice proceeding
- May be invoked while serving time after conviction

Habeas Corpus

- Seeks release from prison because constitutional rights were violated before and during trial
- Example: suspect convicted and the time to appeal has past
- Defendant finds new evidence that police misconduct took place
- Evidence was not made available to the suspect during trial
- Habeas corpus seeks release from prison due to violation of constitutional rights
- However, federal law limits what prisoners can do

Exceptions to the Rule: 4 categories

- Good faith
- Inevitable discovery
- Purged taint
- Independent source

Some states may not allow for exceptions in order to provide more protection to suspect

Good Faith

Evidence is admissible if error or mistake was not committed by police or, if committed by the police, was honest and reasonable

- When error committed by judge
- When error committed by court employee
- When police believed information was true and accurate
- When police believed person had authority to give entry
- When police action was based on law that was later declared unconstitutional

Error by Judge

If error made by judge: Court ruled that evidence is admissible in court because the judge, and not the police, erred. Therefore, the exclusionary rule does not apply because it is designed to control the conduct of police, not judges.

Error by Court Employee

If error made by court employee: Court ruled that evidence is admissible in court because court employee, and not the police, erred. Therefore, the exclusionary rule does not apply because it is designed to control the conduct of police, and there was no evidence that the court employee tried to ignore or subvert the 4th Amendment.

When Police Erred Accidentally

- Constitutionality of police conduct is based on the information that was available to the officer at the time of the action
- Evidence obtained as a result of a mistake is admissible as long as officers thought that their actions were legal and correct
- Based on information officers disclosed or had a duty to discover and disclose to judge
- Police must act within scope of warrant – cannot search dresser drawers for 60" TV

Police Believed had Authority to Enter

- If police have PC to believe that the person has control over property and authority to give consent, then evidence discovered is admissible
- Ex: a woman has a key to an apartment, she states that she lives there with her boyfriend, and states she has furniture and clothes there. Police enter and find drugs. Drugs are admissible in court if police believed woman, even if woman lied to police.

Law later declared Unconstitutional

- If mistake is with law and not police, evidence is admissible
- Ex: Police legally search a car and collect evidence, but the law changes later that would have made the search illegal. Evidence is admissible in court because the act was legal at the time the evidence was collected.

Inevitable Discovery

- States that evidence is admissible if the police can prove that they would have inevitably discovered it anyway by lawful means, regardless of their illegal action.
- Not **could** have led to discovery but **would** have led to discovery

Purged Tainted

- Defendant's subsequent voluntary act dissipates the taint of the initial illegality
- Defendant uses free will
- There is a break in the casual connection
- Decided on case-by-case basis
- Ex: An initial confession was illegal and the suspect was released. If the suspect returns to sign a confession, then the second confession will be admissible.

Independent Source

- Holds that evidence obtained is admissible if the police can prove that it was obtained from an independent source not connected with the illegal search or seizure
- Ex: police conduct an illegal search of a home and find a girl. The girl claims she has been raped by the suspect. Parents had filed a missing report the day before. Informant saw the girl at the location. The girl's statement is not related to illegal search.

When Exclusionary Rule Does Not Apply

- Police violate "knock & announce" rule
- Searches done by private persons
- Grand jury investigations
- Sentencing
- Arrest based on PC that violate state law
- Violations of agency rules
- Noncriminal proceedings
- Parole revocation hearings

Grand Jury

- Person cannot refuse to answer questions from Grand Jury, even if the questions are based on evidence that was obtained illegally
- This would unduly interfere with grand jury's investigative function

Illegally Obtained Evidence - During Sentencing

- May be admissible if state law does not prohibit it
- Evidence may be reliable, even if illegally obtained
- Judge should consider all evidence at sentencing

Reasonable Suspicion

- Quantum of knowledge sufficient to induce an ordinarily prudent and cautious person under similar circumstances to believe criminal activity is at hand. It must be based on articulable facts, which, taken together with rational inferences from those facts, reasonably warrant intrusion.
- Suspicion $\leq$ Reasonable Suspicion $\leq$ Probable Cause

4th Amendment

- Stops, frisks, and stationhouse detention fall under the 4th Amendment
- They are not subject to the same limitations as arrests, searches, and seizures
- Stops, frisks, and stationhouse detention follow different rules than arrests, searches, and seizures
- For legal purposes, even though less intrusive than an arrest, a stationhouse detention should be considered equivalent to an arrest

Stop & Frisk

- Stop: the brief detention of a person when the police officer has reasonable suspicion, in light of his or her experience, that criminal activity is about to take place
- Frisks: the pat-down of a person's outer clothing after a stop to see if the person has a weapon, which can be seized by the officer. A frisk is performed for the protection of the officer and of others.
- Stop & frisk: a police practice that allows an officer, based on reasonable suspicion rather on PC, to stop a person in a public place and ask questions to determine if that person has committed a crime or about to commit a crime and to frisk the person for weapons, if the officer has reasonable concern for his or her own personal safety.
- Two separate acts, not one continuous act
- Intrusion upon a person's freedom
- Requires reasonable suspicion to be valid
- During this scenario, no arrest can be made
- If PC is developed, then may lead to arrest
- Because stop and frisk are less intrusive than an arrest, search, and seizure, all the police need is reasonable suspicion
- Several states have passed laws that allow the practice
- Other state courts and some federal courts have upheld such practices

Seizure

- When does a stop constitute a seizure under 4th Amendment and require RS?
- When is a stop not a seizure under 4th Amendment?
- A person is seized under the 4th Amendment if, **in view of all of the circumstances** surrounding the incident, a **reasonable person** would have believed that he was **not free to leave.**

Not Free to leave

Court gave examples
- Officers display weapon
- Touching of person by officer
- Use of language or tone of voice compelling a suspect's compliance
- Absence of such evidence amounts to less than a seizure

Unprovoked Flight

- Does unprovoked flight constitute reasonable suspicion?
- Yes, and RS may exist to justify a stop
- Headlong flight – wherever it occurs – is an act of evasion: it is not necessarily indicative of wrongdoing, but is certainly suggestive of such.
- RS based on commonsense judgments and inferences about human behavior
- Flight may be innocent, but the stop afterwards does not violate 4th Amendment
- Because of the Court's language, lower courts may render conflicting decisions about whether unprovoked flight alone generates RS

Stops Based on Hearsay

- Are stops based on hearsay information valid?
- Yes, information from a known informant carries enough indicia of reliability to justify the forcible stop of a suspect

Stops Based on Anonymous Tips

- An anonymous tip, corroborated by independent police work, may provide RS to make an investigatory stop **if it carries sufficient indicia of reliability**
- Should provide predictive information that allows police to test the informant's knowledge or credibility
- RS depends on the quality and quantity of the information and both factors are considered in the totality of the circumstances

Flyer from Another Jurisdiction

- Is information based on a flyer from another jurisdiction enough for a stop?
- Yes, the Court decided that the police may stop a suspect on the basis of reasonable suspicion that the person is wanted for investigation in another jurisdiction; must articulate that the suspect is the wanted person.
- A Terry-type stop is permissible

Parolees

- Are stops of parolees without suspicion valid?
- Yes, because a parolee does not have an expectation of privacy that society would recognize as legitimate
- Parolees are still in the legal custody of the DOC until the conclusion of their sentence
- Parolees provide consent to a suspicion-less search at just about any time

Forced to Answer Questions

- Can stopped suspects be forced to answer questions?
- No. However, the failure to answer questions may give the officer RS to frisk the suspect because it may fail to dispel suspicions of danger. It may also lead to PC, if other circumstances are present.

Identification

- Can a stopped person be forced to identify oneself?
- Yes, but only under certain circumstances.
- Balance the intrusion on the individual's rights against the promotion of legitimate governmental interests.
- For example, an officer may identify a person who may have committed a crime or if circumstances lead a reasonable person to believe that public safety requires such identification

Duration of Stop

- May only last as long as necessary to achieve its purpose
- Officer cannot detain a person for as much time is as convenient
- Court ruled a 90 minute delay to get K-9 exceeded permissible limits for an investigatory stop
- Court ruled isolating a suspect at an airport was more intrusive than necessary to carry out a limited investigation permitted under stop and frisk
- Court ruled that detaining a person for longer than necessary to write a ticket was unreasonable (officer ran warrant checks based on hunch)
- In one case, Court ruled detaining a person for 20 minutes was reasonable, considering the particulars of the case
- Reasonableness must take into account the length of time for the stop and the needs of law enforcement
- Determined on a case-by-case basis

Airport Stops

- Are airport stops and searches valid?
- Yes, as long as terrorism is a threat, courts will likely allow practices that do not grossly violate constitutional rights
- Even if racial profiling is employed, legal challenges to this type of profiling may prove difficult because of serious and valid security concerns
- 9th Circuit ruled that airport security may conduct a random check of a traveler's carry-on bag, even if it passed through x-ray without suspicion
- Airport searches are a form of administrative search with lower 4th Amendment protection
- Airport searches are easily justified as a special needs search rather than as a law enforcement activity
- Court has ruled that special needs searches have lower 4th Amendment protection

Degree of Intrusion

- What degree of intrusion is permissible?
- Least intrusive and most reasonably available method to verify or dispel the officer's suspicion
- The greater the degree of police control, the greater the likelihood the court will impose the PC standard

Stop & Frisk

- A **Stop** has only one purpose: to determine if criminal activity has taken place or is about to take place
- A **Frisk** has only one purpose: officer safety
- Terry v. Ohio (1968) is the leading case on stop & frisk
- Sets guidelines that officers must follow for stop and frisk
- Investigatory stop does not constitute an arrest and is permissible if a) the officer observes unusual behavior leading to reasonable suspicion (RS) that criminal activity is about to take place and b) the officer can articulate the facts that lead to RS
- After the stop, the officer may frisk suspects for safety

Terry v. Ohio

The Stop
- The Officer observes unusual behavior leading to reasonable suspicion (RS) that criminal activity is about to take place and the officer can articulate the facts that lead to RS
- Officer must identify self as police officer
- Officer must make reasonable inquiries

The Frisk
- If stop requirements are satisfied, officer may conduct a limited search (i.e., pat-down) of the outer clothing in an attempt to discover dangerous weapons

Summary

Stop
1. Observe
2. Approach and identify
3. Ask questions

Frisk
1. Conduct a pat-down of the outer clothing
2. If weapon is felt, confiscate it and arrest the suspect (optional)
3. Conduct a full body search after the arrest (optional)

Stops

- Stops based on race alone are not valid
- Lower courts disagree on whether race can be taken as one factor in determining reasonable suspicion for a stop
- Persons stopped by the police cannot be forced to answer questions but they may be forced to identify themselves as authorized by state law

Frisks

- A frisk should not automatically follow a stop
- A frisk is valid only if there is reasonable suspicion that a threat to officer safety exists
- A frisk that goes beyond a mere pat-down for weapons is illegal
- Initially limited to pat-down of outer clothing
- May seize the object if it feels like a weapon
- May not seize object if does not feel like weapon; if seized, cannot be admitted in court
- If an arrest is made, then a body search may be conducted
- When actions by police exceed the bounds permitted by RS, the seizure becomes an arrest and must be supported by PC

Plain Touch Doctrine

- If an officer touches or feels something that is immediately recognized as something needing to be seized, the object can be seized as long as such knowledge amounts to PC.
- If the officer has to manipulate the object to determine what it is, then the evidence may be inadmissible in court

Fishing Expeditions

- The frisk cannot be used to fish for evidence
- Its only purpose is to promote safety
- Contraband must be immediately apparent to officer

Consent to Frisk

- Is consent to frisk based on submission to police authority valid?
- If officer does not fear for his safety, then consent is required.
- Validity depends on how consent was obtained.
- Consent to authority may not necessarily be voluntary
- Burden of proof that consent was involuntary lies with person who gave consent

Frisk

Can an officer frisk after a stop without asking questions?
- Reasonable inquires are required before a frisk
- However, in some instances a frisk may be justified without the officer asking questions if the officer believes safety is a concern
- Exception: if state law requires officer to make reasonable inquiries before frisk
- Does a frisk include things carried?
- Court has not directly addressed this issue
- If belongings are easily accessible, then search may be justified
- Burden of proof on police to demonstrate extended frisk was necessary for officer safety
- Cannot be used as a fishing expedition

Stop & Frisk vs. Arrest

	Stop & Frisk	Arrest
• **Degree of certainty**	Reasonable Suspicion	Probable Cause
• **Extent of intrusion**	pat-down for weapons	full body search
• **Purpose**	stop: prevent crime Frisk: safety	to take person into custody, determine if crime occurred
• **Warrant**	not needed	required, unless exception
• **Duration**	no longer than necessary	until legally released
• **Force allowed**	stop: none	reasonable

Motor Vehicles

- Motorists are subject to stop and frisk under the same circumstances as pedestrians
- Motorists may be stopped if there is RS of unlawful activity
- After the vehicle is stopped, the officer may order the driver out of the vehicle, even if the officer has no RS that the driver poses a threat to the officer

Stationhouse Detention

- A form of detention, usually at a police facility, that is short of arrest but greater than on-the-street detention of stop & frisk. It is used by many departments for obtaining fingerprints or photographs, ordering police lineups, administering polygraph tests, or securing other identification or non-testimonial evidence.

Stationhouse Detention – Fingerprinting

- Can stationhouse detention be used to obtain fingerprints?
- Court ruled that RS alone does not permit police to detain a suspect at the police station to obtain fingerprints
- Suspect may consent to stationhouse detention
- Consent may be challenged because police station is intimidating
- Police must tell suspect that he is not under arrest
- Police must tell suspect that he is free to leave at any time
- Police must tell suspect that fingerprinting is voluntary
- Police should get suspect's signature on waiver form
- Police should have witness sign waiver form
- Court implied that detention for fingerprinting might be permissible even without PC to arrest; narrowly circumscribed procedures are required
- Must have objective basis for suspecting person of crime
- Must have legitimate investigatory purpose for detention (such as fingerprinting)
- Must not be an inconvenient time for the suspect
- Must have adequate evidence to justify detention

Field Detention - Fingerprinting

- Court ruled that field detention for purposes of fingerprinting a suspect does not require PC as long as

    1) there is RS that the suspect committed a crime
    2) there is reasonable belief that the fingerprinting will either negate or establish the suspect's guilt
    3) the procedure is promptly effected

Stationhouse Detention – Interrogation

- Court ruled that PC is required for stationhouse detention involving interrogation, even if no arrest is made
- Suspect is not questioned on the street, but transported to police station
- Thus, an arrest has been made, PC is needed at that point, and any statements made afterwards are inadmissible

Border Searches

- Full 4th Amendment protections do not apply at border, particularly at the point of entry
- Border Searches at the point of entry do not come under the 4th Amendment, but searches inside the border do.
- Searches made at the border are based on the longstanding right of a nation to protect itself by stopping and examining persons and property entering the country.
- Searches may be conducted by immigration and border agents without PC, RS, or suspicion
- No amount of certainty is required in border searches, whether the person is a U.S. citizen or not
- There is a compelling state interest involved in stopping illegal immigration and the flow of prohibited goods into the country
- The rules for border stops and searches are governed by immigration laws and policies, subject to minimum rights required by the Bill of Rights
- Since 9/11/2001, border policies have gotten tighter. These rights may be challenged in court, but they should prevail if they do not violate the minimum rights required
- No suspicion is needed to disassemble a fuel tank of a motor vehicle at the border
- Vehicles may be stopped at fixed checkpoints and their occupants questioned, even without RS that the vehicle contains illegal aliens (because it is not arbitrary). Also, no warrant is needed to set up a checkpoint for immigration purposes.
- For vehicle searches away from the border, a warrant or PC is required (roving agents cannot profile occupants to make stop, but they can detain and question occupants of a car as long as they have RS)

Detention of Aliens

- For the purpose of questioning, immigration officers may detain persons against their will if the officers reasonably believe that the persons are illegal aliens.
- The searched person does not have to enter the U.S.
- Any person found in the border area is subject to search based on RS, including employees and visitors
- Search is not limited to actual point of entry; may be conducted in the functional equivalent of the border (e.g., an airport in Illinois)

Factory Surveys of Aliens

- Immigration officers may visit factories and ask employees questions to determine if they are illegal aliens
- Does not constitute a seizure under 4th Amendment so officer does not have to show objective basis for suspecting the worker of being an illegal alien before conducting the survey

Detention of Alimentary Canal Smugglers

- Reasonable suspicion is sufficient for an immigration officer to detain a foreign traveler who is suspected of swallowing contraband. Immigration officers detained a person for 27 hours before the drugs were discovered in the alimentary canal. The Court ruled that the action was reasonable because of the hard-to-detect nature of the crime and because it was at the border.

Border Summary

- Foreigners who attempt to enter the U.S. do not have full 4th Amendment protection at the border
- They can be stopped and searched without RS
- Their vehicles and belongings can be extensively searched without PC
- Once foreigners are legally inside the U.S., they are entitled to constitutional protection
- Advanced technologies are being used in border searches to detect illegal entries and contraband

Constitutional Law (QUIZ)

Circle correct choice

1) T F The only time that the police are required to provide the Miranda warning to a suspect is when the suspect is arrested for a felony offense and the police want to question the person.

2) T F Once the suspect has invoked the right to remain silent, the police cannot question the suspect about any criminal activity unless the suspect initiates further communication with the police.

3) T F Miranda warnings are not required when an uncover police officer poses as an inmate and asks the suspect questions about his crime.

4) T F The police need probable cause to stop a person in a public place to investigate criminal activity.

5) T F Interviewing is the same thing as interrogating.

6) T F Admission is the same thing as confession.

7) T F All contact with the police is considered a type of seizure.

8) T F The police must provide the Miranda warning to drivers during routine traffic stops.

9) T F The police can order a person out of a car even if the police have no reasonable suspicion of criminal activity.

10) T F All confessions must be obtained in writing for them to be valid.

REFERENCES

Del Carmen, R.V. (2014). *Criminal procedures: Laws & practice* (9th ed.). Belmont, CA: Wadsworth.

CHAPTER 2. REASONSING & FLOWCHARTING

REASONING

In criminal justice, it is crucial to practice and enhance the skill of reasoning. If officers operate on flawed assumptions, it could hamper their ability to successfully perform their law enforcement duties. If police officers act on inaccurate assumptions, it could lead to wrongful arrests and wrongful releases.

Deductive reasoning is based on drawing conclusions from statements that are accepted as true (Smith, Eggen, St. Andre, 2006). A person employing deductive reasoning will start with a general principle and will apply the information to a specific case. In other words, deductive reasoning arrives at a specific conclusion based on generalizations. Below is an example of deductive reasoning.

All apples are fruit.
All fruit grows on trees.
Therefore, all apples grow on trees.

If the initial assumptions are incorrect, then the conclusion will be flawed.

Inductive Reasoning is based on an individual making observations and then developing a generality based on those observations (Smith et al., 2006). In other words, the observer detects patterns and then makes predictions based on those patterns. However, if the observations are proved false only one time, then the conclusions will be flawed. Below is an example of inductive reasoning.

Inductive reasoning: Predict next response.

•   ••   •••   _____

It is easy to see how inductive reasoning can be used to predict future criminal behavior. For example, law enforcers have used inductive reasoning as a part of the totality of circumstance to profile possible terrorists. Having limited resources, police departments may try to focus their efforts on the greatest risks.

FLOWCHARTING – FOLLOWING DIRECTIONS
("Flow Chart", 2002).

Definitions of flowchart symbols.

Terminal (start or stop)

Process (do something)

Input or output

Decision

Flow line

Connector (jump)

The terminal symbol indicates the starting point and ending point of the algorithm (*"Flow Chart"*, 2002). The process symbol is used to represent arithmetic functions and data movement instructions. The input/output symbol is used to denote any function of an input/output device. For example, data may be collected from a disk (input) or delivered to a printer (output). The decision symbol is used to indicate a point where a decision is made and there are two or more consequences. Flow lines simply provide the path of travel for the flow of operation. The on-page connector allows a point to jump elsewhere. This is useful if the flow lines become congested and start to crisscross in a particular area.

Describe the numbers that are printed in each of the algorithms below.

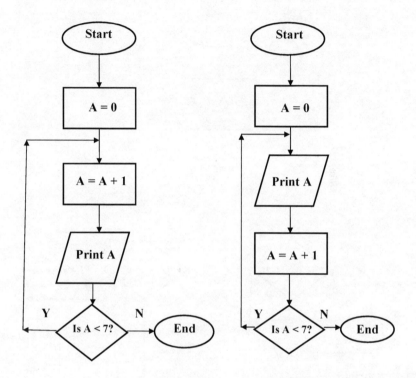

Below is an algorithm that prints the largest of three numbers.

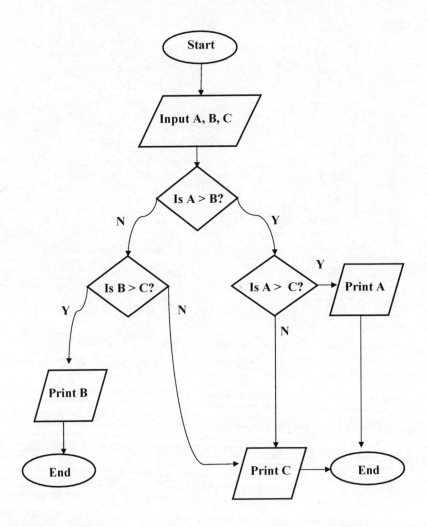

On the next page is a program in which the police select every fifth car to perform a Driving Under the Influence (DUI) investigation. The officers stopping the vehicles are on the Initial Contact Team (ICT). The officers conducting the Field Sobriety Tests are the FST Team (FSTT). (V = V+ 1 means to take the current value of V, add 1, then make that the new value of V.)

Rules:
1) The project will run for 4 hours.
2) The ICT will monitor traffic, will stop every fifth vehicle, and will administer an alco-sensor test to the driver.
3) If the alco-sensor test at initial contact is less than 0.05% BAC, then the driver will be released.
4) If the alco-sensor test at initial contact is at least 0.05% BAC, then the driver will be passed off to the Field Sobriety Test Team, who will continue the investigation via field sobriety tests (FSTs). The ICT will return to traffic.
5) If the alco-senor test is at least .05% BAC but less than .08% BAC, and if the driver passes the FSTs, then the FSTT will release the driver.
6) If the alco-sensor test at initial contact is at least 0.08% BAC, then the driver will automatically be given a Datamaster test after the field sobriety tests.
7) If the driver fails the field sobriety tests, then the driver will be given a DataMastrer test.
8) If the DataMaster test is less than .08% BAC, and if the driver fails the FSTs, then the FSTT will charge the driver with public intoxication.
9) If the DataMaster test is at least .08% BAC, then the FSTT will charge the driver with DUI misdemeanor for the driver's first offense and DUI felony for the driver's second offense.

Driving Under the Influence (DUI) Investigation.

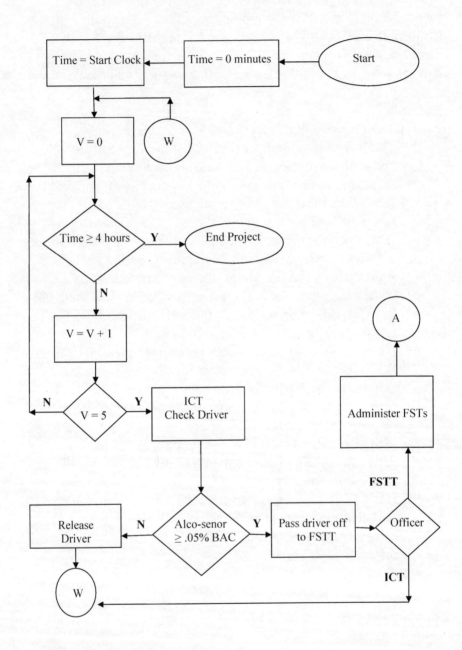

Driving Under the Influence (DUI) investigation (continued).

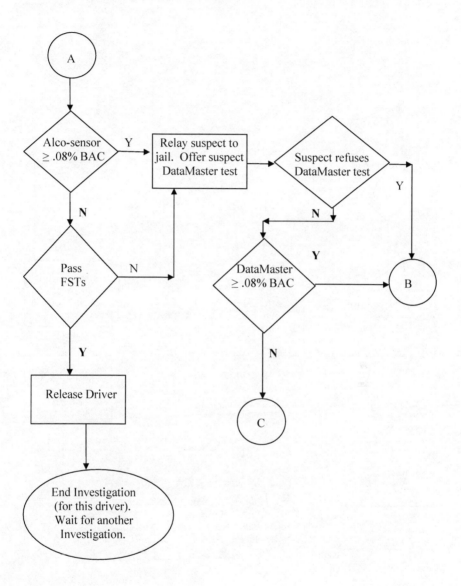

Driving Under the Influence (DUI) investigation (continued).

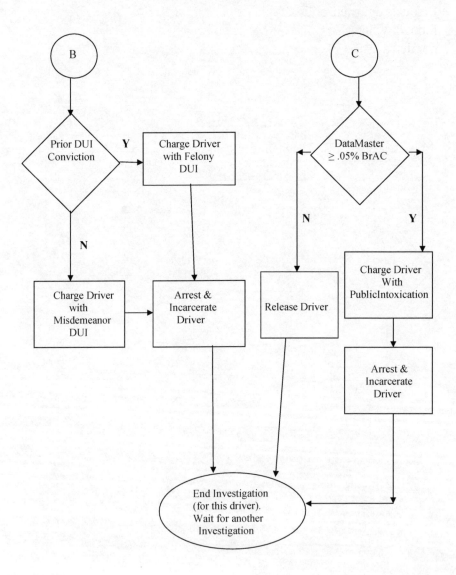

INTERVIEWING, INTERROGATION & COMMUNICATION for LAW ENFORCEMENT

Stop and Frisk Flowchart

Below is a flowchart that explains the stop and frisk procedure. For the following flowchart, probable cause means that it is more likely than not that a crime has occurred (51% confident for practical purposes).

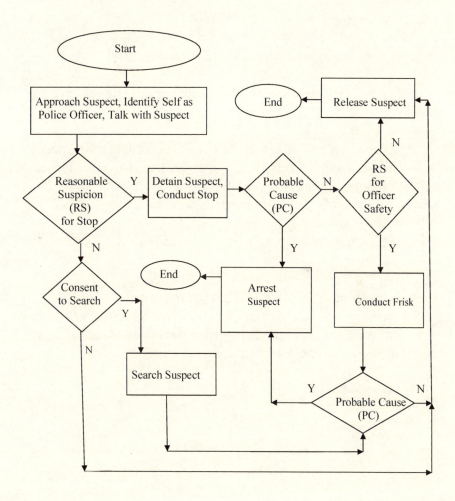

Assignment

Create a flow chart for the following law enforcement situation on a roadway with a maximum speed limit of 65 MPH and a minimum speed limit of 45 MPH.

<u>Make Flow Chart</u>

If car is traveling from 45-65 MPH disregard vehicle.

If car is traveling from 66-79 MPH, write the driver a warning for speed.

If car is traveling $\geq$ 80 MPH, write the driver a citation for speed, unless driver needs an ambulance. If driver needs an ambulance, call an ambulance and disregard enforcement action. If driver does not need an ambulance, write the driver a citation.

If car is traveling from 40-44 MPH, write the driver a warning for speed too slow.

If car is traveling from $\leq$ 39 MPH, write the driver a citation for speed too slow, unless the driver needs a wrecker. If driver needs a wrecker, call a wrecker and disregard enforcement action. If driver does not need a wrecker, write the driver a citation.

REFERENCES

Flow Chart Examples (2002). Retrieved from http://elsmar.com/ pdf_files/ Flow_Charts_for_2000.pdf

Smith, S., Eggen, M., St. Andre, R. (2006). *A transition to advanced mathematics* (6th ed.). Belmont, CA: Thomson Brooks/Cole.

CHAPTER 3. TRUTH TABLES

(Smith, Eggen, & St. Andre, 2006).

The following exercises will require a mathematical/logical mindset. The purpose of this chapter is to challenge your problem solving skills by applying math and English to the law.

Rule: When sentences are presented, variables are always defined in the positive language. For example, if the law states "not intoxicated," then variable A = intoxicated (positive language) while ~ A = not intoxicated (negative language).

Number of combinations = 2^x, where x is the number of variables

Number of combinations using three variables = $2^3 = 8$

∩ = And; U = Or; ~ = not; True = T = 1; False = F = 0

If A = {0, 1, 2, 3, 4, 5} and B = {2, 4, 7, 9},

A ∩ B = {2, 4}

and

A U B = {0, 1, 2, 3, 4, 5, 7, 9}

Examples of Truth Tables for one and two variables.

P	Q	P∩Q	P	Q	P U Q	P	~P	~(~P)
0	0	0	0	0	0	0	1	0
1	0	0	1	0	1	1	0	1
0	1	0	0	1	1			
1	1	1	1	1	1			

P	Q	P∩Q	~(P∩Q)	~P	~Q	~P U ~Q	~P ∩ ~Q
F	F	F	T	T	T	T	T
T	F	F	T	F	T	T	F
F	T	F	T	T	F	T	F
T	T	T	F	F	F	F	F

Examine the pattern of truth values for the combination of variables below. If column F is added, complete the chart. Notice that when all of the different variables are considered, no two rows are identical. In addition, notice that if only two variables are considered, such as A and B, the results will repeat themselves and they will not be influenced by the other variables.

Combination	Variable	A	B	C	D	E	F
1		0	0	0	0	0	
2		1	0	0	0	0	
3		0	1	0	0	0	
4		1	1	0	0	0	
5		0	0	1	0	0	
6		1	0	1	0	0	
7		0	1	1	0	0	
8		1	1	1	0	0	
9		0	0	0	1	0	
10		1	0	0	1	0	
11		0	1	0	1	0	
12		1	1	0	1	0	
13		0	0	1	1	0	
14		1	0	1	1	0	
15		0	1	1	1	0	
16		1	1	1	1	0	
17		0	0	0	0	1	

18	1	0	0	0	1
19	0	1	0	0	1
20	1	1	0	0	1
21	0	0	1	0	1
22	1	0	1	0	1
23	0	1	1	0	1
24	1	1	1	0	1
25	0	0	0	1	1
26	1	0	0	1	1
27	0	1	0	1	1
28	1	1	0	1	1
29	0	0	1	1	1
30	1	0	1	1	1
31	0	1	1	1	1
32	1	1	1	1	1

Truth Tables for three variables.

P	Q	R	~P	~Q	~R	P∩Q	~(P∩Q)	(P∩Q) U ~Q	PU ~Q	(PU ~Q) ∩R	~P ∩ ~Q	P ∩ ~Q
0	0	0	1	1	1	0	1	1	1	0	1	0
1	0	0	0	1	1	0	1	1	1	0	0	1
0	1	0	1	0	1	0	1	0	0	0	0	0
1	1	0	0	0	1	1	0	1	1	0	0	0
0	0	1	1	1	0	0	1	1	1	1	1	0
1	0	1	0	1	0	0	1	1	1	1	0	1
0	1	1	1	0	0	0	1	0	0	0	0	0
1	1	1	0	0	0	1	0	1	1	1	0	0

Make a truth table for each of the following propositional forms.

P ∩ P

P U ~Q

P ∩ (Q U R)

(P ∩ Q) U (P ∩ R)

P ∩ ~Q

P ∩ (Q U ~Q)

Which pairs are equivalent (have the same truth values)?

P ∩ ~P, P

P U P, P

P U P, ~P

P U ~Q, Q ∩ ~P

P U ~Q, Q U ~P

P U Q, Q U ~P

P ∩ Q, Q ∩ P

P ∩ ~Q, Q ∩ ~P

Make a truth table for each of the following propositional forms.
∩ = And; U = Or; ~ = not

~(P ∩ Q ∩ R)

~P ∩ ~Q ∩ ~R

~ (P U Q U R)

~ P U ~ Q U ~ R

If P = T, Q = T, and R = F, state whether the following are true or false?

~ (P ∩ Q ∩ R)   =

~ P ∩ ~ Q ∩ ~ R   =

~ (P U Q U R)   =

~ P U ~ Q U ~ R   =

If P, Q, and R are true while S and T are false, which of the following are true?

Q ∩ (R ∩ S)

Q U (R ∩ S)

(P U Q) ∩ (R U S)

Q U (R ∩ S)

(P U Q) ∩ (R U S)

[(~ P) U (~ Q)] U [(~ R) U (~ S)]

Which combination of variables (laws) are equivalent (i.e., have the same truth values)?

P	Q	R	~P	~Q	~R	P∩Q ∩R	~(P∩Q ∩R)	~P∩~Q ∩~R	P U Q U R	~(P U Q U R)	~P U ~Q U ~R
0	0	0	1	1	1	0	1	1	0	1	1
1	0	0	0	1	1	0	1	0	1	0	1
0	1	0	1	0	1	0	1	0	1	0	1
1	1	0	0	0	1	0	1	0	1	0	1
0	0	1	1	1	0	0	1	0	1	0	1
1	0	1	0	1	0	0	1	0	1	0	1
0	1	1	1	0	0	0	1	0	1	0	1
1	1	1	0	0	0	1	0	0	1	0	0

Make a truth table for each of the following propositional forms.

(P ∩ Q) U ~Q

~ (P ∩ Q)

(P U ~Q) ∩ R

~P ∩ ~Q

P ∩ ~P

If P, Q, and R are true while S and T are false, which of the following are true?

(~P) U (Q ∩ ~Q)

(~P) U (~Q)

[(~Q) U S] ∩ (Q U S)

(S ∩ R) U (S ∩ T)

(P U S) ∩ (P U T)

[(~T ∩ P) U (T ∩ P)

(~P) ∩ (Q U ~Q)

~R ∩ ~S

INTERVIEWING, INTERROGATION & COMMUNICATION for LAW ENFORCEMENT

Competition

Conditions to Compete:
To qualify for the competition, the applicant must be
    1) a female, greater than 21 years of age, and Canadian or
    2) a male, less than 21 years of age, and not Canadian.

Find the row that describes each particular person. Each person will be represented by only one combination of the three variables. Indicate whether each person listed below will qualify to compete by placing *yes* or *no* in the appropriate box that dictates the results.

Row	Combination of Variables			Does this Person Qualify to Compete?			
	A	B	C	Female, age 20, U.S.	Female, age 22, Canadian	Male, age 33, Canadian	Male, age 25, U.S.
	Sex	Age < 21 years of age	Canadian Citizenship				
	Female						
1	T	T	T				
2	F	T	T				
3	T	F	T				
4	F	F	T				
5	T	T	F				
6	F	T	F				
7	T	F	F				
8	F	F	F				

Answer to previous problem.

Conditions to Compete:
To qualify for the competition, the applicant must be
    1) a female, greater than 21 years of age, and Canadian (T F T) or
    2) a male, less than 21 years of age, and not Canadian (F T F).

Row	Combination of Variables			Does this Person Qualify to Compete?			
	A	B	C				
	Sex Female	Age < 21 years of age	Canadian Citizenship	Female, age 20, U.S. (TTF)	Female, age 22, Canadian (TFT)	Male, age 33, Canadian (FFT)	Male, age 25, U.S. (FFF)
1	T	T	T				
2	F	T	T				
3	T	F	T		YES		
4	F	F	T			NO	
5	T	T	F	NO			
6	F	T	F				
7	T	F	F				
8	F	F	F				NO

Only individuals who are in rows 3 and 6 qualify to compete. In this example, only the Canadian female who is 22 years of age qualifies to compete.

Conditional Statements

Conditional statement = If A, then B
Converse of the conditional statement = If B, then A

The converse of a conditional statement is not necessarily true. The Truth Table for a conditional statement is listed below (Smith et al., 2006). Proposition A is the antecedent and B is the consequence.

A	B	A → B
T	T	T
F	T	T
T	F	F
F	F	T

The table above indicates that the conditional statement is true if and only if A is false or B is true.

Suppose you state to your child that if she behaves, then you will give her candy. Let us look at the four possibilities and their associated truth values.

Let **A = child behaves; B = you give child candy**

A	B	A → B
A = False: The child misbehaves	B = True: You give child candy	You are truthful (T), because your guarantee did not address the child's misbehavior
A = False: The child misbehaves	B = False: You do not give child candy	You are truthful (T), because your guarantee did not address the child's misbehavior
A = True: The child behaves	B = True: You give child candy	You are truthful (T), because you honored your guarantee
A = True: The child behaves	B = False: You do not give child candy	You are not truthful (F), because you did not honor your guarantee

Below are conditional statements along with their converse statements.

If the person was aggressive, then the person was arrested.
If the person was arrested, then the person was aggressive.

If you arrested a person, then you seized the person.
If you seized the person, then you arrested the person.

If you interrogated the suspect, then you Mirandized the suspect.
If you Mirandized the suspect, then you interrogated the suspect.

For the conditional statements below, write its converse statement.

If you bought a TV, then you are broke.

If you are the police, then you can arrest.

If you surf, then you are in water.

If I was sad, then I cried.

If you are Catholic, then you are Christian.

<u>Examples to Demonstrate Difference</u>

If you are arrested, then you have been seized. However, if you are seized does not necessarily mean that you have been arrested. If you are sad, then you cry. However, if you cry does not necessarily mean that you are sad.

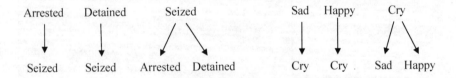

EXAMPLE: LAW H broken down into Levels of Headings

I.
- A.
    1.
        a. and
        b. and
        c.; or
    2.
        a. or
        b.; and
    3.; and
- B.
    1. and
    2.; or
- C.
    1.
        a. or
        b.; and
    2.; or

II.
- A.
    1.
        a. and
        b.; or
    2.
        a.; or
        b. and
        c.; or
- B.   or
- C.
    1.
        a. and
        b.; and
    2.; or

III.
- A.
  1.
     a. or
     b.; or
  2.; or
  3.
     a. and
     b.; or
     c.; and
- B.
  1. and
  2.; and
- C.
  1.
     a. and
     b.; and
  2.; and

IV.

The same LAW H and Levels of Headings using ∩ and U

Law = True if (I. U II. U III. ∩ IV.)	= T
I. = True if (A. ∩ B. U C.)	= T
A. = T if (1. U 2. ∩ 3.)	= T
1. = true if (a. ∩ b. ∩ c.)	= T
2. Is true if (a. U b.)	= T
3. = true if 3	= T
B. = T if (1. ∩ 2)	= T
1. = true if 1.	= T
2. = true if 2.	= T
C. = true if (1. ∩ 2.)	= T
1. = true if (a. U b.)	= T
2. = true if 2	= T
II. = True if (A. U B. U C)	= T
A. = T if (1. U 2.)	= T
1. = True if (a. ∩ b.)	= T
2. = True if [a. U (b. ∩ c.)	= T
B. = T if B. =	= T
C. = T if (1. ∩ 2)	= T
1. = True if (a. ∩ b.)	= T
2. = True if 2	= T
III. = True if (A. ∩ B. ∩ C)	= T
A. = T if [(1. U 2.) U 3]	= T
1. = True if (a. U b.)	= T
2. = True if ?	= T
3. = True if [(a. ∩ b.) U c.]	= T

$\quad$ B. = T if (1. ∩ 2.) $\hspace{6em}$ = T
$\qquad$ 1. = true if 1. = $\hspace{6em}$ = T
$\qquad$ 2. = true if 2. = $\hspace{6em}$ = T

$\quad$ C. = T if (1. ∩ 2) $\hspace{6em}$ = T
$\qquad$ 1. = True if (a. ∩ b.) $\hspace{5em}$ = T
$\qquad$ 2. = True if 2 $\hspace{7em}$ = T

IV. = True if IV. $\hspace{9em}$ = T

Exercise 1

Policy: If you want to legally park your car at the school, you must:

I. Request a parking permit in writing and:
$\quad$ (a_1) Be a registered student and
$\quad$ (b_1) Display a student parking sticker in the car window; or
$\quad$ (c_1) Pay $5 for a daily parking pass; or

II. Be a graduate of the school and:
$\quad$ (a_2) Be a lifetime alumni member of the school; and
$\quad$ (b_2) Be current in fees due; and
$\quad$ (c_2) Display lifetime alumni member sticker in car window.

Use ∩ and U to write the above in a mathematical logical statement.

Suppose:
$\quad$ 1) a_1, a_2, c_1 are all True
$\quad$ 2) b_1, b_2, c_2 are all False

Will the person be able to legally park her car at the school?

Exercise 2

Consider the following statement (elements of the law):

Law = Arrest a person who is intoxicated, has no excuse, and is not on own property, or a person who shoots a gun in public with no excuse.

Let
    A = person is intoxicated
    B = has an excuse
    C = person is on own property
    D = person shoots gun

Use the variables provided and use ∩ and U to write the law in a mathematical logical statement. Evaluate whether you will arrest each of the following suspects if the following conditions exist?

Suspect 1:   A, D = true; B, C = false
Suspect 2:   A, C = false; B, D = true

Exercise 3

Consider the following statement (elements of the law):

Law = Arrest a person who is intoxicated and who shoots a gun, or a person who is not on his own property and shoots a gun with no excuse.

Let
    A = person is intoxicated
    B = has an excuse
    C = person is on own property
    D = person shoots gun

Use the variables provided and use ∩ and U to write the law in a mathematical logical statement.

Evaluate whether you will arrest each of the following suspects if the following conditions exist?

Suspect 1: A, D = true; B, C = false
Suspect 2: A, D = false; B, C = true

Exercise 4

Consider the following statement (elements of the law):

Law = Arrest a person who is intoxicated and in public, or a person who is intoxicated and shoots a gun.

Let
   A = person is intoxicated
   B = has an excuse
   C = person is on own property
   D = person shoots gun

Use the variables provided and use ∩ and U to write the law in a mathematical logical statement.

Evaluate whether you will arrest each of the following suspects if the following conditions exist?

Suspect 1: A, D = true; B, C = false
Suspect 2: A, B = false; C, D = true

REASONING

Deductive reasoning is based on drawing conclusions based on statements that are accepted are true (Smith, et al., 2006). A person employing deductive reasoning will start with a general principle and will apply the information to a specific case. In other words, deductive reasoning arrives at a specific conclusion based on generalizations. Below is an example of deductive reasoning.

All horses are mortal
Sonic is a horse
Therefore, Sonic is mortal
If the initial assumptions are incorrect, then the conclusion will be flawed. Criminal justice games that eliminate potential suspects based on *yes* or *no* answers are based on deductive reasoning.

Inductive Reasoning is based on an individual making observations and developing a generality based on those observations (Smith, et al., 2006). The observer detects patterns and then makes predictions based on those patterns. However, if the observations are proved false only one time, then the conclusions will be flawed. Below is an example of inductive reasoning.

Inductive reasoning: predict next response.

•   ••   •••   ••••   _____

It is easy to see how inductive reasoning can be used to reduce future criminal activity. Law enforcers have used inductive reasoning as a part of the totality of the circumstances to profile possible terrorists. For example, a traveler that comes from a geographical area that has been linked to terrorism, a traveler that has been caught in the past with a modified shipping manifest, the frequency that the traveler crosses the U.S. border, the number of foreign entry stamps that are posted in the traveler's passport, the foreign countries that have been visited by the traveler, a consignor that has been linked to terrorism, and a consignee that has been linked to terrorism are all factors that may be used cumulatively to determine whether a traveler should be inspected.

Totality of Circumstances

Suppose that the driver of a vehicle had bloodshot eyes, had slurred speech, had exhibited poor driving behaviors, had failed the field sobriety tests, had failed the alco-sensor test, and had admitted that he had consumed alcoholic beverages shortly before driving the vehicle. The defense attorney will attack the problem by asking the police officer in court whether a person who admits that he had been drinking is intoxicated. The police officer's answer will be "no." The defense attorney will then ask the police officer if a person is intoxicated because he has bloodshot eyes. The police officer's answer will be "no." The defense attorney will then ask the police officer if a person is intoxicated because he has slurred speech. The police officer's answer will be "no." The defense attorney will then ask the police officer if a person is intoxicated because he was speeding. The police officer's answer will be "no." The defense attorney will then ask the police officer if a person is intoxicated because he failed the one leg stand test. The police officer's answer will be "no." In sum, the police officer will have admitted that every test that the driver failed does not indicate that the driver was intoxicated. The defense attorney will attempt to get the jury to assess each factor individually because each factor, in and of itself, is not enough to show guilt beyond a reasonable doubt.

However, the prosecutor will address the situation by considering the totality of the circumstances (i.e., by linking all of the factors together). For example, if each variable is cumulative and adds 16% toward guilt, then admitting consuming alcoholic beverages, having bloodshot eyes, having slurred speech, speeding at a high rate, failing field sobriety tests, and failing the alco-sensor will all add up to 96% confidence of guilt. This may be enough to find the driver guilty beyond a reasonable doubt. Every factor considered will move the driver inward from one concentric ring to the next concentric ring. Once the driver hits the center of the target, that driver is intoxicated.

The jury may be more likely to convict a suspect if the prosecutor can distinguish the suspect from the jurors in a meaningful way. In other words, the jurors do not want to be arrested for just having bloodshot eyes. Thus, they may not convict a suspect unless the prosecutor can show that the suspect is different from them in a meaningful way. This is exactly what the prosecutor attempts to do as he continually moves inward from one concentric ring to another until he hits the center of the target. See Figure 1.

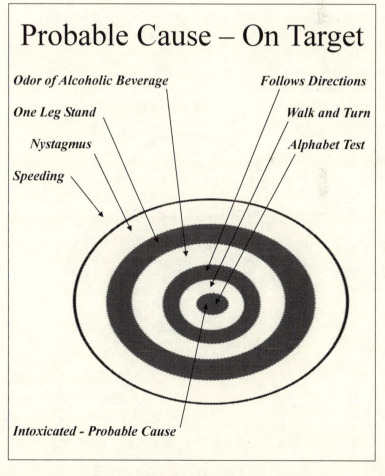

Figure 1. Totality of circumstances.

Venn Diagrams

Venn Diagrams can be used to see how different variables interact. The universe of interest below is designated by the rectangular boundary. In other words, everything inside of the rectangle below represents the population as described by age, sex, and hair color. The circles represent the specific variables of interest and can be considered Boolean variables. For example, either a person has blond hair or not blond hair (e.g., red hair is not blond). With three variables, there are 2^3 different combinations of variables. In other words, with three variables there are 8 different possibilities, which are represented by the 8 different colors in Figure 2. The 8 different colors are red, blue, yellow, orange, green, purple, black, and white (the part of the universe that is not inside any of the circles).

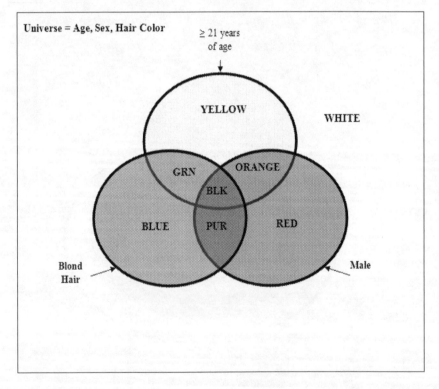

Figure 2. Venn diagram.

Table 1
Interpretation of Figure 2 Venn Diagram

Color	Representation		
Red	Male	< 21 years of age	Not blond hair
Blue	Female	< 21 years of age	Blond hair
Yellow	Female	≥ 21 years of age	Not blond hair
Orange	Male	≥ 21 years of age	Not blond hair
Green	Female	≥ 21 years of age	Blond hair
Purple	Male	< 21 years of age	Blond hair
Black	Male	≥ 21 years of age	Blond hair
White	Female	< 21 years of age	Not blond hair

Exercise: Venn Diagram

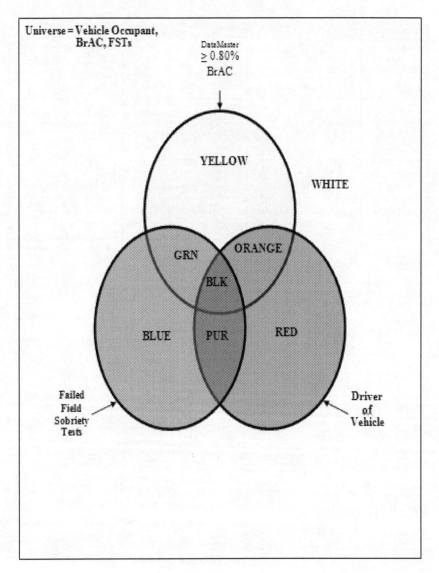

Figure 3. DUI Venn diagram.

INTERVIEWING, INTERROGATION & COMMUNICATION for LAW ENFORCEMENT

Complete the table below based on Figure 3. BrAC = Breath Alcohol Concentration; FSTs = Field Sobriety Tests.

Color	Representation (Driver, BrAC, and FSTs)		
Red			
Blue			
Yellow			
Orange			
Green			
Purple			
Black			
White			

Using Figure 3, indicate the color the matches the description.

Description	Color
Driver, DataMaster = 2.2 BrAC, passed Field Sobriety Tests	
Driver, DataMaster = 0.7 BrAC, passed Field Sobriety Tests	
Driver DataMaster = 0.7 BrAC, failed Field Sobriety Tests	
Driver DataMaster = 1.1 BrAC, failed Field Sobriety Tests	
Passenger, DataMaster = 1.9 BrAC, passed Field Sobriety Tests	
Passenger, DataMaster = 0.4 BrAC, passed Field Sobriety Tests	
Civilian DataMaster = 0.0 BrAC, failed Field Sobriety Tests	
Civilian DataMaster = 1.5 BrAC, failed Field Sobriety Tests	

Venn Diagram Exercises

Draw Venn Diagrams for the following. Define the three variables. Use the same 3 variables for each of the diagrams.

Of all SC residents, people from 21-50 years old, white female

Of all SC residents, people from 21-50 years old, everyone but white females

Of all SC residents, people not 21-50 years old, but who are white male

REFERENCES

Smith, D., Eggen, M., & St. Andre, R. (2006). *A transition to advanced mathematics* (6th ed.). Belmont, CA: Thomson Brooks/Cole

CHAPTER 4. MEANINGS OF TRUTH

What is Truth?

Before police officers can effectively serve the public, they must first understand the public. However, groups of individuals may experience life's events differently from other groups, and one community member may perceive reality differently from another community member. Although not all-inclusive, the following discussion describes several different perspectives of truth. A police officer who understands that there are different interpretations of reality will be able to better serve a greater population. Indeed, a single event may be considered acceptable in one culture yet taboo in another. In short, there are different perceptions of truth based on different references in which to interpret data. If an officer believes that his or her truth is the only truth, then that officer will be at a disadvantage in dealing with other people.

Positivists argue that the world has order and reality is something to be captured, studied, and understood (Hatch, 2002). Positivists rely on facts, laws and theories to make predictions. This can be accomplished via experiments, studies, and surveys. Positivists believe that the researcher is an objective and neutral data analyst.

Logical positivists argue that an objective reality exists and is independent of human mind and human behavior (Crossan, 2003). Logical positivists believe that the human experience of the world reflects an objective, independent reality (Weber, 2004). It is this reality that is used as the foundation for human knowledge in the building of a reality beyond the human mind. Logic positivism argues that people are objects whose behaviors can be reliable predicted (Crossan).

Post positivists argue that reality exists but cannot be fully understood or realized due to limited human intelligence (Hatch, 2002). Post positivists believe that knowledge is produced through generalizations and approximations via rigorously defined qualitative studies and low level statistics. To post positivists, the researcher is the data collection instrument.

Post modernists argue that knowledge is partial, fragmented, and contingent (McLaughlin & Muncie, 2006). Indeed, reality and science are socially constructed (Holliday, 2007). In other words, everything in life that is perceived is conditioned by culture, interactions, and institutions. Life's events occur by chance and, although humans are role-makers, their roles are unstable constructions (McLaughlin & Muncie). To post modernists, discourses are a linguistic coordinate system, and language is very influential.

Constructionists reject scientific realism and argue that there are multiple subjective realities and that absolute realities are unknowable (Glesne, 2006; Hatch, 2002). Constructionists believe that knowledge is symbolically constructed and that various realities are constructed via individual perspectives. Constructivists believe that reality is developed when individuals use their own personal beliefs, attitudes, and experiences to fit new information into what they already know. Reality is affected by the context in which an idea is taught and requires the individual to take an active role in constructing his own reality via reflection and interaction. To constructionists, investigators and participants determine truth through mutual agreement. The rules for various games are examples of individuals using social constructionism to understand unique situations.

Post structuralists argue that there is no truth and that order is created within an individual's mind in order to give meaning to the universe (Hatch, 2002). Post structuralists believe that events happen for no particular reason and that there are multiple realities, each being equally valued. Truth is subjective, local, and constantly changes.

Pragmatists believe that truth is defined by what is effective, useful, and brings about positive consequences (Mertens, 2005). Pragmatists avoid the metaphysical concepts of truth and reality because they involve useless debates and discussions. To pragmatists, truth is measured in terms of accomplishment and resolution.

Critical theorists and **feminists** argue that the world consists of historically situated structures that have a real impact on their lives of individuals based on race, social class, and gender and that knowledge is subjective and political (Hatch, 2002). Critical theorists focus on race and social class while feminists focus on gender. Critical theorists and feminists believe that there is a differential treatment of individuals based on race, social class, and gender and that these factors limit opportunities for certain groups of people. Specifically, the poor, minorities, and females are discriminated against in society and are generally at a disadvantage.

Feminist criminology is "a developing intellectual approach that emphasizes gender in criminology" (Schmalleger, 2007, p. G-11). According to feminists, men have dominated the field of criminal justice and have developed theories and written laws for the explanation and control of crime based on their own perspectives (Akers & Sellers, 2009). Indeed, traditional criminal justice theories make no distinction between men and women (Schmalleger). Although some theories may be applied to both men and women, such as the social bonding theory and the biological theory, the traditional criminology theory inadequately accounts for crimes committed by females (Akers & Sellers). Currently there is no single well-developed theory that explains female crime.

In order to better understand female criminality and to address the root causes of female crime, females need to be incorporated into the development of criminal theories (Schmalleger, 2007). After all, women make up about half of the U.S. population and having first-hand data is optimal (i.e., their perspective is essential). Because women obtain unique understandings of reality based upon their social and personal positions within society, their perceptions of crime may be different from men's perceptions of crime (Hammers & Brown, 2004). Thus, because the criminal justice system is predominately run by men, who use their own realities to make social policies, these policies may be ineffective involving half of the U.S. population (i.e., women) because they may be based on flawed assumptions (i.e., they assume that there is no behavioral difference between men and women). Indeed, women's perception of truth, which is created by their personal experiences involving social class, culture, and race, may not be adequately represented in the current criminal justice system (Weber, 2004).

For females to more effectively influence public policies, they must be equally represented within the state and federal government governments. Although this may be opposed by the men in power, laws could be passed that demand 50% of all positions in the state and federal governments to be held by females. By controlling 50% of the power, females may better influence laws and public policies.

Afrocentrism involves the process of using African principles and standards as the foundation of viewing African customs and conduct (Asante, 2009). Proponents of Afrocentrism state that African cultures and contributions have been downplayed and deliberately kept hidden under the so called *historic records*, which are controlled by Caucasians. The Afrocentrist asks what Africans would do if no Caucasians existed. Afrocentrists claim that African people are underdeveloped as a result of a) the lack of power and b) lack of control of the global economy.

According to Hall (2000), the U.S. Supreme Court's current equal protection doctrine exploits minority groups in America's increasingly multiracial society. The Supreme Court uses the image of a mosaic America to recast Caucasians as just another group competing against other groups. By transforming Caucasians into a victim group with the same moral and legal claims as minority groups, the Court's actions fail to effectively support programs that will help minorities, such as affirmative action, while providing stronger protections for white entitlements.

According to Dotzler (2000), solutions to racial problems can be solved but only if Caucasians face the fact that many of the current racial problems are due to the massive crime of slavery from long ago. By providing the truly disadvantaged people (i.e., African Americans) with major monetary reparations, African

Americans may be able to overcome their hardships. Indeed, African Americans face social environments on a daily basis that are not experienced by Caucasians. Thus, even if a Caucasian has never owned slaves, the U.S. social environment seems to favor and reward Caucasians over African Americans. In other words, Caucasians and African Americans do not experience America in the same manner. Hence, all Caucasians in the U.S. have benefited from slavery and the discrimination against African Americans.

It is difficult to solve past injustices when the injustices continue even today. Benton Harbor, Michigan is a good example of the struggle for resources and power between Caucasians and African Americans. According to Jesse Jackson, Benton Harbor's high unemployment rate, the lack of job opportunities, and African American residents' sense of hopelessness are all believed to have been created by Caucasians. Furthermore, many individuals feel that the judicial system, the police, and the financial system, which are all under white control, continue to abuse African Americans (Stevens, 2003).

Interpretivists argue that a person's perceptions and knowledge are shaped through lived experiences (Weber, 2004). Perceptions are shaped by individual experiences and are unique to each individual. Individuals constantly negotiate their perceptions with other people with whom they associate, reflecting an intersubjective reality.

Technical rationality supporters argue that scientific theory is more important than other theories and that this theory is essential in applying theory to practice (Papell & Skolnik, 1992). Indeed, the solving of professional complex problems depends upon the general principles derived from the basic and applied sciences. However, because professional practitioners often use art and intuition to solve complex and unpredictable problems, knowledge and action are causally connected but are inadequate in describing the competencies demonstrated by professionals. However, through reflection, people obtain information that allows them to continually adapt their behaviors to overcome obstacles.

Phenomenology focuses on lived experiences and the commonalities and shared meanings in those experiences. Phenomenology explores the essence of experience and gains a deeper understanding of an experience by uncovering hidden phenomena (Hatch, 2002). Phenomenology involves the fundamental nature of reality and it questions what can really be known about it (Ponterotto, 2005). In other words, phenomenology is concerned with human experience and it attempts to reveal phenomena that have been given meaning (Wimpenny & Gass, 2000). Because people are an integral part of the environment and each person has his or her own perspectives, reality is co-created with other individuals.

Hermeneutics study the interpretation of both verbal and nonverbal forms of communication. Hermeneutics interpret life's events through lived experiences and language (Dowling, 2004). Supporters of hermeneutics believe that investigators have biases that are an essential part in the evidence collection, analysis, and interpretation processes because the biases may serve as reference (Ponterotto, 2005). These will allow the investigator to effectively probe individuals for further information during an interview process, perhaps in the form of examples. Indeed, it is believed that these biases will improve an investigator's understanding of the information received from individuals (Dowling, 2004). However, because everyone has different lived experiences, they develop different truths (Chessick, 1990). Indeed, two investigators may evaluate the same information and may arrive at two different conclusions.

Ethnography seeks to describe a culture from the local or indigenous people's point of view (Berg, 2007). Data collection includes participant observation, participant interviewing, and artifact examination in order "to understand the cultural knowledge that group members use to make sense of the everyday experiences" (Hatch, 2002, p. 21). Examining the writings and the types of markers used in gravesites are examples of artifact data.

Table 2
Different Lenses of Truth

Lens	Beliefs
Positivists	World has order and reality is something to be captured, studied, and understood
Logical positivists	An objective reality exists and is independent of human mind and human behavior
Post positivists	Reality exists but cannot be fully understood or realized due to limited human intelligence
Post modernists	Everything in life that is perceived is conditioned by culture, interactions, and institutions; life's events occur by chance and, although humans are role-makers, their roles are unstable constructions
Constructionists	Reject scientific realism and argue that there are multiple subjective realities; absolute realities are unknowable
Post structuralists	There is no truth and order is created within an individual's mind in order to give meaning to the universe
Pragmatists	Truth is defined by what is effective, useful, and brings about positive consequences
Critical theorists and feminists	World consists of historically situated structures that have a real impact on the lives of individuals based on race, social class, and gender; knowledge is subjective and political
Afrocentrism	Uses African principles and standards as the foundation of viewing African customs and conduct; asks what Africans would do if no Caucasians existed
Interpretivists	A person's perceptions and knowledge are shaped through lived experiences; truth is unique to each individual
Technical rationalist	Scientific theory is more important than other theories and this theory is essential in applying theory to practice

Phenomenologist	Explores the essence of experience and gains a deeper understanding of an experience by uncovering hidden phenomena; reality is co-created with other individuals
Hermeneutics	Interprets life's events through lived experiences and language; because everyone has different lived experiences, each person develops a different truth
Ethnography	Describes a culture from the local or indigenous people's point of view

Deviance

Deviance is the source of innovation that results when a person takes one measurable step away from the normally accepted policies and infects the status quo. Deviance is an innovation virus that attacks traditional thinking at the core level. In other words, do not simply do something a particular way because it has always been done that way. Furthermore, what is classified as deviance may be influenced by culture.

In order to evaluate what is normal behavior and what is deviant behavior, some reference point is needed (Liska & Messner, 1999). Consequently, different interest groups struggle for power and the group that comes out on top, the dominate group, establishes what is considered normal behavior. Some actions are guided by what is defined as proper (acceptable) social etiquette and cultural customs, and some are defined by laws. Although many people may violate accepted cultural customs of etiquette at one point or another, this is considered normal if the behaviors are not continued for prolonged periods of time. If the behaviors are practiced over prolonged periods, then those people are labeled deviant.

Some rules are considered serious enough to write down and to enforce, punishing those who do not conform to these specific guidelines. The problem with laws is that they are not universally and evenly applied to all persons (Liska & Messner, 1999). Even though law enforcement knows that certain persons commit crimes, charges are not always filed. Even if charges are files, there is a good chance that prosecutors will dismiss some of the cases for one reason or another (caseload, personal acquaintance, etc.). Finally, even if a person is arrested and convicted of a crime, there is no consistency in sentencing. Outside factors, such as jail space availability, the status of the convicted person within the community, and the community's reaction to the conviction may all affect a judge's decision on a case-by-case basis.

Ethical Systems: What is Good Behavior?

According to the Declaration of Independence, the U.S. government derives its power from the individuals that it governs (U.S. Citizenship and Immigration Services, 2008). Indeed, because there are about 400 U.S. residents for every full-time sworn police officer, law enforcement requires that people voluntarily comply with the law and assist with law enforcement efforts (Reaves, 2007; U.S. Department of Labor, 2009). Furthermore, because the Posse Comitatus Act of 1878 generally prohibits the U.S. military from engaging in domestic law enforcement, and because the U.S. Constitution protects the public against unreasonable searches and seizures (i.e., protects privacy), local police are ill equipped to handle criminal problems alone (Leventhal, 2005). Residents are stakeholders in maintaining a peaceful society and they must take an active part in promoting pro-social behaviors (Carter, 2002). However, the definition of good behaviors is relative. In short, before individuals can promote pro-social behaviors, a reference point is needed to define good behavior.

Ethics is the study of human conduct in the light of set ideas of right and wrong (i.e., morals) (Pollock, 2004). However, there are different ideas of right and wrong in which to judge good behavior. Consequently, different ethical systems answer the question, "What is good?" in different manners. **Moral principles** are set ideas of right and wrong that form the basis of ethical behaviors.

Deontological ethical system is concerned with the intent of the actor or goodwill as the element of morality (Pollock, 2004). The consequence of the action is unimportant. For example, the assassination of Hitler might be unethical under a deontological system because killing is always wrong. For police officers, shooting a murderer who is about to kill again is unethical.

Teleological ethical system is concerned with the consequences of an action to determine goodness (Pollock, 2004). For example, the assassination of Hitler might be ethical under a teleological system because the consequence may save many lives. For police officers, shooting a murderer who is about to kill again is ethical because it may save an innocent life.

Each ethical system answers the question, "What is good?" (Pollock, 2004). In other words, good behavior is relative and depends on the reference system (i.e., morals) used to judge behavior. For example, a behavior may be considered good according to one ethical system and bad according to another ethical system. However, not all behaviors are subject to ethical judgment; only those behaviors that are performed by humans acting with free will and that impact other people are subject to ethical judgment. In addition, a particular act may be defined as bad behavior for one person but not bad behavior for another person. For example, a child under the age of reason and a person that is mentally incapacitated may lack the knowledge and intent of wrong doing. Therefore, good behavior is relative. In addition, although personal values may influence individual moral beliefs and behaviors, not all personal values have ethical components. For example, the act of valuing one color automobile over another is ethically neutral and is based solely on personal opinion.

Criteria are used to decide what is right or wrong (Pollock, 2004). There are various ethical systems that use different criteria to evaluate the morality of an action. An action that may be considered moral by one ethical system may be considered immoral according to the standards of another ethical system. For example, although some people may go out their way to kill spiders and think nothing of it, others may view such acts as cruelty to animals and demand criminal punishment. Some of the basic ethical systems that shape moral and ethical principles include a) ethical formalism, b) utilitarianism c) act utilitarianism, d) rule utilitarianism, e) religious ethics, f) natural law, g) ethics of virtue, h) ethics of care, i) egoism, j) enlightened egoism, k) ethical relativism, l) cultural relativism, and m) situational ethics.

Ethical formalism ethical system states that good is defined by a person's goodwill and by doing one's duty (Pollock, 2004). Good actions are based on categorical imperatives: (a) act as if the behavior will become a universal law, (b) do not use people for one's own purposes, and (c) act consistent with universal laws. For example, a lie is only a lie if the recipient is led to believe or has a right to believe that he or she is being told the truth. For instance, not telling a car thief that a bait car is being used to capture car thieves is not unethical. However, ethical formalism is problematic when there are conflicting duties (e.g., judge's order versus department policy).

Utilitarianism ethical system determines the goodness of an act by a benefit-to-cost ratio (Kraska, 2004; Pollock, 2004). The needs of the many outweigh the needs of the few. In other words, as the benefit-to-cost ratio increases, the better the act will be perceived. For example, it is okay to arrest innocent people by mistake if it solves a bigger problem.

Act Utilitarianism ethical system determines the goodness of a particular act by measuring the utility of the specific act without regard for future acts (Pollock, 2004). For example, it is not unethical to steal food when a person is hungry and has no other way to get food.

Rule Utilitarianism ethical system determines the goodness of an act by measuring the utility of the act when made into a rule for behavior (Pollock, 2004). For example, it is unethical to steal food when a person is hungry and has no other way to get food because this will result in lawlessness if people are allowed to steal food anytime that they are hungry and cannot afford food. In addition, it may be unethical not to engage in high speed chases because this may encourage people to flee.

Religious ethics ethical system determines the goodness of an act based on the concepts of good and evil and what is good is based on God's will (Pollock, 2004). Ethics are determined by individual conscious, religious authorities, and Holy Scripture. However, problems with religious ethics are that no one may ever know exactly what the will of God is and there are current controversies within and between religions. For example, it may not be unethical or illegal for Native Americans to consume contraband mushrooms for religious practices.

An example of a controversy within a religion is the use of deceit to save a life. For example, should a person lie to save an innocent child who is being sought by a gunman? Some Christian thinkers may argue for the existence of a higher ethic, namely love, and that lying to save a life is okay because it is based on good intent and love (Father F. Rogers, personal communication on 6/26/2014). If one looks at this situation as the *lesser of two evils*, then the greatest evil would be to contribute to the intended victim's death. In this case, if a lie allows the intended victim to get away safely, or if the gunman's threat can be neutralized, then a lie would be the *lesser of two evils*. The lie would have the effect of preserving life, which is a greater good and, therefore, justified.

However, from a biblical perspective, one does not have to answer the gunman's question at all (Father F. Rogers, personal communication on 6/26/2014). A person can choose to remain silent and to face the consequences. In this case, a person may choose to die rather than to sin (e.g., by lying or by contributing to the harm of another person). Hence, one need not lie. In Christian ethics, self-preservation is not the ultimate good. Indeed, death is preferable to sin.

Natural law ethical system states that there is a universal set of rights and wrongs but without reference to specific supernatural beings (Pollock, 2004). What is good is determined by what is natural to humans (e.g., socialization and the right to life) and is free of passion. Indeed, the founding fathers might be described as natural law practitioners. However, identifying what is consistent and congruent with natural inclinations of humankind is a fundamental problem of this ethical system. This is evidenced by the changing of laws and the developing of new laws (e.g., use of force policies).

Ethics of virtue ethical system determines the goodness of an act based on the attempt to achieve happiness, such as living a good life and achieving life's goals (Pollock, 2004). Good behavior is based on the golden mean, which is the median between extreme states of character. For example, absolute police powers and civil liberties oppose one another. Effective law enforcement must compromise between the two. It is based on a person's character and includes factors such as honesty, humility, and temperance.

Ethics of care ethical system determines goodness of an act based meeting needs and preserving and enriching relationships (Pollock, 2004). Actions are taken based on connecting with other people, caring for the needs of other people, and being aware of other people. For example, involving a single event in which battery threats were made, instead of arresting the offender for intimidation (a felony), the police officer may arrest the offender for disorderly conduct (a misdemeanor), provocation (a civil infraction), or simply separate the parties (a warning). By taking the minimum enforcement action necessary in order to achieve peace, relationships will be enhanced and labeling may be prevented.

Egoism ethical system claims that good results from pursuing self-interests (Pollock, 2004). However, every person acting in his or her own best interests is not logical or feasible and this will result in great conflict. An example of egoism in law enforcement is when police officers write unnecessary tickets in order to meet quotas for good performance reviews.

Enlightened egoism claims that it is in one's long-term best interest to help others so that they will learn to help themselves (Pollock, 2004). For example, a police officer may refuse to change a flat tire on a car occupied with capable adults and may instead instruct them on how to change the tire themselves. Having the occupants change the tire themselves may prove valuable in the future if they get another flat tire and no assistance is available. However, community members may expect the police to provide full and immediate service and this may result in complaints. As a way to comply with departmental policy, police officers in the field may offer full service in terms of providing a wrecker service. If drivers are dissatisfied with that response due to time and cost, this may damage police-community relations.

Ethical relativism ethical system determines what is good or bad based on the individual or group (Pollock, 2004). For example, community members in a poor region may hunt and fish without purchasing the proper licenses. Also, prostitution may be encouraged and institutionalized in certain societies.

Cultural relativism defines good as that which contributes to the health and survival of society (Pollock, 2004). For example, men in certain cultures may kill their spouses if their wives expose their faces to strangers. However, U.S. law enforcers may sometimes need to identify these females. This situation is often encountered at the U.S. borders.

Situational ethics ethical system states that there are few universal truths and that different situations call for different responses (Pollock, 2004). Thus, the same action may be right in some situations and wrong in other situations. For example, it may be ethical for a person to violate the speed laws if he or she is racing an injured person to the hospital. However, the same action may be unethical if no such emergency exists.

Ethics in Law Enforcement		
Utilitarianism Good is based on a benefit-cost ratio. Example of good behavior: arresting an innocent person in order to deter crime in general. 	**Types of Ethical Systems** • **Ethical Formalism** • **Utilitarianism** • **Religious** • **Natural Law** • **Ethics of Virtue** • **Ethics of Care** • **Egoism** • **Cultural Relativism** • **Situational Ethics**	**Ethics in Law Enforcement** What is good behavior? *Ethics is the study of set ideas of right and wrong. However, there are different ideas of right and wrong in which to judge good behavior. Consequently, different ethical systems answer the question, "What is good?" in different manners.*
Religious Good is based on God's will. Example of good behavior: always providing complete and truthful information, regardless of the cost. 	**Ethical Formalism** Good is based on goodwill and intent. Example of good behavior: catching a fleeing felon, even if the violator gets hurt. 	

Figure 4. Types of ethical systems.

Ethics in Law Enforcement		
Natural Law Good is based on a universal set of rights (i.e., what is natural). Example of good behavior: acting in accordance with the U.S. Constitution. 	**Ethics of Care** Good is based on the needs of those concerned. Example of good behavior: always arresting males who are involved in domestic violence in order to protect female victims. 	**Cultural Relativism** Good is based on what promotes the health and survival of society. Example of good behavior: Middle Eastern women refusing to show their faces in public.
Ethics of Virtue Good is based on compromise. Example of good behavior: using non-intrusive X-Ray machines to search for contraband.  X-Ray	**Egoism** Good is based on what benefits the actor. Example of good behavior: writing a lot of tickets to meet the monthly quota for a good performance review. 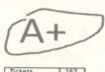	**Situational Ethics** Good is based on the particular situation at a particular time. Example of good behavior: speeding in order to get to the hospital to save a life. 

Figure 1 (continued). Types of ethical systems.

Deceiving Suspects: Is it Ethical for Police?

Ethical Formalism: condemned, due to violation of categorical imperative; lying would become rule for all people

Religious: condemned, due to lying; God is truth; possibly justified, if can argue lesser of two evils

Rule Utilitarianism: condemned, because it may undermine long-term system of laws

Utilitarianism: justified, if benefits outweigh costs to society as a whole

Natural Law: justified, as long as civil rights are not violated

Ethics of Virtue: justified, if crimes are severe and if methods are moderate

Ethics of Care: justified, if it protects victims

Egoism: justified, if profitable to police officer

Act Utilitarianism: justified, if benefits outweigh costs of methods employed (serious crimes may be more accepting of deceit)

Enlightened Egoism: justified, if long-term benefits are greater than loss of trust in police

Cultural Relativism: justified, as long as accepted by culture

Situational Ethics: justified, if police officer can effectively articulate reasons for deception in the particular case (evaluated on a case-by-case basis)

Ethics

Canons of Ethics

- Officers shall uphold the Constitution
- Officers shall use ethical procedures
- Officers shall discharge duties as a public trust
- Officers shall conduct their private lives with integrity
- Officers shall hold freedom as a paramount precept
- Officers shall maintain the integrity and competence of the profession
- Officers shall cooperate with other officials to achieve law enforcement objectives
- Officers shall observe confidentiality
- Officers shall not compromise their integrity by accepting gratuities

Test of Ethics

There is a test of ethics. First, the end must be justified as good (e.g., the conviction of criminals) (Pollock, 2004). Second, the means must be a plausible way to achieve the ends (e.g., police officers must articulate their actions). Third, there is no less intrusive method to achieve the same end (e.g., radiation portal monitors at the U.S. border). Finally, the means must not undermine some other equal or greater end (e.g., community members losing faith in the legal system).

Ethical Dilemmas

Ethical dilemmas arise as a result of conflicting core ethical values and may be inherent in some situations (Perez & Moore, 2002). Situations that involve unfair advantage, conflicts between personal values and institutional goals, power differentials, abuse of power, breaches of confidentiality, hidden agendas, impropriety or boundary violations, multiple roles, and differences in perceptions may generate ethical dilemmas. Ethical dilemmas can sometimes be foreseen by evaluating if particular signals exist.

These signals may involve whether laws or professional standards are violated, whether there is internal conflict and doubt about the issue, whether anyone can be harmed as a result of the decision, whether the decision is objective, whether there is strong opposition to the decision, whether the decision can be revealed without hesitation, and whether anyone else would be willing to make the decision. When conflict arises, professional, social, and economic pressures can make ethical decision-making difficult.

Integrity has many gray areas and is a complex subject that is not always easily defined. Generally, however, integrity is a positive, proactive system of values that is constant over time and consists of fairness, honesty, sincerity, and doing what seems to be the proper thing (Dreisbach, 2008; Harberfeld, 2006; Hess & Bennett, 2007). Several standards that may be used to evaluate the integrity of police conduct are a) fair access, b) public trust, c) safety and security versus enforcement, d) teamwork, and e) objectivity. Fair access relates to fair and open access of police services to all citizens. Public trust relates to the trust that the civilians give to the police officers in exchange for their right to enforce laws. Safety and security versus enforcement relates to police officers using discretion in balancing the goal of maintaining order with the goal of enforcing the law. Teamwork relates to police officers who are expected to coordinate, communicate, and cooperate with others in the law enforcement system. Objectivity relates to police officers who are expected to be impartial and a disinterested party.

English, Logic, and Quantifiers

Quantitative v. Qualitative Studies

Quantitative investigations are scientific, objective, and effective in describing phenomena in terms of magnitude (Balian, 1988). Quantitative investigations use numeric values and statistics to identify patterns, to objectively quantify relationships between variables, and to make predictions. In addition, because larger sample sizes are used, data can be generalized to larger populations. However, numeric values are ineffective in describing the subjective interpretations of human emotions (Wakefield, 1995). Because individuals have unique lived experiences and their realities are based on their own perceptions, a single objective truth is unattainable; indeed, there are multiple realities when dealing with perceptions. Thus, quantitative investigations are ineffective for the reconstruction of meanings. In short, quantitative studies ask **how** variables are related but not **why** they are related. For example, a quantitative research question may ask, *Is there a relationship between ice cream sales and the murder rate?* By the way, there is a positive relationship.

When investigating a topic that cannot be quantitatively predicted, such as human nature, qualitative investigations are most effective. Indeed, qualitative investigations are preferred for describing and interpreting experiences in context specific settings because each person's reality is construed in his or her own mind; qualitative research attempts to reveal the meanings that participants have given to various phenomena (Adams, 1999; Ponterotto, 2005). This kind of information cannot be attained through quantitative analysis and requires probing the participants for greater detail through in-depth interviews using open ended questions. In short, qualitative studies ask **why** variables are related but not **how** they are related. For example, a qualitative research question may ask, *Why do you feel that ice cream sales are related to the murder rate?*

Falsification

Theories are an organized body of principles and concepts intended to explain specific phenomena (Leedy & Ormrod, 2005). A police officer can test a theory to determine if it is a viable explanation of a phenomenon by developing and statistically verifying a conjecture concerning the relationship between the variables. However, because human knowledge is limited, hypotheses cannot actually be proved true (Shields, 2007). For example, we will never know for sure if any of the many extraneous variables have impacted a particular relationship between known variables (a person may appear to have committed a crime, but appearances can be deceiving). However, we can demonstrate that relationships do not exist between variables (the person was already dead at the time of the crime and could not have committed the crime). Thus, because relationships cannot be proved true, an attempt is made to prove them false. This is called falsification. For example, instead of proving that a defendant is truly guilty of a crime, a prosecutor attempts to prove with a certain confidence level that the defendant is not innocent of the crime. For example, if there is a 95% confidence level that a defendant is not innocent, then jurors may find the defendant guilty. In other words, if hypotheses are not proved false, then they are accepted as true at a certain confidence level. This implies that there is an acceptable level of being wrong. Thus, innocent people may sometimes be wrongly convicted.

For a trial verdict, there are two possible ways to make a mistake. One way is to convict an innocent person. The other way is to set a guilty person free. A juror can ensure that one type of error is never made, but this will require either a) always setting defendants free or b) always convicting defendants. For either case, there is no need for a trial. On the one hand, if one juror wants to ensure that he never makes a mistake by letting a guilty person go free, then that juror must always vote guilty. His reasoning may be that the police do not arrest innocent persons. With this reasoning, there is no need for a trial because everyone arrested will be convicted by this type of juror. On the other hand, if another juror wants to ensure that she never makes a mistake by sending an innocent person to jail, then that juror must always vote not guilty. With this reasoning, there is no need for a trial because everyone arrested will be set free by this type of juror. Thus, in both cases, there is no need for a trial. However, there are trials in the U.S., which means that there is compromise and the chance of making mistakes.

Negotiations are required among jury members. If a mistake is made, then the question is whether U.S. jurors want to error on the side of convicting innocent individuals or to error on the side of setting guilty individuals free. By design, the U.S. legal system is set up to error on the side of letting guilty persons go free. A conviction is based on guilt beyond a reasonable doubt; an acquittal is not based on innocence beyond a reasonable doubt. As indicated in *Figure 5*, because decisions are based on confidence levels and negotiations, innocent individuals will sometimes be convicted. This is an inherent part of the U.S. legal system. Notice that this argument is not influenced by the penalty of the conviction, such as the death penalty. In other words, it is expected that innocent persons will sometimes be convicted and will be put to death.

Levels of Proof

Probable Cause (51%)	Clear and Convincing Evidence	Beyond Reasonable Doubt		Absolute Guilt (100%)
↑	↑	↑	←——→	↑
Arrest	Overturn Warrant	Conviction	Acceptable chance of wrongful convictions	Truly Guilty

Figure 5. Acceptable chance of wrongful conviction. (not to scale)

Assumptions

Most decisions depend on assumptions, and we will never know if all of the assumptions are 100% accurate. Although we may be confident about a decision, we cannot know with absolute certainty that the decision is correct. However, understanding the assumptions that were relied upon in making a decision is important because the assumptions may change, which may impact an objective decision. In law enforcement, if the assumptions change, then police officers must be willing to modify their position.

Correlation does not mean causation (Leedy & Ormrod, 2005). Just because two events are highly correlated does not mean that one event causes the other. For example, it does not get dark at night because the sun is on the other side of the earth (Verma, 2005). The sun is an additional light source, but it is not the only light source in the sky. Thus, in this case, a wrong assumption may lead one to believe that the lack of sunlight causes it to get dark at night.

Being not false is not the same thing as being true. In order words, if something is not negative, this does not mean that it is positive (i.e., it may be neutral). For example, if a basketball team has played 10 games and is undefeated, what is the team's record? It is unknown because the team may have tied any number of the 10 games. If by some chance the team had tied all 10 games, a defense attorney may claim that the team has never lost, while the prosecutor may claim that the team has never won. Both statements are true, yet they seem to be contradictory. However, the two statements do not necessarily conflict with one another. This is how statistics can be misleading. Should consumers buy the same shoes used by the team? Either decision may be argued and supported with statistical data.

Police officers need to detect diversionary flares (i.e., deception) that are intended to lead the officer off track. The way to do this is to get the sought after answers to their questions via active voice questions and answers. For example, if an individual answers questions via double negatives or through misplaced modifiers, the officer must clarify the answers by asking direct questions that elicit active voice responses. See *Table 3*.

Table 3
Interpretation of Sport Statement

	Interpretation of Results		
	Won (+)	**Tied (neutral)**	**Lost (-)**
Suspect statement			
I have not lost =	x	x	
I have not won =		x	x
I have won =	x		
I have lost =			x

It should be pointed out in Table 3 that *I have won ≠ I have not lost*. For a second example, suppose you state that the sky was not cloudy all day. All day means 100% of the time. Therefore, you are stating that it was not cloudy 100% of the time; it could have been cloudy 0% of the time up to 99% of the time. In other words, it could have been sunny 1% of the time up to 100% of the time. If you are writing a police report and it is important that the sky was sunny during the crime, stating that the sky was not cloudy all day may be detrimental to your case. See *Table 4*.

Table 4
Interpretation of Weather Statement

	Interpretation of Statement		
	Sunny all day	**Cloudy up to 99% of time**	**Cloudy all day (100% of time)**
Not cloudy all day =	x	x	

Now suppose that a police officer arrives at a crash scene. A car that was parked near a curb pulled out into traffic and was struck by another car headed in the same direction. If the police officer asks a witness to the crash what she saw, and if she states that she did not see the driver in the parked car look before he pulled out into traffic, the statement is basically valueless. See *Table 5*.

Table 5
Interpretation of Witness Statement

	Interpretation of Witness Statement		
	I saw driver look	I was not looking	I saw driver not look
Witness statement provided =		X	X
Answer sought (two good responses) =	X		X

Notice the first four words: *"I did not see."* This is problematic because the police officer wants to know what the witness did see. Indeed, the witness statement never claimed that the driver of the parked car did not look before he pulled out into traffic. The witness statement would be true even if the witness was not looking in the right direction at the time of the crash. It would be wrong to assume that the witness was looking in the right direction. To argue in court that the witness saw the driver of the parked car not look would be changing the truth value of the witness statement. In short, a police officer needs to be careful about relying on assumptions. Get responses that provide direct and positive answers.

In addition, police officers must not assume that all individuals define words in the same way. For example, consider the following statements.

Unclear: Where were you during dinner?
Clear: Where were you during supper?

The above sentence that mentions dinner is problematic because dinner is not time dependent. Although supper is the last meal of the day, dinner is the largest meal of the day. Thus, for some people, dinner may not be the same as supper. In other words, if you were to question a suspect about his or her alibi during dinner time, you may be thinking about 5:00 pm and the individual may be speaking about noon. Therefore, seek precise times of day that do not have different meanings to different individuals.

Misplaced and dangling modifiers

Grammar is important in police writing because an officer's credibility is linked to his or her written reports. If police officers make mistakes in their reports, the officers should expect defense attorneys to ask them if they have performed their jobs to the best of their ability. On the one hand, if the officers claim that they have done their best work, then mistakes in their reports will make them appear incompetent or dishonest. On the other hand, if the officers claim that they have not done their best work, then mistakes in their reports will make them appear lazy and uncaring. Thus, police officers need to use proper grammar when writing police reports.

Although some mistakes in grammar may make police officers look incompetent, lazy, or dishonest in court, other mistakes in grammar may significantly change the meaning of a police report. For example, because a misplaced modifier incorrectly modifies the wrong word, and because a dangling modifier has no referent in a sentence, misplaced and dangling modifiers may alter the meaning of a sentence. Thus, adjectives and adverbs should be placed as closely as possible to the words that they are supposed to modify and active voice should be employed (American Psychological Association, 2010). This may help eliminate any unintended meanings. In this case, the police officers should expect defense attorneys to ask them if they write true and accurate reports. If the officers state that their reports are true and accurate, then the defense attorney may argue that the reports should be accepted at face value, especially if misplaced modifiers change the meanings of sentences in the police reports to mean what the defense attorneys want them to mean. However, if the officers state that their reports are not true and accurate, then the reports will have little value, the officers' credibility will be ruined, and the officers could be criminally charged with filing false police reports.

Consider the following example. Suppose a man and his wife are at school and he tells her that he loves her.

Incorrect statement: He told his wife that he loves her at the school.
Correct statement: While at the school, he told his wife that he loves her.

The incorrect statement does not indicate that he loves his wife, but it does indicate that he loves his wife's presence at the school. This would be appropriate, for example, if his wife worked at a school and he did not want her to quit her job and to leave the school.

Incorrect statement: Running out of gas, she walked to the gas station.
Correct statement: She walked to the gas station because her car ran out of gas.

The incorrect sentence indicates that she ran out of gas (not her car). This may imply that she was jogging, became tired, and started to walk.

Logic: Conditional Statements

Although an if-then statement may be true, the converse of an if-then statement may not necessarily be true (Smith et al., 2006). In other words, the converse of a conditional statement is not necessarily true. For example, research shows that aggressive behaviors in children are good predictors of adult criminality (Huesmann & Eron, 1992; Huesmann et al., 2002; Miller-Johnson et al., 2005). Thus, if aggression is present then there is crime. However, if crime is present does not necessarily mean that there is aggression (e.g., there may be other reasons why people are arrested).

Suppose a father states to his daughter that if she behaves, then he will give her candy. Then suppose his daughter misbehaves. The only guarantee that the father made was that he will act in a certain way if his daughter behaves. However, the father never addressed what he will do if his daughter misbehaves. Thus, if his daughter misbehaves, the father's actions will be truthful whether or not his gives his daughter candy. The father will only be untruthful if his daughter behaves and he does not give her candy. See *Table 6*.

Table 6
Interpretation of Conditional Statement

Guarantee	If my daughter behaves...	If my daughter misbehaves...
If my daughter behaviors, then I will give her candy	Then a truthful statement dictates that I give her candy	Then a truthful statement allows me to either give her candy or to not give her candy

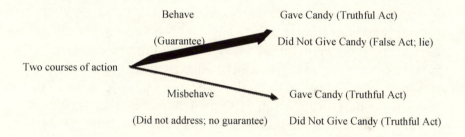

Figure 6. Interpretation of conditional statement.

Let us apply this argument to a law. A U.S. visa is an entry document issued by the U.S. government that allows a non-citizen to seek entry into the U.S. (LexisNexis, 2005). A non-American passport is issued by the person's native country and is a travel document that is used for identification and proof of citizenship. **Suppose federal law states that a particular person cannot enter the U.S. without a passport.** Thus, if the person has entered the U.S., then the person must have had a passport (this is a true statement). However, it is not necessarily true that if the person has a passport, then the person will be allowed to enter the U.S. The law states that not having a passport will prevent the person's entry into the U.S., but the law does not address what will happen if the person does have a passport. See *Table 7*. Thus, understanding the converse of conditional statements is important in law enforcement.

Table 7
Interpretation of Law

| | Passport Law ||
	If have, then may enter	If do not have, then may not enter
Foreign Passport		x

Quantifiers

Because conditional statements can be objectively assessed by turning them into mathematic equations, police officers need to understand the difference between existential and universal quantifiers. It is important for a police officer not to change the meaning of a statement by changing an existential-quantifier statement into a universal-quantifier statement and vice versa. For an open sentence that uses an existential quantifier, the sentence is true if the truth set is nonempty (Smith et al., 2006). This means that a statement is true if the statement is true at least one time. However, for an open sentence that uses a universal quantifier, the sentence is true only if the truth set is the entire universe. This means that a statement is true only if the statement is true all of the time. For example, if a suspect stated that he likes beer, this statement is true if the suspect likes at least one type of beer. Thus, for the suspect to be lying, an officer will have to prove that the suspect dislikes all types of beer. However, if the suspect stated that he likes all beer, then the officer only needs to show that the suspect dislikes one type of beer for the suspect to be considered untruthful.

Suppose that the signs on a roadway indicate that speed is controlled via RADAR. Then suppose you receive a speeding ticket but the officer used VASCAR to clock your speed. Your argument is that the ticket is invalid because the officer used

VASCAR and the signs indicate that RADAR will be used. **What will you have to do in court to show that the signs are not truthful and what does the officer have to do to show that the signs are truthful?** The signs are truthful if at least one officer in the area uses RADAR. Thus, the officer only has to show that one officer in the area uses RADAR. You, on the other hand, will have to show that every officer in the area does not use RADAR.

Subsets

A set is a group of objects that follow a rule or that have something in common (Large, 2007). A subset is a set that belongs to a larger set. Suppose a friend states to you on January 1 that you may borrow his car any day of the year, whenever you want. Then suppose you borrow the car on July 7 and get pulled over by the police. The police charge you with driving another person's car without permission. The police officer asks you, "Did you have permission to drive the car specifically on July 7?" The police officer wants a *yes* or *no* answer. The correct answer is yes, because July 7 is a part of the year. In other words, the year includes July 7 and you had permission to drive the car on every day of the year.

Suppose John has $20. True or false, John has $10. The answer is true because $10 is a subset of $20. If John has $20, then John has $10.

Consequence of Wrong Assumptions

Magic shows are successful because they challenge the viewers' assumptions. The viewers are led to believe that something is true when it is not true. The next time that you watch a magic trick, try to determine what assumptions you are making.

Assumptions are important because a solution that is based on the wrong assumptions may be ineffective. For example, the effectiveness of the sex offender community notification process relies on the assumptions of the labeling and deterrence theories. Authorities rely on labeling and deterrence in order to get sex predators to **rationally** decide not to commit additional sex crimes due to the high cost. First, people learn to identify other individuals in the way that they are labeled (Vold, Bernard, & Snipes, 2002). Thus, the labeling theory indicates that sex offenders will be easily recognized by local community members if sex offenders are publically labeled and if their crimes are advertised. In regards to Megan's law, it is assumed that all sex offenders are alike and, consequently, they are all labeled as a homogenous group of sex predators (Corrigan, 2006). However, different types of sex offenders are not all motivated by the same reasons. Hence, a single program designed to modify their various behaviors will not work. Second, Megan's law relies on the idea that most sex offenders are strangers to their victims and that offenders are **mentally disturbed** predators who attack without warning or reason. In other words, mentally disturbed predators are expected to make rational decisions (i.e., rationally decide that the cost of crime is too high). In addition, most sex crimes against children are committed by friends or family members and not by strangers. Thus, community notification efforts are ineffective because they are not in alignment with the problem. Because the research findings do not support the argument that community notification deters stigmatized sex offenders from committing repeat sex offenses, then perhaps programs that rely on theories that support the argument that sex offenders are mentally disturbed need to be investigated (Langevin et al., 2004; Zevitz, 2006). In other words, limited resources may be better spent on programs that address mental illnesses instead of labeling and rational choice. As stated earlier, the solution to the problem must be in alignment with the theory used to explain the crime. See *Table 8* for various criminal theories and their limitations.

Table 8
Various Theories and their Limitations (Akers & Seller, 2009; Fay, 1987; Sower, & Gist, 1994; Sower, Holland, Tiedke, & Freeman, 1957; Turvey & Petherick, 2009)

Theory	Description	Critique
Rational Choice Theory / Deterrence Theory	People freely choose their behaviors. Individuals evaluate the benefits versus costs ratio for each potential course of action. If the benefits are greater than costs, then the decision to perform that act is favorable. Rational choice emphasizes the benefits and deterrence theory emphasizes the costs. Deterrence Theory relies on three factors: Celerity, Severity, & Certainty of Punishment	Overemphasizes importance of individual choice; social factors, such as poverty, are dismissed; does not adequately consider emotions; target hardening causes displacement of crime; factors of deterrence may promote crime if all three factors are not effectively implemented simultaneously (certain, severe, and swift punishment)
Routine Activities Theory	Crime occurs when three elements converge: motivated offenders, attractive targets, and the absence of capable guardians.	Level of motivation is not well defined; because attractive targets and the absence of capable guardians are emphasized more than the motivated offender, identifying and measuring the motivation of offenders is avoided.
Neoclassical Theory	Being tough on crime and retribution will curtail future crime.	Does not explain why crime decreases in areas without tough on crime policies; crime rate reductions may be due to demographic changes in the population.

Biological Theory	First, human beings are biological creatures who are born with certain hardware, such as a brain that controls thought and behavioral development. Because the brain uses a complex chemical-electrical process during the processing of information, any impairment in this process may interfere with the effective operation of the brain. Body shape, diet, hormones, environmental pollution, and chemical factors cause crime.	Denies role of free will; not everyone who is exposed to the same chemicals behave in the same way; why is there no specific diet to cure crime? Increased exposure to pollution and chemicals has not increased the crime rate; cannot explain crime in different parts of the country.
Age-graded Theory	There is a positive relationship between social capital and pro-social behaviors; positive relations are developed over time and lead to pro-social behaviors and reduced crime.	Positive relationships are subjective; some positive relations may provide greater opportunity to commit crime; does not explain why social capital does not prevent everyone from committing crime.
Sociobiology Theory	Behaviors are embedded in the process of natural selection and human survival; crime is the result of territorial struggles.	Fails to consider culture, social learning, and personal experiences; equates humans to animals.
Psychoanalytic Perspective Theory	Crime is the result of poorly developed superegos.	Lacks scientific support; elements of theory were not applied to a wide context for society as a whole.

Modeling Theory	Individuals learn behaviors by observing others who are in the vicinity; individuals are rewarded for aggressive behaviors.	Lacks comprehensive explanatory power.
Behavior Theory	The surrounding environment impacts behavior.	Dismisses cognition in human behavior; punishments may not deter martyrs; some groups believe that punishments are status-enhancing.
Self-control Theory	Individuals have low self-esteem and seek immediate gratification; individuals have little patience and are frustrated easily, which lead to conflict.	Dismisses external factors during different stages of life; oversimplifies the causes of crime.
Ecological Theory	Crime associated with urban transition zones; crime is higher in low income zones near city.	Too much credence to spatial location; does not explain crime outside of socially disorganized areas; correlation does not mean causation.
Strain Theory	Crime is the result of frustration due to blocked opportunities, which prevent success.	The U.S. provides opportunities for all Americans to financially succeed; delinquent juveniles do not report being more stressed than law abiding juveniles; claims that wealth is the single most important goal in life; does not adequately explain the lack of crime for women, who may be stressed as a result of continual discrimination.

Theory	Description	Critique
Cultural Conflict Theory	Those individuals in power pass laws to protect their own interests.	Can be tautological and may lack explanatory power; may be racist because minorities (who have little power) are labeled as criminals.
Differential Association Theory	Criminal behaviors are learned through communications with intimate others; definitions favorable to crime exceed definitions unfavorable to crime; frequency, duration, intensity, and importance impact the learning of behavior.	Does not sufficiently explain crime; does not consider free choice; does not explain why those surrounded by crime do not commit crime; only accounts for the communication of criminal values, not the emergence of criminal values.
Containment Theory	Crime results when internal (e.g., positive self-esteem) and external (e.g., social groups) control mechanisms fail to protect the individual; like an illness in which only some people who are exposed to social pressures commit crime.	May be feelings of the moment that have been conditioned through individual thought mechanisms.
Social Bond Theory	Weaken bonds between an individual and the social group results in crime; crime is reduced if a person has a strong bond with society, has strong attachments, is committed, and is involved.	Individuals commit crime even when they know that it is wrong; social bonds do not appear strong enough to negate criminal behavior.

Social Control Theory	Delinquent behavior occurs when social constraints on antisocial behaviors are weakened; Control ratio predicts criminal behavior; Control ratio = amount of control personally experienced versus amount of control exercised over others; Too much or too little self-control are equally dangerous.	Assumes that all individuals are automatically deviant unless socialized through control mechanisms; dismisses learned behavior and human motivations.
Labeling Theory	If individuals are arrested, they may become labeled. This may result in a negative stigma being attached to them. This may consequently disrupt their personal relationships and may block their future legitimate economic opportunities, which may lead to more crime.	Does not explain the origin of crime; does not explain secret deviants.

Broken Window Theory	Broken windows, graffiti, litter, abandoned vehicles, homeless persons, and public drinking indicates disorder and a lack of caring. If people do not care about what happens in their neighborhood, then this attracts crime.	May be artifact of police decision-making practices; may bear little objective relationship to the actual degree of crime in area; police may focus more efforts in poor areas and this may mislead media. For example, if the department patrols a certain area with more officers, police will make more arrests in that area (Do more arrests mean safer streets or a more dangerous area?).
Life Course Theory	Human lives are embedded in social relationships across the life span; the impact of various experiences depend on when they occur in life; each person makes choices, which impact each person's life course; a life course is shaped by historic times and places.	Many important life course determinants are experienced during childhood, which means adults may not be accountable for their crimes; individuals may select components of their life course and may influence their own trajectories.
Interactional Theory	Crime is the result of a weakened bond between an individual and society combined with the learning of anti-social behaviors that are rewarded.	Does not fully appreciate childhood maltreatment as an important factor, which leads to crime.

Social Conflict Theory	People in power pass laws to protect their own interests. There is a struggle for power and laws are passed that penalize the disadvantaged.	Overstresses social change and dismisses other well-developed theories of crime; fails to recognize that most people believe crime should be controlled.
Normative Sponsorship Theory	Indicates that people who have a convergence of interest may cooperate with one another in order to satisfy their needs.	Community members will only work together as long as the goals are within the normal limits of established standards.
Dual Taxonomic Theory	Most antisocial children do not become criminals; there are two types of offenders: life course persistent offenders (due to family dysfunction, poverty, neurophysiological deficits, failure in school) and adolescence limited offenders (due to structural disadvantages).	Family and psychological dysfunction are not shown to be directly correlated to parent control or individual trajectories.
Postmodern Criminology	Skeptical of science and scientific method; crime is an integral part of society.	Challenges other theories of crime prevention and control, but fails to offer feasible alternatives.
Convict Criminology	Prisons are too big, hold too many people, and do not reduce crime; to control crime upon release from prison, prisons should focus more on treatment and less on security; based on the lived experiences of convicted felons and ex-inmates.	Most of the authors of the theory are white males, but not all are ex-convicts; authors are biased with agendas; non-convict feminists have been adding to the field, moving the theory from its roots.

Victim Precipitation	Victim unconsciously exhibits behaviors or characteristics that instigate or encourage the attacker; explains multiple victimizations.	Relevant only to violent crime or to particular forms of unlawful violence; assumes that victims and offenders interact prior to crime occurring.
Critical Social Theory	Practical social science that encourages individuals to become socially and politically active in order to change and improve their current social conditions; endorses the enlightenment, empowerment, and emancipation of the people: people are enlightened when they obtain empirical knowledge about their states of oppression and their potential capacity to improve their situations, people are empowered when they are galvanized to engage in a socially transformation action, people are emancipated when they know who they are, what they genuinely want, and when they have collective autonomy and power to freely and rationally determine the nature and course of their collective existence.	Must raise the people's awareness of their current oppression; must demonstrate the possibility of a qualitatively different future; must hold community members responsible for actively getting involved and creating their own liberation.

Situational Crime Prevention / Crime Prevention Through Environmental Design	SCP is a crime prevention strategy that attempts to eliminate or reduce the opportunities to commit specific crimes in specific locations by making crime more risky to attempt and more difficult to accomplish. Instead of relying upon law enforcers, the SCP strategy depends on public and private organizations. Furthermore, SCP does not focus on the persons committing the crimes or the underlying causes of crime, such as unjust social and economic conditions, but focuses instead on the settings for crime.	Only protects a limited geographical area; crime may be displaced.
Developmental Pathways	Anti-social behaviors are age dependent; as children age, they develop verbal coping skills, which help them manage conflict.	Fails to explain free choice in human development.
Delinquent Development Theory	Persistence in crime is influenced by many risk factors, such as broken homes, low family income, and harsh discipline. Desistance in crime has four factors: deceleration, specialization, de-escalation, and reaching a ceiling (plateau).	Aging causing desistance is meaningless because the theory fails to explain why desistance occurs.

Peacemaking Criminology	Crime can be managed, not by stopping crime, but by making peace; citizens and social control agencies need to work together through education, social policies, human rights, and community involvement.	Is utopian and fails to recognize the realities of law enforcement and crime control limitations.
Feminist Criminology	Men have dominated the field of criminal justice and have developed theories and written laws for the explanation and control of crime based on their own limited perspectives.	Inadequately accounts for crimes committed by females. Currently there is no single well-developed theory that explains female crime.

Conclusion: Why Theory Is Important

Theories help explain problems and provide possible solutions to the problems. However, all theories rely on assumptions, which may impact the effectiveness of decisions based on those theories. Understanding criminal theories is important because police officers need to make best-practice decisions to solve current problems. Applying the wrong theory to solve the problem at hand will be less than optimal. As stated earlier, this is why Megan's Law is proving to be less than effective. According to research on Megan's Law, the deterrence theory and labeling theory are being used to solve a biological-based problem (Corrigan, 2006). Thus, the proposed solution is not in alignment with the theories used to explain the problem and, consequently, Megan's Law is not effectively working.

Theories also control the types of questions that should be asked on research surveys. Data collecting surveys need to ask questions that are in alignment with the theory used to describe the problem. Otherwise the survey itself may not be valid. For example, if the biological theory is used to explain a problem, it does not make sense to ask questions about social learning experiences. For the instrument to be effective, it must collect information that is relevant to the study.

In short, every criminal theory has a limitation and there is always an exception to the rule when trying to explain human behavior. Law enforcers must understand the various limitations of information so that they can defend their actions. Understanding information will also help prevent police officers from being deceived. **In order to assess risk and vulnerability, the law enforcer must understand information.**

Questions to ponder....

Q1: Why does the sky get dark at night?

If you believe that the sky gets dark at night because the sun is on the other side of the earth, then you have made a flawed assumption (Verma, 2005). The flawed assumption is that the sun is the only light in the sky and that the lack of sunlight causes darkness. Getting dark at night and the sun being on the other side of the earth are correlated, but it is not causal relationship. **There is another reason why it gets dark at night.** Thus, a research based on wrong assumptions may produce poor results. Therefore, students should always assess the validity of information by asking certain questions. Some of the factors that should be evaluated include a) the data collection process, b) the data analysis, c) the participants, d) the assumptions, and e) the limitations.

Q2: I have three coins, which total 25 cents. However, one of them is not a nickel. What are the three coins? Clue: one of them is not a nickel ≠ not one of them is a nickel.

REFERENCES

Adams, W. (1999). The interpretation of self and world: Empirical research, existential phenomenology, and transpersonal psychology. *Journal of Phenomenological Psychology, 30*(2), 39-65.

Akers, R., and Sellers, C. (2009). *Criminological theories: Introduction, evaluation, and application* (5th ed.). New York, NY: Oxford University Press.

American Psychological Association. (2010). *Publication manual of the American Psychological Association* (6th ed.). Washington, DC: Author.

Asante, M.K. (2009). What is Afrocentricity? Retrieved from http://www.asante.net/ scholarly/afrocentricityarticle.html

Balian, E.S. (1988). *How to design, analyze, and write doctoral or master's research* (2nd ed.). New York, NY: University Press of America.

Berg, B. (2007). *Qualitative research methods for the social sciences* (6th ed.). Boston, MA: Pearson Education, Inc.

Carter, D. (2002). *Issues in police-community relations: Taken from The Police and the community* (7th ed.). Boston, MA: Pearson Custom.

Chessick, R. (1990). Hermeneutics for psychotherapists. *American Journal of Psychotherapy, 44*(2), 256-273.

Corrigan, R. (2006). Making meaning of Megan's law. *Law & Social Inquiry, 31*(2), 267-312.

Crossan, F. (2003). Research philosophy: Towards an understanding. *Nurse Researcher, 11*(1), 46-55.

Dowling, M. (2004). Hermeneutics: An exploration. *Nurse Researcher, 11*(4), 30-39.

Dotzler, R.J. (2000). Getting to reparations: A response to Fein. *Sociological Practice: A Journal of Clinical and Applied Sociology, 2*(3), 177-182.

Dreisbach, C. (2008). *Ethics in criminal justice.* Boston, MA: McGraw-Hill Irwin.

Fay, B. (1987). *Critical social science.* Ithaca, NY: Cornell University Press.

Glesne, C. (2006). *Becoming qualitative researchers: An introduction* (3rd ed.). Boston, MA: Pearson.

Hall, A.A. (2000). There is a lot to be repaired before we get reparations: A critique of the underlying issues of race that impact the fate of African American reparations. *St. Mary's Law Review, 1,* 22-32.

Hammers, C., and Brown, A. (2004). Towards a feminist-queer alliance: A paradigmatic shift in the research process. *Social Epistemology, 18*(1).

Harberfeld, M.R. (2006). *Police leadership.* Upper Saddle River, NJ: Pearson Prentice.

Hatch, J. (2002). *Doing qualitative research in education settings.* Albany, NY: State University of New York Press.

Hess, K.M., & Bennett, W.W. (2007). *Management and supervision in law enforcement* (5th ed.). Belmont, CA: Wadsworth Thomson.

Holliday, A. (2007). *Doing and writing qualitative research* (2nd ed.). Thousand Oaks, CA: Sage.

Huesmann, L.R., & Eron, L.D. (1992). Childhood aggression and adult criminality. In J. McCord (Ed.), *Facts, frameworks, and forecasts: Advances in criminology theory* (p. 137-156). New Brunswick, NJ: Transaction.

Huesmann, L.R., Eron, L.D., & Dubow, E.F. (2002). Childhood predictors of adult criminality: Are all risk factors reflected in childhood aggressiveness? *Criminal Behaviour and Mental Health, 12*(3), 185-208.

Kraska, P. (2004). *Theorizing criminal justice: Eight essential orientations.* Long Grove, IL: Waveland Press, Inc.

Langevin, R., Curnoe, S., Federoff, P., Bennett, R., Langevin, M., Peever, C., et al. (2004). Lifetime sex offender recidivism: A 25-year follow-up study. *Canadian Journal of Criminology and Criminal Justice, 46*(5), 531-552.

Large, T. (2007). *The Usborne Illustrated Dictionary of Math.* Tulsa, OK: Usborne.

Leventhal, M.G. (2005). *The Posse Comitatus Act of 1878.* Retrieved from http://www.doj gov.net/posse_comitatus_act.htm

Leedy, P., & Ormrod, J. (2005). *Practical research: Planning and design* (8th ed.). Upper Saddle River, NJ: Pearson Merrill Prentice Hall.

LexisNexis (2005). *Immigration law handbook.* Longwood, FL: Gould.

Liska, A. and Messner, S. (1999). *Perspectives on Crime and Deviance* (3rd ed.). Upper Saddle River, NJ: Prentice Hall.

McLaughlin, E., & Muncie, J. (2006). *The Sage dictionary of criminology* (2nd ed.). Thousand Oaks, CA: Sage.

Mertens, D.M. (2005). *Research and evaluation in education and psychology: integrating diversity with quantitative, qualitative, and mixed methods* (2nd ed.). Thousand Oaks, CA: Sage Publications.

Miller-Johnson, S., Moore, B.L., Underwood, M.K., & Cole, J.D. (2005). African-American girls and physical aggression: Does stability of childhood aggression predict later negative outcomes? In D. Pepler, K. Madsen, C. Webster, & K. Levene (Eds.), *The development and treatment of girlhood aggression* (p. 75-101). Mahwah, NJ: Lawrence Erlbaum.

Papell, C., and Skolnik, L. (1992). The reflective practitioner: A contemporary paradigm's relevance for social work education. *Journal of Social Work Education, 28*(1), 18-26.

Perez, D.W., & Moore, J.A. (2002). *Police ethics: A matter of character.* Incline Village, NV: Copperhouse.

Pollock, J.M. (2004). *Ethics in crime and justice: Dilemmas & decisions.* Belmont, CA: Thomas-Wadsworth.

Ponterotto, J. (2005). Qualitative research in counseling psychology: A primer on research paradigms and philosophy of science. *Journal of Counseling, 52*(2), 126-136.

Reaves, B.A. (2007). Census of state and local law enforcement agencies, 2004. *Bureau of Justice Statistics Bulletin.* Retrieved from http://bjs.ojp.usdoj.gov/index.cfm?ty =dcdetail&iid=249

Schmalleger, F. (2007). *Criminal justice today: An introductory text for the 21st century* (9th ed.). Upper Saddle River, NJ: Pearson Prentice Hall.

Shields, L. (2007). Falsification. *Pediatric Nursing, 19*(7), 37.

Smith, S., Eggen, M., St. Andre, R. (2006). *A transition to advanced mathematics* (6th ed.). Belmont, CA: Thomson Brooks/Cole.

Sower, C., & Gist, G.T. (1994). *Formula for change: Using the urban experiment station methods and the normative sponsorship theory.* East Lansing, MI: Michigan State University Press.

Sower, C., Holland, J., Tiedke, K., & Freeman, W. (1957). *Community Involvement: The webs of formal and informal ties that make for action.* Glencoe, IL: The Free Press.

Stevens, L. (2003, June 20). Jackson: All must help the city in wake of violence. *The Herald Palladium* (Benton Harbor, Michigan). Retrieved from http://www.herald palladium.com

Turvey, B. E., & Petherick, W. (2009). *Forensic victimology: Examining violent crime victims in investigative and legal contexts.* Burlington, MA: Academic Press.

U.S. Citizenship and Immigration Services (2008). *The Declaration of Independence & the Constitution of the United States.* Retrieved from http://www.uscis.gov/sites/ default/ files/USCIS/Office%20of%20Citizenship/Citizenship%20 Resource%20Center%20Site/Publications/PDFs/M-654.pdf

U.S. Department of Labor, Bureau of Labor Statistics (2009). *Occupational outlook handbook, 2010-11 edition.* Retrieved from http://www.bls.gov//oco/ocos/60.htm

Verma, S. (2005). *The little book of scientific principles, theories, & things.* New York, NY: Sterling.

Vold, G., Bernard, T., & Snipes, J. (2002). *Theoretical criminology* (5th ed.). New York, NY: Oxford University Press.

Wakefield, W. (1995). When an irresistible epistemology meets an immovable ontology. *Social Work Research, 19*(1).

Weber, R. (2004). The rhetoric of positivism versus interpretivism: A personal view. *MIS Quarterly, 28*(1), iii-xii.

Wimpenny, P., & Gass, J. (2000). Interviewing in phenomenology and grounded theory: is there a difference? *Journal of Advanced Nursing, 31*(6), 1485-1492.

Zevitz, R.G. (2006). Sex offender community notification: Its role in recidivism and offender reintegration. *Criminal Justice Studies, 19*(2), 193-208.

CHAPTER 5. COMMUNICATION THEORY

The Need to Communicate

Although the United States has less than 5% of the world's population, it has nearly 25% of the world's total prison population (Liptak, 2008). Having such a large incarceration rate is due, in part, to get tough policies and longer prison sentences (Kelley, Mueller, & Hemmens, 2004). Indeed, at the end of 2007 in the U.S., there were about 2.3 million people incarcerated, 4.2 million people on probation, and 800,000 people on parole (Fears, 2008; McCarthy, 2009). Hence, there is a need for police reports.

Since September 2001, federal resources, which were previously used to fund local law enforcement, have been redirected toward homeland security (Kingsbury, 2006). With a 45% cut in funds, many local law enforcement agencies have reduced their manpower, with some midsize cities reducing their manpower by about 25%. In addition, U.S. prisons are releasing about 630,000 inmates each year, and the recidivism rate from state prisons is about 67%. Thus, with fewer police officers on the streets and more criminals on the streets, this is a public safety concern. Indeed, the FBI has indicated that violent crimes rates, such as murder, robberies, and aggravated assaults, are on the rise in the U.S. (Edwards, 2006). As more crimes occur, more arrests will be made. Therefore, police officers can expect to find themselves in the courtroom more often. Indeed, the public's safety depends upon prosecutors and police officers performing effectively within the courtroom.

To effectively serve the public, a police officer must be a credible witness in the courtroom during a trial. Part of the job of police officers is to arrest criminals, to complete the proper paperwork, and then to testify in the courtroom. If police officers make arrests, they must properly complete the paperwork because the paper work may be presented in court. Poor paperwork may indicate in court that the officers are lazy or incompetent. Officers who fail to write effectively have failed to do their jobs and have failed to adequately protect the public. Thus, police officers must learn how to properly testify and effectively persuade the jurors.

For example, if a defense attorney discovers mistakes in a police report, the defense attorney may ask the officer if the officer has performed the work to the best of his or her ability. At this point, the officer is in trouble because the officer must admit that he or she is incompetent or deceitful (if officer applied best effort) or that he or she is lazy or uncaring (if officer did not apply best effort).

History of Communication and Persuasion Theories

Communication theory as it relates to persuasion theory started around the 5th century BCE (Schiappa, 1991). During this time, Protagoras (490-421 BCE), a philosophical thinker in Athens, became the pioneer of the study of language; he invented a new way of thinking and speaking. Protagoras, the father of debate and a promoter of democracy, organized dialogue and invented the lecture between teachers and students, where each side presented an argument in an informal discussion group, then had to defend it. About the same time, in 466 BCE, the Sicilian government was overthrown. That government, consequently, changed from tyranny to democracy. As a result, there was a high demand for people to be able to speak their minds in assemblies and to be able to testify for themselves in court (because there were few lawyers at the time). Meeting this demand, Corax and Tisias, two Sicilians, developed the argument from probability. Thus, persuasive arguments had begun.

In 1776, the American Revolution took place. During this era, the U.S. Constitution was written, which affords each person charged with a crime the right to a trial by jury. Like Great Britain, trials in the U.S. are based on an adversarial model; debate is expected (Resnick & Knoll, 2007). Thus, the founding fathers have promoted communication theory and persuasive arguments within the courtroom; it has always been a part of U.S. history.

In modern times, there have been several landmark theories involving communication theory and interpersonal persuasion

(Reardon, 1981). These landmark theories include: 1) the **Balance Theory**, 2) the **Attribution Theory**, 3) **Congruity Principle Theory**, 4) the **Cognitive Dissonance Theory**, 5) the **Learning Theory**, 6) the **Functional Theory**, 7) the **Inoculation Theory**, and 8) the **CounterAttitudinal Advocacy Theory**. Indeed, communication theory is a very broad field of study (Stremler, 1982).

Four of the landmark theories were developed in the 1950s. First, Fritz Heider developed the **Balance Theory** (Crandall, Silvia, N'Gbala, Tsang, & Dawson, 2007; Reardon, 1981). This theory states that people like consistency and they resist change. Because people like to remain static, successful persuasion must create a degree of imbalance from the status quo. Second, Heider developed the **Attribution Theory**, which states that people seek reasons to justify someone else's behavior (Reardon). An example may include a police officer or juror seeking a motive when a person commits a crime. Third, Osgood and Tannenbaum developed the **Congruity Principle Theory**. This theory states that when a person is confronted with two or more incompatible concepts, the person will change his or her attitude so that the two concepts are congruent. For example, if John supports the death penalty and Lisa does not, then every time John thinks of Lisa he will have negative feelings toward her due to her stance on the death penalty. Finally, in 1957, Leon Festinger developed the **Cognitive Dissonance Theory**. This theory states that two relations, dissonant and consonant, are associated with cognitive elements. Dissonant relations between two cognitive elements produce negative feelings; thus, people behave in ways that reduce dissonance. An example of a dissonant relation between two elements is when a person goes into debt when buying a house (this can be stressful). On the other hand, consonant relations imply an appropriate match of two cognitive elements, such as not buying a home because one is already in debt.

Three of the landmark theories were developed in the 1960s. First, Staats developed the **Learning Theory**, which describes how people are conditioned to respond in particular ways (Reardon, 1981). People can be trained to provide certain responses based upon certain information provided to them. A classic example of conditioning is the experiment conducted by Pavlov when he conditioned a dog to saliva at the sound of a bell. Second, Katz developed the **Functional Theory**. According to the Functional Theory, people tend to behave and perform only those actions that they find favorable, they refuse to humble themselves and admit their faults, they act in ways to foster preferred impressions, and they tend to act in ways that provide certainty. Finally, McGuire developed the **Inoculation Theory**. This theory states that the best persuasion is one that supports one side of an argument and, at the same time, refutes the other side of the argument. By explaining both the benefits for doing something and costs for doing something else, the argument will be more persuasive; it is like being pushed and pulled in the same direction at the same time. Furthermore, by reinforcing the message with multiple sources, credibility will be enhanced and, thus, the argument will be more persuasive (Tucker, Donovan, & Marlatt, 1999).

During the 1970s, Miller and Burgoon developed the **CounterAttitudinal Advocacy Theory** (Reardon, 1981). This theory states that people will best construe their own beliefs and behaviors when rewards are not associated with their activities. This theory is the opposite of the theory based on incentives, which states that people will perform those acts that are rewarded.

Communication Theory in the Courtroom

U.S. democratic principles rely upon truth being discovered through open debates within the courtroom (Bank, 2001). Therefore, communication theory is critical in law enforcement, especially within the courtroom. Indeed, how police officers communicate within the courtroom will influence the jurors' decisions. The basic assumptions of communication theory indicate that jurors will perceive information that impacts their attitudes, which will result in decisions that can be significant (Tucker, et al., 1999). For example, based upon the information that they receive and perceive, the jurors may set a killer loose, or, on the other hand, they may convict an innocent person. Thus, prosecutors and police officers, who are the message sources, use persuasion to affect the attitudes and opinions of the jurors in order to arrive at an appropriate verdict (Tucker, et al, 1999.). Although most police officers receive very little training in courtroom testimony, the jurors believe otherwise and have high expectations for them (Smith & Hilderbrand, n.d.). Thus, the jurors already have a misconception about how well the police officers should testify. Consequently, police officers must learn how to effectively communicate in the courtroom so that their testimonies are credible. In short, persuasion is directly related to credibility.

Persuasion

In trying to convince someone to perform particular acts, there are three different modes of persuasion. The three modes of persuasion are **ethos**, **pathos**, and **logos** (Honeycutt, 2004). **Ethos** is based on credibility, which is the attitude or perception that the customer has of the speaker; in other words, it is based on the speaker's reputation. **Pathos**, on the other hand, is based on emotional appeals. Using emotions in the heat of the moment, pathos is very effective and is commonly used by salespeople. Salespeople's goal is to make emotional appeals to potential customers and then to close deals before the customers have time to cool down and reason things out. Finally, **logos**, which maintains personal beliefs the longest, is based on critical thinking and reasoning. Although police officers may need to use all three modes of persuasion as they perform their duties, they also need to understand when they are being manipulated (i.e., persuaded) by others.

Verbal Persuasion

A police officer's verbal communication in the courtroom impacts the police officer's credibility as a witness. Verbal communication can be either written or spoken. If it is written, then it takes the form of police reports, which may include arrest reports. If it is vocal, then it takes the form of oral testimony. Indeed, both types of verbal communication impact the office's credibility as a witness. In all cases, any communication that is less than truthful is illegal and unacceptable. This being said, it is assumed that the police officers have made justifiable arrests in which they are testifying.

A police officer's written report is a reflection of the police officer's competence. First of all, a police report must have good content, and the officer must be familiar with its content (Stewart, 2007). Because it is not uncommon for a trial to take place years after the arrest, the police officer should review the report prior to the trial. In other words, a police officer should never take the stand without knowing what is in his or her report. Otherwise, the defense attorney will make the officer look like a fool, and this is not the image that the officer wants to portray to the jury. Furthermore, the police report must contain all pertinent information; if it is not written down in the report, then it cannot be used in court. In other words, there is no pulling a rabbit out of a magic hat. Second, the report must be objective, complete, accurate, and clear. For example, if a hockey team played 10 games and is undefeated, this does not mean that the team has won ten games; they could have tied some of the games.

Misleading the juror is unethical, and an officer must present a true representation of the facts. In addition, the police officer should use active statements instead of passive statements. This can be achieved by focusing on what witnesses saw, rather than by focusing on what witnesses did not see. For instance, the statements, "I did not see the driver look back before he backed his car," is not equivalent to, "I saw the driver not look back before he backed his car." The former statement is problematic because it may indicate that the witness saw nothing, but the latter statement is valuable and describes what the witness actually saw. Third, in order to keep the jury's attention, the report must be organized and structured. It is just like watching television; in order to keep the jurors interested and to help them understand the flow of events, the report must not keep changing channels (Boccaccini, 2002). The report should flow smoothly, and this requires proper grammar. If there are grammar mistakes within the report, the jurors will perceive the officer as either lazy and uncaring or incompetent. If the officer is perceived as unprofessional, uncaring, or incompetent, then the jurors may transfer that negative perception to the validity of the report. In the jurors' minds, if they believe that the officer is a fool, then they will consider themselves bigger fools if they agree. Finally, because defense attorneys are experts at finding weaknesses in police officers' reports, police officers must put the necessary time and effort into writing good reports. Indeed, the credibility of police officers will be determined by the evidence that they present in the courtroom, which is contained, in part, in their written documentations.

A police officer's oral testimony is a reflection of the police officer's competence. Testifying on the stand can be intimidating and can cause anxiety, but police officers must maintain their professionalism and objectivity (Klimon, 1985). When testifying, it is more important to make a lasting impression rather than to present a perfect testimony (Maxey & O'Connor, 2007). Specifically, if an officer makes a mistake or cannot remember a particular event, the officer must admit it as soon as it is realized. The jurors understand that no one is perfect and that people make mistakes. By a police officer admitting a mistake right away, the jurors will perceive that officer as human and honest, rather than one who is trying to cover things up.

When police officers are testifying in court, they should never start a sentence with, "To be honest" or "To tell the truth," because this will give the impression to the jurors that the rest of the testimony is less than truthful. In addition, if the truth is to be discovered, the officers must persuade the jurors using plain language (Navarro, 2004; Stewart, 2007). If a police officer uses slang or police jargon, then the jurors may either become confused, not understanding what is being said, or they may perceive that the officer is insulting them, by trying to make them feel dumb and inferior. Both cases will impede persuasion. For example, suppose an officer said, *"District 11, 11-43, 10-23, 7 south, Signal 6."* Although this meaning may be quite clear to a police officer in District 11, this is meaningless to the average civilian or juror.

As indicated, the officer must present the information in a normal conversational manner.

Testifying in the courtroom is an art and the police officer is a performer (Navarro, 2004). A good way to think about this is to consider the courtroom as an amusement park and the jurors as customers who love thrills. If the police officer rehearses and memorizes the testimony, the jurors will perceive the testimony as a boring and lame merry-go-round (Boccaccini, 2002). In addition, if an officer continually pauses during the testimony, jurors will perceive this as a frustrating Ferris wheel, which keeps stopping every few seconds (Navarro). However, by speaking moderately fast with variations in pitch and volume, the jurors will perceive this as a roller coaster, something interesting and exciting. Moreover, the officers must project their voices with confidence, like a big screen television. This will eliminate any perception of doubt in their voices (Defoe, 2007). The bottom line is, just as in written communications, weaknesses in a police officer's oral testimony will be exposed. Hence, police officers must practice their oral presentations so that they will be perceived as being credible witnesses.

Nonverbal Persuasion

In addition to communicating verbally, police officers also communicate in many nonverbal manners. Indeed, similar to verbal communication, nonverbal communication in the courtroom also impacts the police officer's credibility as a witness. First of all, a police officer's appearance sets the stage for the perception of his or her credibility as a witness. Because the jurors make judgments on the outward appearances of the police officers, the officers must dress appropriately and professionally (Navarro, 2004; Stewart, 2007). The jurors may make the analogy that a dirty yard equals a dirty house. In other words, if the officers do not even care enough to take care of themselves, then they probably do not care about their work. Second, a police officer's conduct impacts the police officer's credibility as a witness. Indeed, police officers must have postures that show interest (Boccaccini, 2002; Navarro, 2004). For instance, if a boy is interested in a girl and is about to kiss her, he learns forward toward her and he focuses his eyes upon her. This is an example of a person showing interest, and it is obvious when it is observed. On the other hand, negative body language, such as fidgeting, crossing the arms, looking at one's watch, and looking at the ceiling, gives the impression that the officer has more important things to do than to be in court (Navarro, 2004; Tower, 2011). Thus, if the officers are perceived as being disinterested, the jurors will perceive the officers as less than sincere.

Implementing Communication Theories within the Courtroom

Because, according to the **Balance Theory**, people like consistency and they resist change, people must be motivated to change (Reardon, 1981). In this case, a prosecutor can achieve persuasion by distancing the criminal from the jurors. For example, if a person was being tried for public intoxication, the jurors may be strongly resistant to convict the person. The jurors may feel that they themselves have all drank too much at one time or another and that this could be one of them on the stand. However, to overcome this perception, the prosecutor must distinguish the criminal from the jurors in a meaningful way. First of all, by drawing a target with concentric circles around it, the prosecutor could start at the outer most ring and state that this level represents the subject's bloodshot eyes. Second, the prosecutor could move to the next circle inward, which represents a person with bloodshot eyes and slurred speech. Third, the prosecutor could move to the next circle inward, which represents bloodshot eyes, slurred speech, and staggering. Fourth, the prosecutor could move to the next circle inward, which represents all of the previous symptoms plus the subject urinating upon the roadway. This continues onward until the target in the center is reached. In this way, the jurors can clearly distance themselves from the defendant and this may persuade them to change their attitudes.

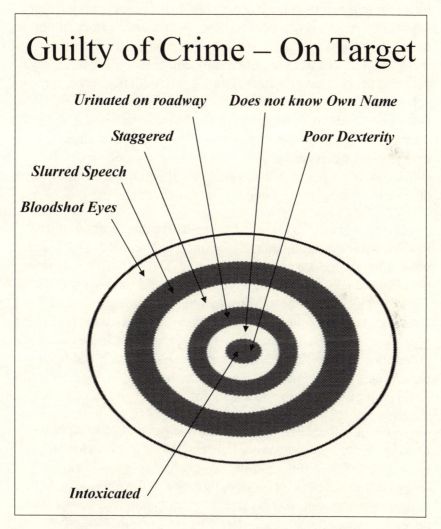

Figure 7. Balance theory - totality of circumstances.

The **Attribution Theory** states that people seek reasons to justify someone else's behavior; they try to find a motive when a person commits a crime (Reardon, 1981). Suppose a person commits a benevolent act but it is perceived by someone else to be a criminal act, then the motive may be the determining factor whether a crime has been committed. Because the jurors do not want to convict an innocent person of a crime, and because they themselves do not want to be wrongly convicted of a crime, they desire to find reasons for the actions. Thus, with no motive for committing a crime, the jurors will be less likely to convict a defendant. Thus, as part of the criminal investigation, it is the police officer's job to determine a motive. Once the motive is determined, it is included as part of the written case report. It is then up to the police officer to explain the motive, in simple language, to the jurors so that they will understand it.

The **Congruity Principle Theory** states that jurors will try to align two or more incompatible concepts (Reardon, 1981). The prosecutor and police officer can take advantage of this by aligning the criminal activity to a negative concept held by the jurors. For example, if the county is dry and the jurors disapprove of alcoholic beverages, then a person who is being tried for marijuana possession can be associated to being an alcoholic. In this case, the prosecutor can say that marijuana causes intoxication and leads to car crashes, killing innocent people. Furthermore, marijuana could be an addictive habit, just like alcohol.

The **Cognitive Dissonance Theory** states that people behave in ways that reduce dissonance between two cognitive elements (Reardon, 1981). In this case, the prosecutor could associate the idea that if the accused is set free, then one of the jurors may be the defendant's next victim. This stressful perception will persuade the jurors to convict the accused; they will associate the defendant's freedom to negative feelings. Furthermore, by persuading the jurors that justice and democracy demand fair payment for the defendant's actions, and that jail is the perfect place for the accused, the jurors will appropriately match the two cognitive elements.

The **Learning Theory** describes how people are conditioned to respond in particular ways (Reardon, 1981). The county prosecutor is an elected official and knows the local community issues. By associating the particular crime to something that the jurors, who are local community members, find upsetting, the prosecutor can direct their anger toward the accused. For example, if the jurors are upset about paying higher taxes, the prosecutor can illustrate how the accused could not care less about their money problems, as is evidenced by the commission of the criminal act, and that the accused is now mocking them by using their tax paying dollars to get away with it.

According to the **Functional Theory**, people refuse to humble themselves and tend to perform only those actions that they find favorable (Reardon, 1981). In this case, the prosecutor can use the jurors' pride against them by linking the conviction of the accused to the jurors' intelligence. This can be achieved by indicating to the jurors that they are too smart to be fooled by a common criminal (who was not smart enough to avoid getting caught). By stating that the jurors are community pillars whom the local residents are relying upon to protect them, the jurors may find it beneficial to convict the accused.

The **Inoculation Theory** states that the best persuasion is one that supports one side of an argument and, at the same time, refutes the other side of the argument (Reardon, 1981). In this case, the prosecutor can argue that in order to reduce crime, the accused needs to be locked up. On the other hand, if the jurors fail to convict, their safety is at risk. Thus, the jurors can reduce crime and promote safety at the same time. In order to reinforce this argument and to make it as persuasive as possible, all submitted evidence related to the crime should be emphasized, including victim statements, witness statements, photographs, and laboratory reports (Tucker, et al., 1999).

Finally, the **CounterAttitudinal Advocacy Theory** states that people will best construe their own beliefs and behaviors when rewards are not associated with their activities (Reardon, 1981).

In this case, the prosecutor can remind the jurors that by serving on the jury, they are serving their community. Convicting the perpetrator is not for personal gain, but it is their patriotic duty as U.S. citizens. Democracy and freedom depend upon law and order. For without law and order, there can be no democracy.

Conclusion

As mentioned earlier, democracy and truth rely upon open debate within the courtroom (Bank, 2001). However, jurors select their own truths based on their perceptions of the credibility of the information that they receive (Peterson, 1954). One way that this credibility is determined is through the jurors' assessment of the way police officers communicate, both verbally and nonverbally. Thus, police officers must communicate well, be credible, and learn to effectively persuade. A second way that credibility is determined is by the way the prosecutor presents information in the courtroom. By using multiple communication theories, and simultaneously employing as many of them as possible, prosecutors can align information in ways that will be well received by the jurors. Being well received, the information will be more credible. Being more credible, the information will be more persuasive. In short, for both police officers and prosecutors, persuasion through communication is the basic concept of courtroom testimony.

Courtroom Procedures (Gaines & Miller, 2009)

Opening Statement by Prosecutor
• Acquaints jury with nature of charge • Describes evidence that will be offered

Presentation of Prosecutor

- Direct examination (by prosecutor)
- Cross- examination (by defense attorney)
- Redirect examination (by prosecutor)
- Re-cross-examination (by defense attorney)

- Goal: prosecutor seeks to prove case beyond a reasonable doubt
- Direct evidence = based on firsthand knowledge
- Circumstantial evidence = based on deductions and inferences
- Studies show eyewitness testimony are highly unreliable

Presentation of Defense Attorney

- Does not have to show anything for acquittal
- Beyond reasonable doubt is subjective

Rebuttal Evidence

- After both sides present their main case, each side has the chance to present evidence to destroy the credibility of witnesses or evidence relied upon by the opposing side

> **Closing Arguments**
>
> - Prosecution summarizes evidence first
> - Defense replies
> - Prosecution rebuts defense
>
> - Prosecution gives two closing arguments because bears greater burden of proof
> - Closing arguments are limited to evidence presented during trial

Deposition

A deposition is a court proceeding used by lawyers to collect the testimony of witnesses, such as police officers, prior to trial (Nicholas, n.d.). Depositions are part of the discovery process and may be employed by either the defendant's lawyer or the plaintiff's lawyer. The deponent must answer questions truthfully under oath, which will be transcribed by a court recorder. The oral testimony locks-in the officer's story, which may be used against the officer later in court. If a police officer changes her story in court, the defense lawyer will discredit the officer. Thus, police officers must not provide general responses that will prevent the introduction of valuable evidence later in court. For example, when asked if there is anything else to add, the officer would be wise to state, "I cannot recall anything else at this time," instead of saying, "No." Below is an outline for deposing a police officer for an operating while intoxicated investigation. The police officer should expect the defense attorney to ask about the following topics.

A. Experience
        Law enforcement experience
        Training in specific area
        Proficient with equipment
        Was the officer engaging in normal police practice?

B. Location
        Direction of travel (both suspect and officer)
        Position of the officer's vehicle
        Roadway – specific location
        Lighting

C. Contact
        Reason for initial contact
        Normal police practice
        Time of day
        Hours on duty

D. Ambience
        Visibility
        Weather
        Road surface
        Volume of traffic

E. Witnesses
        Witnesses present with the police officer
        Witnesses present with the suspect
        Video in car
        Video at jail

F. Evidence
        Suspect's driving behavior
        Suspect's statements
        Police statements made to the suspect - coercion
        Physical evidence in vehicle (or lack thereof)
        Chain of custody
        Any other evidence

G. Arrest
        Implied Consent – right to refuse DataMaster
        Handcuffed – before the officer placed the suspect under arrest
        DataMaster test – proper procedures
        Time of arrest (e.g., before or after DataMaster test)

Case Report & Related Deposition Examples

On 8-7-2013 at about 2:00 a.m., I (Trooper Olga Hernandez) was stationary on Telegraph road near Lane 375 Walled Lake and I used radar and clocked a blue Chevy truck at 50 MPH headed WB on a posted 30 MPH zone. I initiated my commission's emergency lights and stopped the vehicle at Telegraph road and Lincoln road. The vehicle had Ohio registration OH133A. I approached the vehicle and talked with the driver, who was the only occupant in the vehicle. I noticed that his speech was slurred and I could smell the strong odor of an alcoholic beverage on his breath. I asked the driver if he had anything to drink and he stated 'More than enough.' I then asked the driver for his driver's license. The driver identified himself as John Doe having OH DL# 8234-518 (W/M DOB=4-22-68). I asked John DOE to tell me his age. He stated he was 43 (this was incorrect). I then asked him what his social security number was and he was only able to provide the first five numbers, after thinking about it for about ten seconds. I gave John DOE an also-sensor test at about 2:05 am and the result was 0.21% B.A.C. At this time, I read to him the Indiana Implied Consent Law. John Doe exited the vehicle and staggered. I double-locked handcuffed him and secured him in the front passenger seat of my commission. I then secured the Chevy truck. At about 2:17 am, I observed that nothing was in John Doe's mouth and I transported him to the Wixom county jail. I arrived at the jail at about 2:42 am.

At the Wixom County jail, I stated to John Doe that I was going to offer him some field sobriety tests. John Doe immediately stated that he would not cooperate and would not perform any tests. I again read to John Doe the Indiana Implied Consent law, informing him of the consequences for refusing the chemical test. Mr. Doe stated that he still would not cooperate and that he would not submit to a chemical test. At that time, at about 3:13 am, John Doe was placed under arrest for operating a vehicle while intoxicated-refusal, and incarcerated.

At about 3:54 am on 8-7-2013, King Wench of Bad Axe, IN arrived at the scene and removed the vehicle as indicated on Vehicle Impound form VR3872.

Attachments: 　1) Face sheet
　　　　　　　2) Copy of UTT # W6150 and #W6151 (Uniform Traffic Tickets)
　　　　　　　3) Copy of affidavit to establish probable cause (PC affidavit)
　　　　　　　4) Copy of charging form (information)
　　　　　　　5) Copy of Vehicle Impound form #VR3872
　　　　　　　6) Copy of suspect's driving record

Trooper Olga Hernandez
Indiana State Police

Below is a fictional deposition of Trooper Olga Hernandez on the above case report.

STATE OF INDIANA)	IN THE WIXOM CIRCUIT COURT
COUNTY OF WIXOM)	ss.
IN THE MATTER OF:	CAUSE NO. 11C03-1212-CM-9393

STATE OF INDIANA)
              Plaintiff,)
vs.)
John Doe,)
<u>Defendant.</u>   )

             <u>The Deposition of TROOPER OLGA HERNANDEZ</u>
             <u>DATE</u>:   February 1, 2014
             <u>TIME</u>:   9:00 o'clock a.m.
             <u>PLACE</u>:   The Law Office of Sue M. Good, LLP
                          111 Lane of Gold Wixom, IN

             Called as a Witness herein, in
             Accordance with the Rules of Civil Procedure.

Before Suzan Short
Certified Shorthand Reporter

             CRYSTAL CLEAR REPORTING
             Certified Shorthand Reporters
             Wixom, IN
             1-803-555-1313

APPEARANCES: 2

Prosecuting Attorney
2321 District Attorney Ave
Wixom, IN

On behalf of the State of Indiana
Plaintiff;

Ms.
Sue M.
Good

111 Lane of Gold Wixom, IN

On behalf of John Doe,
Defendant.

3

INDEX

THE DEPOSITION OF TROOPER OLGA HERNANDEZ

DIRECT EXAMINATION By Ms. Good .... Page 4

1		TROOPER OLGA HERNANDEZ,	4
2		Called as a Witness herein,	
3		Having been first duly sworn,	
4		Was examined and testified as follows:	
5			
6		<u>DIRECT EXAMINATION</u>	
7	BY MS. GOOD:		
8	Q.	Officer, would you give us your full name and business address, please?	
9	A.	Olga Hernandez, Indiana State Police. Address, I think,	
10		is 111 Police Alley in South Bend, IN.	
11	Q.	Okay. And are you assigned to which district, please?	
12	A.	Eighty-four.	
13	Q.	What is your appointment date with the department?	
14	A.	12-15-2007	
15	Q.	And has District 84 always been your assignment?	
16	A.	Yes.	
17	Q.	What is the extent of your law enforcement background, please?	
18	A.	About seven years law enforcement, as an auxiliary police officer in the	
19		City of Wayne, Michigan and I just started with the Indiana State	
20		Police in December of '07.	
21	Q.	What did you do in Wayne, Michigan?	
22	A.	Pretty much I patrolled with another officer all the time and had	
23		full police powers when I was with the other officer, road patrol,	
24		every now and then I did special events, parades and watched	
25		security around parks and stuff.	

INTERVIEWING, INTERROGATION & COMMUNICATION for LAW ENFORCEMENT

1	Q.	Okay. In your training with the Indiana State Police,
2		was held where, please?
3	A.	Plainfield, Indiana.
4	Q.	And how long were you there at the academy?
5	A.	I believe it was 21 weeks.
6	Q.	Twenty-one?
7	A.	Twenty-one, maybe twenty-two. I think it was 21.
8	Q.	During your training at the academy or after the academy, for that
9		matter, have you received any specialized training in any particular
10		area of law enforcement?
11	A.	Since then, I've gone to Breathalyzer school so I could administer
12		breath tests.
13	Q.	Okay. When was that?
14	A.	I don't remember. It was about 2 years ago.
15	Q.	In 2012?
16	A.	About.
17	Q.	And how long a school was that?
18	A.	That was one week.
19	Q.	And following that one week's training then, what are you authorized to
20		do as a result of that school?
21	A.	To use the DataMaster and Breathalyzer on individuals.
22	Q.	DataMaster?
23	A.	Yes.
24	Q.	And did you say another kind of equipment?
25	A.	For the breath tests.

1	Q.	All right. Anything other than the DataMaster?	6
2	A.	There was another piece of machinery there. I don't see it	
3		very often. I don't remember what it was.	
4	Q.	Is the old Breathalyzer not being used anymore?	
5		MR. SAM: DataMaster.	
6		Intoxilyzer and DataMaster.	
7	By MS. GOOD:		
8	Q.	Did you take a written exam, Trooper Hernandez, following this breath --	
9	A.	I did.	
10	Q.	-- test training?	
11	A.	Yes.	
12	Q.	And do you recall what grade you received on that?	
13	A.	No.	
14	Q.	Did you receive a grade or a numerical grade?	
15	A.	I don't remember how they scored it, but I did well enough to pass.	
16		I usually do pretty well, so I don't remember doing poorly on it.	
17	Q.	All right. It was more of a pass/fail sort of thing?	
18	A.	I don't remember how they graded us.	
19	Q.	Since your graduation from the breath test school in 2012, how many	
20		Breath tests do you believe you've administered now?	
21	A.	I've done about maybe thirty.	
22	Q.	And have these primarily been yours?	
23	A.	Yes.	
24	Q.	Do you run then for other departments as well?	
25	A.	I have not, to date.	

INTERVIEWING, INTERROGATION & COMMUNICATION for LAW ENFORCEMENT

1	Q.	If I may direct your attention to the morning of August - - 7
2		is that August 7, - -
3	A.	Yes.
4	Q.	- - 2013, what were your hours of employment that day?
5	A.	I believe, since I was, it looks like I stopped him at 2:00 am, I
6		probably started at 10:00 o'clock p.m. the day before and then
7		6:00 am when I got off.
8	Q.	10:00 p.m. to what please?
9	A.	Probably 6:30 a.m. on the 7th.
10	Q.	All right. And again, on that date you were assigned to the turnpike?
11	A.	Yes.
12	Q.	What section on the turnpike?
13	A.	Zone 13, mile post 89 to the state line, Ohio State Line, 133.
14	Q.	Okay. And your report reflects that you stopped him at 2:00 a.m.,
15		Is that correct?
16	A.	Yes.
17	Q.	You stopped John Doe at 2:00 a.m.?
18	A.	Yes.
19	Q.	Tell me, if you would please, where you were when you first
20		observed Mr. Doe's vehicle?
21	A.	I was on Telegraph Road stationary, just west of Lane 375,
22		Walled Lake.
23	Q.	And what is it that you were doing there?
24	A.	Using radar to clock vehicles coming westbound and eastbound.
25	Q.	Were you with any other police officers?

1	A.	No.
2	Q.	I apologize, but I'm confused. If I understand correctly, you
3		were assigned to the turnpike by mile post 89 to 133, but at
4		2:00 a.m. you were set up on the Telegraph Road to run radar?
5	A.	That's right.
6	Q.	What was the purpose of that? I guess I don't understand.
7	A.	I live right across the street. I stopped in front of it, clocked
8		a vehicle. Every now and then when I go home for lunch, I will clock
9		vehicles right in front of my house. That's what I was doing.
10	Q.	You had come back from lunch --
11	A.	I was going to it.
12	Q.	You were going to lunch. And do you recall what time you arrived
13		at your home?
14	A.	Approximately just prior to that.
15	Q.	Five minutes, ten minutes before.
16	A.	I don't know.
17	Q.	And when you arrived at home, you - -
18	A.	This was right across from my house, is what I said.
19	Q.	All right. So you backed in or how did you set up?
20	A.	No, across the street. I live at - - well, I don't anymore, but - -
21	Q.	At that time?
22	A.	Yeah. I don't know the name of the apartment complex it was.
23		It was 454 Telegraph Road.
24	Q.	Okay.
25	A.	And you have to pull into a parking lot to pull into my trailer.

1		I did not do that. I pulled on the other side of the street, 9
2		up on a hill, and I was using my lunch hour to clock traffic.
3	Q.	Okay. You were actually going home for lunch, you were just
4		using your lunch hour to clock traffic?
5	A.	Right.
6	Q.	Okay.
7	A.	I was on my lunch hour clocking traffic.
8	Q.	Okay. Did you have lunch then that morning?
9	A.	No.
10	Q.	And then after, what, did you just come off the road for an
11		hour and then return to the road, is that essentially what you did?
12	A.	Right.
13	Q.	Did you make any other arrests that morning during your lunch
14		hour other than Mr. Doe?
15	A.	No.
16	Q.	At the time you were stopped, set up with your radar unit, you
17		were facing what direction?
18	A.	I was facing eastbound.
19	Q.	And could you describe your patrol car, please?
20	A.	It's a black Indiana State Police car.
21	Q.	Fully lit?
22	A.	Yes, light bar on top.
23	Q.	Would you describe the traffic that morning on Telegraph Road?
24	A.	Very light.
25	Q.	What drew your attention to Mr. Doe's Chevy pickup truck?

1	A.	I can tell - - I could see the headlights. Of course, I can	10
2		tell that it looks like it was coming pretty fast. The speed	
3		limit there is posted 30 MPH and I can tell how long it takes them	
4		to get to me and he was moving a lot faster than 30.	
5	Q.	Okay. So that was essentially what drew your attention to - -	
6	A.	The speed.	
7	Q.	- - Mr. Doe, was his speed?	
8	A.	Right.	
9	Q.	Did you ultimately determine what his speed was?	
10	A.	I did.	
11	Q.	What was that, please?	
12	A.	Fifty miles an hour.	
13	Q.	In a 30 zone?	
14	A.	Right.	
15	Q.	Now, would you typically write a ticket for 50 in a 30 MPH zone	
16		at 2:00 a.m. in the morning with light traffic?	
17	A.	I would.	
18	Q.	If you would, describe Mr. Doe's vehicle, please?	
19	A.	It was a blue Chevy pickup truck.	
20	Q.	Okay.	
21	A.	After I stopped it, I looked at the registration.	
22	Q.	Okay. Was Mr. Doe alone in the vehicle?	
23	A.	He was.	
24	Q.	Tell me, if you would, now you're sitting stationary, eastbound on	
25		Telegraph Road, and Mr. Doe was traveling what direction, please?	

1	A.	Westbound.	11
2	Q.	And how quickly after he passed you, you got your reading, did you	
3		begin to follow him?	
4	A.	Immediately.	
5	Q.	And describe for me, if you would, what you did as soon as you	
6		began the pursuit?	
7	A.	I turned on - - I initiated my emergency lights.	
8	Q.	Right away?	
9	A.	Yes.	
10	Q.	And then what happened?	
11	A.	And then he ended up pulling into the parking lot at Sunset Inn,	
12		which is at Telegraph Road and Lincoln Road.	
13	Q.	How far did you follow him before he pulled into the Sunset?	
14	A.	A very short distance. Maybe several hundred yards.	
15	Q.	No more than several hundred?	
16	A.	Very short.	
17	Q.	During the time that you've followed him during that several hundred	
18		yards, could you describe for us any violations of state or - -	
19	A.	In addition to the speed, I saw no other violations.	
20	Q.	All right. Was his vehicle otherwise in good condition?	
21	A.	It looked fine.	
22	Q.	Okay. Now, as you stopped the vehicle and pulled in behind Mr. Doe,	
23		did it appear that he accelerated after you initiated your lights?	
24	A.	No.	
25	Q.	When you say he pulled on down the road and into the parking lot of the	

1		Sunset Inn, you're not suggesting that he was trying to elude	12
2		you in any fashion, was he?	
3	A.	There's a stop sign there at that intersection.	
4	Q.	Okay. And he yielded to your right of way?	
5	A.	Yes.	
6	Q.	And did you flash him with your spotlight or did he respond	
7		to your - - I guess you've got red and blue lights now?	
8	A.	He responded to my lights.	
9	Q.	All right. As he stopped, tell me if you would please, what next occurred?	
10	A.	I approached the vehicle and I asked him, I told him why I	
11		stopped him. I said, "I clocked you at 50 in a 30 MPH zone and that's	
12		why I'm stopping you."	
13	Q.	Okay.	
14	A.	I said, "Have you had anything to drink today?" And he said, "No."	
15		I smelled the alcoholic beverage on his breath, plus his eyes looked kind	
16		of glassy and blood shot. And then he said, "More than enough." So	
17		then I'm going to investigate further. "Let me see your driver's license."	
18	Q.	Did he produce it for you?	
19	A.	He did.	
20	Q.	Did he have any trouble getting it out?	
21	A.	Nothing special, no.	
22	Q.	Okay. What next occurred?	
23	A.	He handed it to me and I was looking at it. And I said, "I'm	
24		going to ask you some questions." Of course, I asked him what his	
25		birthday was. I said, "How old are you?" He gave me the wrong age.	

1		I think he said he was 43. But that was wrong. He was 45.	13
2		I'm also looking at his - -	
3	Q.	Sometimes you don't feel your age when the police have you. You know,	
4		I thinks that's the case.	
5	A.	His driver's license had his social security number on it too.	
6	Q.	All right.	
7	A.	So I asked him, "what's your social security number?" He	
8		sat there for a while and was thinking and couldn't come up with	
9		it after about 10 seconds. He gives me the first five numbers and	
10		he can't complete it.	
11	Q.	Okay.	
12	A.	So I wrote that down.	
13	Q.	Did you see any open beverage containers in the vehicle?	
14	A.	No.	
15	Q.	Any empties in the vehicle?	
16	A.	No.	
17	Q.	Did you have occasion to look inside the vehicle after he was out	
18		for any kind of - -	
19	A.	Yeah.	
20	Q.	- - beverage containers?	
21	A.	Yes	
22	Q.	Would you describe Mr. Doe's demeanor for us, please?	
23	A.	In the vehicle, he replied that he just came from a bar, he drank - -	
24	Q.	Did he tell you what bar?	
25	A.	I didn't even mark it down. I don't remember.	

1	Q.	He would have been - - I'm sorry. You told me he
2		was westbound on Telegraph Road?
3	A.	Yeah. I didn't record what bar he said he - - all I remember
4		was he said more than enough, so that's what I wrote down.
5	Q.	Okay.
6	A.	When I asked him to get out of the car, he staggered. I read
7		him the implied consent. I don't remember how he responded then,
8		but it wasn't that critical to me because I always give them
9		another opportunity at the jail.
10	Q.	Okay.
11	A.	And so - - but he did stagger. I double-locked handcuffed,
12		he didn't resist. And once I got him in my vehicle, of course,
13		I could continue to smell the alcoholic beverage coming from him.
14		I did give him an Also-Sensor, though. Before I handcuffed him
15		and that did read .21, I believe it was, and that was more
16		probable cause indicating he's been drinking.
17	Q.	Now, did you ever give him any of these field sobriety tests,
18		the one leg stand, the walk and turn, point your finger to your
19		nose and those sort of things?
20	A.	I was going to do that at the jail, but he refused.
21	Q.	Okay. You say the Also-Sensor - -
22	A.	Yes.
23	Q.	Tell me, after you got him in the vehicle, in your police vehicle,
24		did you transport him to the county jail yourself?
25	A.	I did.

1	Q.	Tell me, if you would please, what conversation, if any,	15
2		you had on the way to jail with Mr. Doe?	
3	A.	Nothing really of any significance. He wasn't under arrest and	
4		I wasn't planning to ask him anything at that time, anything	
5		in addition to what I already had recorded.	
6	Q.	Even though he wasn't under arrest, you had already handcuffed	
7		him though, right?	
8	A.	For officer safety, we do, when we transport. I was going to	
9		take him down and investigate further because he blew a .21 on the alco-sensor.	
10		That automatically means I'm going to take him down and investigate	
11		further. For office safety, double-locked handcuffed him and put him	
12		in my vehicle and that's standard practice.	
13	Q.	Okay. Now, did you notice any damage to Mr. Doe's vehicle?	
14	A.	I would have recorded the damage on my impound sheet. Just,	
15		I got, he did have his gearshift broken, his dash was cracked,	
16		dent on the left side of the vehicle.	
17	Q.	Was that recent damage?	
18	A.	I didn't notice it. I didn't really try to put a time and date	
19		when it was damaged.	
20	Q.	Did you ask him about it or anything?	
21	A.	No.	
22	Q.	It appears to be an older vehicle of some sort, is that - -	
23	A.	Yeah. I put down a '76 Chevy.	
24	Q.	Let me ask you, during your tour of duty that evening from	
25		10:00 p.m. until 2:00 a.m. when you stopped Mr. Doe,	

			16
1		Were you in your car primarily that whole four-hour period?	
2	A.	Yes.	
3	Q.	During that four-hour period, did you receive or overhear any	
4		dispatches from either local county, local city, or state police to be	
5		on the lookout for a 1976 Chevy pickup truck,	
6		reported as being intoxicated?	
7	A.	No.	
8	Q.	As you got to the county jail, tell me about that. You folks arrived,	
9		no doubt, and got Mr. Doe out of the car and got inside. I've seen	
10		your video that was taken. Tell me about what happened there, when	
11		you guys get inside.	
12	A.	I told him I was going to offer him some field sobriety tests	
13		and he immediately said he was not going to perform any tests.	
14		So at that point, he wasn't going to give any breath tests, so he was	
15		automatically under arrest because of refusal because I had	
16		probable cause to believe that he was intoxicated.	
17	Q.	Now, when he refused the field sobriety test, did you tell him that that	
18		would be okay, he was entitled to refuse?	
19	A.	I read him the implied consent and explained to him the	
20		consequences. He still refused.	
21	Q.	And how many times did you ask him to take the test at the county jail?	
22	A.	I believe I only asked once and then he refused and I	
23		explained the consequences. He still refused and it was over at that time.	
24	Q.	So would it be fair to say, at the county jail in the presence of the	
25		DataMaster, you asked him to take the breath test one time?	

1	A.	I wasn't in the room where the Data Master was.
2	Q.	No, but I mean the DataMaster was on station?
3	A.	Right.
4		What was the original question?
5	Q.	Do I understand correctly that at the county jail where the Data Master
6		is located, you asked Mr. Doe to take the test one time and he refused?
7	A.	Right.
8	Q.	Did he ever make any statements to you at all explaining why
9		he wanted to refuse or where he had been or what he had been
10		drinking? Did you ever discover what it was he had been drinking?
11	A.	No, I don't know what he was drinking.
12	Q.	Okay.
13	A.	But I did run a driving history on him, so I know that he's
14		been arrested before, so he's probably experienced or knew not to
15		take it or believed that it was better for him.
16	Q.	What record did you discover?
17	A.	I have a printout where or the post might have told me. When
18		I called him in, the post provided certain information. But
19		they told me it wasn't a felony, so four to five years ago.
20	Q.	That was done in Wayne County in 2007?
21	A.	I'm not sure what county. I would have to look.
22	Q.	Okay. I just noticed here on his ten-year record it shows it was
23		Wayne County.
24		Very well. Did there ever come a time after you stopped Mr. Doe
25		and talked to him at the vehicle and got him out and obtained his

1		License and registration and got him to the county jail, did
2		he appear to you to be able to understand your instructions?
3	A.	Yes.
4	Q.	Are there any other observations or is there any other information that
5		you have to indicate that Mr. Doe was intoxicated on that night?
6	A.	I cannot recall any other information at this time.
7		
8		Ms. GOOD: Thank you.
9		That's all I have for this officer.
10		Mr. SAM: That's all I have.
11		(Whereupon, the deposition was completed
12		and the Witness was excused at 9:28 a.m.)
13		
14		
15		----------------------------------
16		TROOPER OLGA HERNANDEZ
17		SUBSCRIBED AND SWORN to me before
18		This _____ day of _____, A.D., 2014
19		----------------------------------
20		Notary Public, State of: _____
21		County of Residence: _____
22		My commission expires: _____
23		
24		
25		

INTERVIEWING, INTERROGATION & COMMUNICATION for LAW ENFORCEMENT

19

<u>ERRATA</u> <u>SHEET</u>

DEPONENT: TROOPER OLGA HERNANDEZ

DATE OF DEPOSITION: FEBRUARY 1, 2014

CASE NAME: STATE V. DOE

PAGE LINE	CORRECTION	REASON

I HEREBY CERTIFY under the penalties of perjury that I have read the above and foregoing deposition, and that the testimony contained therein, together with any corrections in form or substance as above set out, is a true, correct and complete record of my testimony given at said deposition on the above-shown data.

_____

TROOPER OLGA HERNANDEZ

Deponent

DATED: _____

REFERENCES

Bank, S. (2001). From mental health professional to expert witness: testifying in court. *New Directions for Mental Health Services, Fall*(91), 57-66.

Boccaccini, M. (2002). What do we really know about witness preparation. *Behavioral Sciences and the Law, 20* (1/2), 161-189.

Crandall, C., Silvia, P., N'Gbala, A., Tsang, J., and Dawson, K. (2007). Balance theory, unit relations, and attribution: the underlying integrity of heiderian theory. *Review of General Psychology, 11*(1), 12-30.

Defoe, T. (2007). The truth is, you gave a lousy talk. *Chronicle of Higher Education, 54*(17). Retrieved from http://chronicle.com/article/The-Truth-Is-You-Gave-a-Lo/46627/

Edwards, S. (2006, June 13). Violent crime rates rising in U.S., FBI says: Murder, assault, robbery. *CanWest News Service*. Retrieved from http://www.lexisnexis.com

Fears, D. (2008, June 12). New criminal record: 7.2 million. *The Washington Post*. Retrieved from http://www.washingtonpost.com/wp-dyn/content/article/2008/06/11/AR2008061103458.html

Gaines, L.K., & Miller, R.L. (2009). Criminal justice in action (5th ed.). Belmont, CA: Wadsworth.

Honeycutt, L. (Ed.). (2004). *Aristotle's rhetoric*. Retrieved from http://rhetoric.eserver.org/aristotle/index.html

Kelley, L., Mueller, D., & Hemmens, C. (2004). To punish or rehabilitate revisited: An analysis of the purpose/goals of state correctional statutes, 1991-2002. *Criminal Justice Studies, 17*(4), 333-351.

Klimon, E. (1985). "Do you swear to tell the truth?" *Nursing Economics, 3*(2), 98-102.

Kingsbury, K. (2006). The next crime wave. *Time, 168*(24), 70-77.

Liptak, A. (2008, April 23). U.S. prison population dwarfs that of other nations. *International Herald Tribune.* Retrieved from http://www.iht.com/articles/ 2008/04/23/america/23prison.php

Maxey, C., and O'Connor, K. (2007). Dealing with blunders. *T+D, 61*(3), 78-79.

McCarthy, K. (2009). *Growth in prison and jail populations slowing: 16 states report declines in the number of prisoners.* Retrieved from Bureau of Justice Statistics Web site: http://bjs.ojp.usdoj.gov/index.cfm?ty=pbdetail&iid=361

Navarro, J. (2004). Testifying in the theater of the courtroom. *FBI Law Enforcement Bulletin, 73*(9), 26-30.

Nicholas, A. (n.d.). How to depose a police officer. *eHow.* Retrieved from http://www.ehow.com/print/how_8506257_depose-police-officer.html

Peterson, R. (1954). I swear to tell. *Saturday Evening Post, 227*(10), 88.

Reardon, K. (1981). *Persuasion: Theory and context.* Beverly Hills, CA: Sage Publications.

Resnick, P. and Knoll, J. (2007). Being an effective psychiatric expert witness. *Psychiatric Times, 24*(6). Retrieved from http://www.psychiatrictimes.com/ showArticle.jhtml?articleID=202602098

Schiappa, E. (1991). *Protagoras and logos.* Columbia, SC: University of South Carolina Press.

Smith R., and Hilderbrand, D. (n.d.). Courtroom testimony techniques: Success instead of survival. Retrieved from http://www.ronsmithand associates.com/CTT.htm

Stewart, S. (2007). Effective courtroom performance by Indiana law enforcement. *Clark County Prosecuting Attorney for Police Officers.* Retrieved http://www.clark prosecutor.org/html/police/police2.htm

Stremler, F. (1982). Introduction to communication systems (2nd ed.). Reading, MA: Addison-Wesley publishing Company.

Tower, W. (2008). Courtroom demeanor. *Kidjacked.* Retrieved from http://kidjacked.com/ defense/courtroom_demeanor.asp

Tucker, J., Donovan, D., and Marlatt, G. (Eds.). (1999). Changing additive behavior: Bridging clinical and public health strategies. New York: Guilford Press.

CHAPTER 6. POLICE OFFICER COMMUNICATIONS

Audience

- Police officers must learn how to communicate to different audiences
- Police management/administration
- Fellow police officers
- Media
- General public (non-violators)
- School children
- Prosecutors and Defense Attorneys
- Violators
- Victims
- Witnesses
- Jury
- Judge
- Intellectually Disabled

Police Communications

- Police officers develop friendships with one another
- Officers often share tragic experiences together
- Police officers are required not to disclose confidential information
- Media may view this lack of openness as a conspiracy
- Police develop shop talk = police jargon
- Police jargon = efficient communication in field
- Police officers must learn how to communicate with different audiences
- Police dispatch $\neq$ jury $\neq$ media $\neq$ school children $\neq$ violators $\neq$ …
- Speak to the jury in plain English

Radio Communication

- Police officers must learn how to effectively and efficiently use the radio
- Officers will be dispatched and will make inquiries over the radio
- Many people listen to the radio (important to talk professionally)
- Media, police chief, other departments, political activists, FCC, civilians
- Practice enhances professional communications over the radio

10 Codes & Signal Codes (*"9-Code, 10-Code"*, n.d.; Sleewee, 2013)

- 10 Codes not consistent among departments
- Signals not consistent among departments
- Lack of interagency communication

10 Codes (Examples of Differences)

	Dept. 1	**Dept. 2**
10-0	Person is dead	Signal weak
10-10	Fight in progress	Off duty
10-79	Coroner requested	Bomb threat

Signal Codes (Examples of Differences)

	Dept. 1	**Dept. 2**
Signal 7	Extreme emergency	Dead person
Signal 40	Stolen	Alarm
Signal 60	Drugs	Hostage situation

Just like the 10 codes and signal codes, there are many different versions of the phonetic alphabet. See the following for two commonly used phonetic alphabets in law enforcement.

Phonetic Alphabet 1

- A = Adam   B = Boy   C = Charles   D = David   E = Edward
- F = Frank   G = George   H = Henry   I – Ida   J = John
- K = King   L = Lincoln M = Mary   N = Nora   O = Ocean
- P = Paul   Q = Queen   R = Robert   S = Sam   T = Tom
- U = Union   V = Victor   W = William   X = X-Ray   Y = Young
- Z = Zebra

Phonetic Alphabet 2

- A = Alpha   B = Bravo   C = Charlie   D = Delta   E = Echo
- F = Foxtrot   G = Golf   H = Hotel   I = India   J = Juliet
- K = Kilo   L = Lima   M = Mike   N = November   O = Oscar
- P = PaPa   Q = Quebec   R = Romeo   S = Sierra   T = Tango
- U = Uniform   V = Victor   W = Whiskey   X = X-Ray   Y = Yankee
- Z = Zulu

Computer Communication

- Permanent record
- Officers need to communicate professionally or they may get fired
- Police departments may require police officers to use computers to run checks
- An officer must learn how to use the computer

Communicating with Defense Attorney – Purpose of the Cross Examination

- To show that the officer is in error
- To show that the officer is forgetful
- To show that the officer is unobservant
- To show that the officer is opinionated
- To show that the officer is untrustworthy
- To show that the officer is emotional and easily angered
- To show that the officer is discourteous

Communicating with Individuals - Accident Investigation

- To gain quick assessment of scene
- To request assistance, if needed
- To assist the injured
- To protect persons and property at the scene
- To protect the public
- To remove any situations that caused the crash
- To contain all witnesses, drivers, suspects
- To document the crash in a report

Communicating with Witnesses & Suspects – Voluntary Statement Forms

- Voluntary statements are an important part of many investigations
- They provide clues as to what happened
- They dissuade persons from changing their stories
- They refresh memories
- They allow for the determination of facts
- Police should talk to each person privately (individuals may be reluctant to talk to police if others are listening; spectators may interrupt with their own ideas)
- Police officers should first ask witnesses what happened
- If any points are not covered, officers need to ask specific questions
- Once all points are covered, officers should have the witnesses write their statements down on the voluntary statement forms
- Another person (e.g., the police officer) will need to sign as a witness that the witness completed the voluntary statement
- If a witness refuses to sign the statement, officer should not insist that the witness sign it (signature is not that important)

Police Reports

Table 9
Police Reports and their Purpose

Report Name	Purpose
Voluntary Statement	Form used to document the statements of witnesses or suspects
Miranda Rights	Form used to protect the suspect's constitutional rights; form used to waive constitutional rights
Case Report	Form used to record criminal activity with probable cause; if have suspect, will include an information and probable cause affidavit
Probable Cause Affidavit	Sworn statement of criminal violation (clues of crime)
Information	Criminal charge filed by prosecutor's office
Indictment	Criminal charge filed by grand jury
Property Record & Receipt	Form used to document the chain of custody of the evidence
Lab Request	Form used to request tests to be performed on the evidence by lab personnel
Vehicle Impound	Form used to remove a vehicle from the scene and to record of vehicle's damage and contents
Intelligence Report	Form used to document possible criminal activity but with no probable cause; police will record detailed information about a suspect that will be placed in the police database.
Show-up Report	Form used when witnesses identify possible suspects in the field
Line-up Report	Form used when witnesses identify possible suspects at police station
Photographic Line-up	Form used when witnesses identify possible suspects via photographs in police environment

Jail Intake Form	Form used to record arrested suspect's administrative information
Correctional Medical Survey	Form used to record arrested suspect's medical needs/conditions
Field Interview Card	Form used by police to collect information from individuals in the field
Crash Report	Form used to record vehicle damage and personal injuries related to vehicle crashes
Salvation Army Form	Form used to provide food and shelter to needy individuals free of charge
Public Speaker Form	Form used to describe information that the officer presented to the local community
Public Service Form	Form used to describe the help that an officer provided to the local community
Personal Illness Form	Form submitted to department and used to describe why an officer missed work due to health reasons
Application for 72 hour Medical Detention	A non-criminal application for the 72 hour detention of a person who may be mentally ill and needs to be evaluated by medical personnel
Custody Order/Custody Hold Form	Form used by an officer and submitted to the jail that indicates the criminal charges being filed against the suspect and that gives the jail the authority to detain the suspect
Temporary Hold Form	Form used by officers to hold suspects for 24 hours without charging them of a crime

Following are several of the forms described above. For additional police report forms, see *Report Writing for Police Officers* (Davis, 2013).

INTERVIEWING, INTERROGATION & COMMUNICATION for LAW ENFORCEMENT

VOLUNTARY STATEMENT This is page _____ of ___.

_____ Police Department

Date_____ Place _____ time started _____
I, _____, am _____ years of age, being born on _____ have been warned by _____, with the _____ police department, that I do not have to make any statement at all, nor answer any questions. I was also warned and advised of my right to a lawyer of my own choice before or at any time during questioning, and if I am not able to hire a lawyer, I may request to have a lawyer appointed to me. I do not now want a lawyer, and I waive my right to the advice and presence of a lawyer, knowing that anything I say can and will be used against me in a court of law. I now want to make a statement.

_____
_____
_____
_____
_____
_____
_____
_____
_____

Draw a diagonal line through all unused space. Have person place initials at end of statement.

This form was completed at (time) _____.

Signature of person providing statement _____

Witness_____ Signature_____ Badge # _____
      Print name

Witness_____ Signature_____ Badge # _____
      Print name

Page____of_____ Type of Report _____ Report #_____

Interview Statement

_____
_____
_____
_____
_____
_____
_____
_____
_____
_____
_____
_____
_____
_____
_____
_____
_____
_____
_____
_____

Draw a diagonal line through all unused space and initial at end of statement.

_____ _____ _____
Print Name   Signature   Date/Time

Witness_____ Signature_____
         Print name

Witness_____ Signature_____
         Print name

MIRANDA WARNING

_____*POLICE DEPARTMENT*

Subject's Name: _____ SS#_____
Location of Interview: _____
Date: _____ Beginning Time of Interview_____ Ending Time of Interview_____

MIRANDA RIGHTS

Before we ask you any questions, you must understand your rights. Initial each line to indicate your understanding of, and agreement with, that line.

_____ You have the right to remain silent.

_____ Anything you say can and will be used against you in a court of law.

_____ You have the right to talk to a lawyer for advice before we ask you any questions and to have him with you during questioning.

_____ If you cannot afford a lawyer, the court will appoint one to represent you without cost if you wish.

_____ If you decide to answer questions now without a lawyer present, you will still have the right to stop answering at any time. You also have the right to stop answering at any time until you talk to a lawyer.

_____ I have read this statement of my rights and I understand what my rights are.

WAIVER OF RIGHTS

_____ I am willing to make a statement and answer questions. I do not want a lawyer at this time. I understand and know what I am doing. No promises or threats have been made to me and no pressure of any kind has been used against me.

_____ _____ Date: _____ Time: _____
Print Name   Signature

Witness: _____   _____
  Print Name   Signature

Witness: _____   _____
  Print Name   Signature

When interrogating juveniles, legal guardian signatures also required.

Legal Guardian of Juvenile

As parent or legal guardian of _____, I have read the rights as set out above and understand them. Neither the juvenile nor I want a lawyer at this time and the juvenile is willing to answer questions.

Signed_____

Witness:_____

Witness:_____

Date_____ Time_____ _____.M.

AFFIDAVIT FOR PROBABLE CAUSE (General)

State of _____   IN THE _____ COURT
County of _____   CAUSE NO. _____

STATE OF _____
VS.
_____
DOB: _____
SSN: _____

FOR OFFENSE (title): _____ Code: _____

COMES NOW, _____, who being duly sworn upon oath, says that:

1. He/She is an officer with the _____ Department, and believes the following to be true.

2. On or about: (date of offense) _____ 20____, at the following location: _____, which is in _____ County, _____ (State), one (defendant) _____

3. Did then and there commit the following violation (code) _____, by (describe the specific act that supports the criminal charge via **elements of the crime**)
_____
_____
_____

4. This officer believes the above facts to be true because (check all that apply)

   ⊣ I personally observed the activity described herein.

   ⊣ The above was told to me by another sworn law enforcement officer, upon whom I have relied on in the past for information and found his/her information to be credible without exception.

- ⚓ The above was told to me by the victim of a crime, who has no apparent motive to lie, and said statement was given in a straightforward and non-evasive manner, which indicated that the statement was credible.

- ⚓ The above was told to me by a witness of a crime, who has no apparent motive to lie, and said statement was given in a straightforward and non-evasive manner, which indicated that the statement was credible. Further, witness' statement was corroborated by independent evidence.

- ⚓ The above was told to me by the defendant, which was a statement made against his/her penal interests. Further, Defendant's statement was corroborated by independent evidence.

I swear or affirm under penalty of perjury that the foregoing representations are true.

Dated on this _____ day of _____, 20____

_____
Arresting Officer's Name & Badge #

Approved by: _____
Prosecutor

INFORMATION FOR VIOLATION OF LAW

State of _____   IN THE _____ COURT
County of _____   CAUSE NO. _____

STATE OF _____
VS.

_____
DOB: _____   SSN: _____

INFORMATION FOR (OFFENSE TITLE): _____
CODE _____ **CLASS** _____ ☐ **MISDEMEANOR** ☐ **FELONY**
COMES NOW, _____ (name of officer), who being duly sworn upon oath, says that on or about : (date of offense) _____, 20___, at (location of offense) _____, in _____ County, _____ (State), one (defendant) _____ of (Defendant's address) _____ did then and there RECKLESSLY, KNOWINGLY, or INTENTIONALLY: **(elements of the crime)**
_____
_____

All of which is contrary to the form of the statute in such cases made and provided, and against the peace and dignity of the State of _____.

I swear or affirm under penalty of perjury that the foregoing representations are true.

Dated on this _____ day of _____, 20___

_____
ARRESTING OFFICER'S NAME & BADGE #

Witness List:
Approved by: _____
PROSECUTOR

DAVIS, LESLIE, DAVIS

POLICE PROPERTY RECORD & RECEIPT FORM

$(\alpha \rightarrow \sum \Delta \rightarrow \Omega)$ PRR # _____

Name of Investigating Officer	Badge Number	Report # / Citation #
Name of officer submitting evidence to lab	Badge Number	Lab # (issued by lab)
Date of Evidence Collection	Time of Evidence Collection	Who was evidence collected from

Location of recovery	County
Witnesses to recovery	
Specific detail or title of offense (use law book if a crime)	Offense code (only if criminal case)

Evidence Description for Lab (quantity, serial #, color, etc.)

Item #	
Item #	
Item #	

Chain of Custody (If no subjects involved, use word "recovered" in "From" box.)

Item #	Date/Time	From: Signature & Badge #	To: Signature & Badge #	Code	Location	Remarks

Code: T = Transferred; S = Stored; R = Released; D = Destroyed

REQUEST FOR POLICE LABORATORY EXAMINATION

☐ New Case   ☐ Supplemental Case   Lab Assigned Report # _____

Name of Investigating Officer	Badge Number	Case #	PRR #
Police Agency & Address		Phone #	ORI #
Date		Time	County of Occurrence

Type of Case Investigation (most serious criminal violation)	Police Case Report #
Suspect Name	Victim Name
Delivered to lab by / Badge #	Received in lab by / Date & time

Evidence Description for Lab (quantity, serial #, color, etc.)

Item #	Description of Items being submitted to lab

Lab Exam Request (Specify each item number to be tested (e.g., "Test item X for ......")

_____
_____
_____
_____

Field Interview Card

_____ Police Department

County	Date	Time
Department Incident Number	Reason for contact	
Location of Contact	Pedestrian Stop ☐ Y ☐ N	Traffic Stop ☐ Y ☐ N ☐ Driver ☐ Passenger
Disposition		

Name of Subject				Nickname			
Address				Phone			
State ID or Driver's License #			State	SSN			
Age	Sex	Race	Height	Weight	Build		Complexion
DOB	POB	Hair	Eyes	Marks/Tattoos (Type & Location)			
Subject's Parents' Names							
Clothing Description							
Persons with Subject at Scene							
Gang Affiliation							
Vehicle Make		Model		VIN#			
Color		Tag		State			
Owner of Vehicle				Owner at Scene ☐ Y ☐ N			

INTERVIEWING, INTERROGATION & COMMUNICATION for LAW ENFORCEMENT

SUSPECT REPORT

_____ POLICE DEPARTMENT

Case # _____   PAGE____OF____

CRIME	CRIME TITLE		CODE	LOCATION		DATE
SUSP. VEH	LICENSE#	STATE / YEAR / MAKE	MODEL	BODY STYLE __2DR __4DR __CONVERT __P/U __STRAIGHT TRUCK __VAN __RV __M/C __OTHER		
	COLOR/COLOR	OTHER CHARACTERISTICS		DISPOSTION OF VEHICLE		
	REGISTERED OWNER					
SUSPECT	SUSPECT NAME	SEX	RACE: __UK __HISP __NATIVE AM. __ASIAN __WHT __BLK __OTH			
	AKA	DOB	AGE	HT	WT	BUILD: __THIN __MEDIUM __UK __HEAVY __MUSCLR
	HAIR: __BLK __BRN __RED __BLN __GRAY __WHITE __N/A __OTHER __UK		EYES: __BLK __GRN __GRAY __UK __BRN __BLU __HAZEL __OTHER			
	RESIDENCE ADDRESS	STATE	ZIP	RES. PHONE	SSN	
	BUSINESS ADDRESS	STATE	ZIP	BUS PHONE	OCCUPATION	
	CLOTHING	ARRESTED ▫YES ▫NO	STATUS ▫DRIVER ▫PED ▫PASS	GANG AFFILIATION: HOW KNOWN:		
	DL STATE & #					

DAVIS, LESLIE, DAVIS

AMOUNT OF HAIR	HAIR STYLE	COMPLEXION	TATTOOS/SCARS	WEAPON(S)
__UNKNOWN	__UNKNOWN	__UNKNOWN	__UNKNOWN	__UNKNOWN
__THICK	__LONG	__CLEAR	__FACE	__CLUB
__THIN	__SHORT	__ACNE	__TEETH	__HANDGUN
__RECEDING	__COLLAR	__POCKED	__NECK	__OTHER UNK GUN
__BALD	__MILITARY	__FRECKLED	__R/ARM	__RIFLE
__OTHER	__CREW CUT	__WEATHERED	__L/ARM	__SHOTGUN
	__RIGHT PART	__ALBINO	__R/HAND	__TOYGUN
	__LEFT PART	__OTHER	__L/HAND	__SIMULATED
	__CENTER PART		__R/LEG	__POCKET KNIFE
	__STRAIGHT		__L/LEG	__BUTCHER KNIFE
	__PONY TAIL		__R/SHOULDER	__HANDS/FEET
	__AFRO		__L/SHOULDER	__BODILY FORCE
	__TEASED		__FRONT TORSO	__STRNGULATION
	__OTHER		__BACK TORSO	__TIRE IRON
			__OTHER	__OTHER

TYPE OF HAIR	FACIAL HAIR	GLASSES	UNIQUE CLOTHING	HAD WEAPON IN OR ABOUT
__UNKNOWN	__UNKNOWN	__UNKNOWN	__UNKNOWN	__UNKNOWN
__CLEAN	__N/A	__NONE	__NONE	__N/A
__DIRTY	__CLN SHAVEN	__YES	__CAP/HAT	__BAG/BRIEFCASE
__GREASY	__MOUSTACHE	__REG GLASSES	__GLOVES	__NEWSPAPER
__MATTED	__FULL BEARD	__SUN GLASSES	__SKI MASK	__POCKET
__ODOR	__GOATEE	__WIRE FRAME	__STOCKING MASK	__SHOULDER
__OTHER	__FU MANCHU	__PLASTIC FRAME	__OTHER	__HOLSTER
	__LOWER LIP	__COLOR		__WAISTBAND
	__SIDE BURNS	__OTHER		__OTHER
	__FUZZ			
	__UNSHAVEN			
	__OTHER			

R/L HANDED	VOICE	WEAPON FEATURE
__UNKOWN	__UNKNOWN	__UNKNOWN
	__N/A	__ALTERED STOCK
__RIGHT	__LISP	__SAWED OFF
	__SLURRED	__AUTOMATIC
__LEFT	__STUTTER	__BOLT ACTION
	__ACCENT	__PUMP
	__DESCRIBE_____	__REVOLVER
	__OTHER	__BLUE STEEL
		__CHROME/NICKEL
		__DOUBLE BARREL
		__SINGLE BARREL
		__OTHER

Officer's Name (printed)	Officer's Signature & Badge #	Date	Approved by Supervisor ☐ Yes ☐ No

INTERVIEWING, INTERROGATION & COMMUNICATION for LAW ENFORCEMENT

POLICE DEPARTMENT - INTELLIGENCE REPORT

DATE:_____ TIME:_____ OFFICER & BADGE #:_____

SUBJECT NAME:_____ ALIAS:_____

DOB:_____ AGE:_____ RACE:_____ SEX:_____

SSN:_____ DL#_____ STATE:_____

HEIGHT:_____ WEIGHT:_____ HAIR:_____ EYES:_____

SCARS, MARKS, TATTOOS: _____

OCCUPATION: _____

ADDRESS: _____ PHONE: _____

VEHICLE DESCRIPTION: _____

SUBJECT'S ASSOCIATES: _____

STATUS OF SUBJECT (CIRCLE ONE) **SUSPECT   WANTED   ARRESTED**

INFORMATION SOURCE: _____

NOTES (Articulate reason for suspicion):
_____
_____
_____
_____

DAVIS, LESLIE, DAVIS

IN FIELD SHOW-UP REPORT

_____ Police Department

CASE NO._____   PRIORITY __YES __NO

OFFENSE	LOCATION OF OCCURRENCE	
VICTIM	DATE OF OCCURRENCE	COUNTY

ADMONITION OF VICTIMS AND WITNESSES:
It is requested that you look at an individual who has been temporarily detained by police. You are under no obligation to participate. This person may or may not have committed the crime. It is just as important to eliminate innocent persons from suspicion as it is to identify the perpetrator. Do not let handcuffs or police presence influence your decision. Please do not discuss the case with any other witnesses.

BY SIGNING THIS FORM, I AM INDICATING THAT I FULLY UNDERSTAND THE ADMONITION PRESENTED TO ME BY OFFICER _____, REGARDING THE IN FIELD SHOW-UP.

_____   _____   _____
Printed Name of Witness   Signature of Witness   Date

IDENTIFICATION:

    ⁋ I CANNOT IDENTIFY THIS INDIVIDUAL AS THE SUSPECT.
    ⁋ I CAN IDENTIFY THIS INDIVIDUAL AS THE SUSPECT.

ADDITIONAL COMMENTS OF VICTIM/WITNESSES:

_____

SIGNATURE OF WITNESS: _____ DATE: _____
WITNESSED BY OFFICER: _____ DATE/TIME: _____
LOCATION OF IN FIELD SHOW-UP_____

DATE & TIME OF IN FIELD SHOW-UP_____
NAME AND DOB OF PERSON VIEWED_____

Officer's Name (printed)	Officer's Signature & Badge #	Date	Approved by Supervisor ☐ Yes ☐ No

PHOTOGRAPIC LINEUP PROCEDURES

A LINE-UP THAT IS SUGGESTIVE IS INADMISSIBLE IN COURT. TO BE SURE YOUR LINEUP IDENTIFICATION WILL NOT BE EXCLUDED AT TRIAL AS UNFAIR, FOLLOW THESE GUIDELINES.

1. THE PHOTOGRAPIC LINEUP MUST CONSIST OF AT LEAST (6) PHOTOGRAPHS.
2. USE ALL COLOR OR ALL BLACK AND WHITE PHOTOGRAPHS, DO NOT MIX.
3. EVERYONE IN THE DISPLAY SHOULD BE OF THE SAME SEX, RACE, APPROXIMATE AGE AND GENERAL FEATURES.
4. TRY TO USE PHOTOGRAPHS OF THE SAME APPROXIMATE SIZE, DEPICTING THE SAME APPROXIMATE SHOTS OF THE FACES (SUCH AS ALL CLOSE UPS OR NOT CLOSE UPS).
5. LABEL EACH PHOTOGRAPH WITH A NUMBER FROM ONE (#1) THROUGH SIX (#6).
6. IF YOU HAVE TWO OR MORE WITNESSES, SEPARATE THEM BEFORE VIEWING THE LINEUP, SO THAT ONE WITNESS DOES NOT IMPROPERLY INFLUENCE ANOTHER WITNESS (WE WANT INDEPENDENT OPINION).
7. READ THE ADMONITION STATEMENT TO THE WITNESS AND HAVE THE WITNESS SIGN THE ADMONITION PART OF THE REPORT.
8. DISPLAY THE PHOTOGRAPHIC LINEUP TO THE WITNESS.
9. IF POSSIBLE, RECORD THE WITNESS' EXACT WORDS, SUCH AS, "MAYBE IT'S HIM", "I GUARANTEE THAT'S HIM."

PHOTOGRAPHIC LINE-UP

_____ Police Department

CASE NO._____   PRIORITY __YES __NO

Offense	Code	County
Location of offense	Victim	Date of occurrence

PHOTOGRAPHIC LINE-UP:

ON_____(DATE/TIME),

AT (Location) _____(Victim/Witness)_____WAS READ THE FOLLOWING ADMONITION, AND THEN ALLOWED TO VIEW THE PHOTOGRAPH LINE-UP

ADMONITION OF VICTIMS AND WITNESSES:
It is requested that you look at a group of photographs. You are under no obligation to pick out any photographs. The suspect may or may not be in the photographic line-up. It is just as important to eliminate innocent persons from suspicion as it is to identify the perpetrator. Please do not discuss the photographs with any other witnesses.

I FULLY UNDERSTAND THE ADMONITION PRESENTED TO ME BY OFFICER_____,
REGARDING THE PHOTOGRAPHIC LINE-UP   ☐YES   ☐ NO

_____   _____ _____
Printed Name of Witness   Signature of Witness   Date

IDENTIFICATION: ☐ I CANNOT MAKE ANY IDENTIFICATION
☐ I CAN IDENTIFY PHOTOGRAPH# _____ AS THE SUSPECT.

STATEMENT OF WITNESS/VICTIM:
_____
_____

SIGNATURE OF WITNESS: _____ DATE/TIME_____
WITNESSED BY OFFICER: _____ DATE/TIME_____
PHOTOGRAPH# _____ IS THAT OF: _____

Officer's Name (printed)	Officer's Signature & Badge #	Date	Approved by Supervisor ☐ Yes ☐ No

Jail Intake Form

_____ Police Department Booking Record

Booking Number	Arresting Agency	ORI #	State ID	MUG #	Inmate's Photograph
Name	Sex	Race	Height	Weight	
Date of Birth	Hair	Complexion	Build	Eyes	
SSN	Home Phone	Work Phone	Marital Status	Resident Status	
Driver's License #	State of DL	Home Address		Place of Birth	

Information Given at time of Booking   DOB   SSN   Address
Name:

Gang Affiliation	Tattoos	Place & Address of Employment

Emergency Contact Information
Name: Address: Home phone #:

Ill or Injured __YES __NO	TYPE OF ILLNESS OF INJURY	Type of Medication Taking

Special Management for Inmate __Medical __Mental __Suicidal __High Security __Other (Describe):

Arresting Officer	Arrest Date/Time	Arrest Location
Booking Officer	Booking Date/Time	Booking Status (Complete/Pending)
Received by Officer	Custodial Search by	
Charge 1 (Title)	State Code	Charge Level (M or F) & Class (A-F)
Charge 2 (Title)	State Code	Charge Level (M or F) & Class (A-F)

Arresting Officer's Signature	Arresting Officer's Badge #	Arresting Officer's Department	
Fine	Bail	Disposition	
Inmate Tracking #	Intake Date	Block	Cell
Scheduled Release Date	Actual Release Date	Release Type	

INTERVIEWING, INTERROGATION & COMMUNICATION for LAW ENFORCEMENT

CORRECTIONAL MEDICAL SURVEY

INTAKE SCREENING AND TRIAGE

Date Booked In _____ NAME_____ BOOKING#_____ DOB____ SEX __

STATEMENT OF BOOKING OFFICER		
DOES THE INMATE SEEM TO BE UNDER THE INFLUENCE OF DRUGS, IMPAIRED, OR INJURED IN ANY WAY? ___YES ___NO Comments _____		
OFFICER'S SIGNATURE: DEPT: DATE:		
MEDICAL/MENTAL QUESTIONNAIRE 1. DO YOU HAVE ANY OF THE FOLLOWING PROBLEMS? __ASTHMA __ENT PROBLEMS __HERNIA __INTESTINAL DISORDERS __BACK INJURIES __FX/SPRAINS __HIV/AIDS __MENATL PROBLEMS __DEFORMITIES __HEART TROUBLE __HIGH BLOOD PRESSURE __PSYCH. HOSPITAL __TUBERCULOSIS __DENTAL PROBLEMS __STD __HEPATITIS: TYPE____ __DIABETES __SEIZURES __PREGNANT/DUE DATE_____ DATE:_____ __OTHER_____ ALLERGIES_____		
	Y	N
2. ARE YOU TAKING OR DO YOU NEED TO TAKE ANY PRESCRIBED MEDICATIONS (INCLUDING PSYCHIATRIC, BIRTH CONTROL PILLS)?		
3. HAVE YOU EVER BEEN TREATED FOR TUBERCULOSIS?		
4. HAVE YOU HAD A COUGH FOR MORE THAN THREE WEEKS WITH ANY OF THE FOLLOWING: FEVER, WEIGHT LOSS, FATIGUE, NIGHT SWEATS?		
5. HAVE YOU HAD A HEAD INJURY/TRAFFIC ACCIDENT OR ALTERCATION IN THE PAST 7 HOURS?		
6. ARE YOU AN ALCOHOLIC? DATE OF LAST DRINK: HOW MUCH DO YOU DRINK?		
7. ANY SEIZURES OR DTS?		
8. DO YOU USE ANY STREET DRUGS SUCH AS HEROIN, COCAINE, METHAPHETAMINE, MARIJUANA OR ANY OTHER DRUGS?		
9. ARE YOU RECEIVING METHADONE? __DETOX OR __MAINTENANCE		
10. DO YOU HAVE ANY RASHES, CUTS, BOILS, ABSCESSES, OR OTHER SKIN DISEASES?		
11. DO YOU HAVE ANY ARTIFICIAL LIMBS, BRACES, DENTURES, HEARING AID, CONTACT LENSES OR EYEGLASSES?		
12. HAVE YOU EVER TRIED TO HARM YOURSELF OR TAKE YOUR OWN LIFE? WHEN:		

13.	ARE YOU THINKING OF HARMING YOURSELF NOW?	
14.	ARE YOU CURRENTLY RECEIVING PSYCHIATRIC TREATMENT?	
15.	HAVE YOU BEEN A PATIENT IN A HOSPITAL WITHIN THE LAST 3 MONTHS?	
16.	HAVE YOU EVER BEEN TREATED AT A REGIONAL CENTER OR DIAGNOSED WITH DEVELOPMENTAL PROBLEMS?	
17.	DO YOU KNOW OF ANY MEDICAL REASON WHY YOU CANNOT WORK IN JAIL?	

TRIAGE DISPOSITION	WORK STATUS
__ACCEPTABLE FOR BOOKING	__GENERAL
__MEDICAL	__KITCHEN
__REFER TO MENTAL HEALTH	__LITE DUTY/NO KITCHEN
__REFUSED ASSESMENT	__NO WORK
__E.R. REASON	__HOLD FOR FOLLOW-UP/RECHECK ON:

Field Interviews and Suspect Information

Field Interviews

- Police may identify local needs and assist residents
- Police may talk to informants and gather intelligence
- Police may make arrest once probable cause is attained
- Interview = general questioning; no probable cause to suspect person of crime
- Interrogation = formal, adversarial; person is suspected of crime

Key Items in Suspect Identification

- Sex
- Height
- Weight
- Build
- Age
- Race
- Face
- Complexion
- Hair
- Forehead
- Eyebrows
- Eyes
- Nose
- Ears
- Mustache
- Mouth
- Lips
- Teeth
- Beard
- Chin
- Neck
- Distinctive marks and features (e.g., scars, tattoos)
- Peculiarities
- Clothing
- Voice
- Distinctive behaviors (e.g., walk)
- Weapon
- Jewelry

Table 10
Difference between Interview and Interrogation (Swanson et al., 2009)

Factor	Difference between interview and interrogation	
	Interview	Interrogation
Purpose	Obtain information	To test information
Relationship between interrogator and suspect	Cooperative	Adversarial or hostile
Level of Certainty	Less than probable cause of guilt	Probable cause of guilt
Planning	Moderate	Extensive
Environment	Private or semi-private	Private
Person Under Arrest	No	Yes
Miranda Warning given	No	Yes

Table 11
Qualities of Good Interviewers and Interrogators
(Swanson et al., 2009)

Qualities of Good Interviewers and Interrogators
• Sensitive to constitutional rights • Adaptable • Culturally sensitive • Culturally informed • Optimistic • Know elements of crime • Role player • Patient • Confident • Objective

Police-Individual Encounters

When a police officer interviews a suspect in the field, the officer must maintain a safe position. The police officer should be in front of the suspect and at about 45 degrees off to the side (Siddle, 2005). See Figure 8. For safety reasons, the police officer should not be at the suspect's inside position or within 6 feet of the suspect. The police officer should be bladed in such a manner that the firearm is away from the suspect. If the police officer needs to take notes, the officer should hold the clipboard between him and the suspect so that the officer can use his peripheral vision to monitor the suspect's actions.

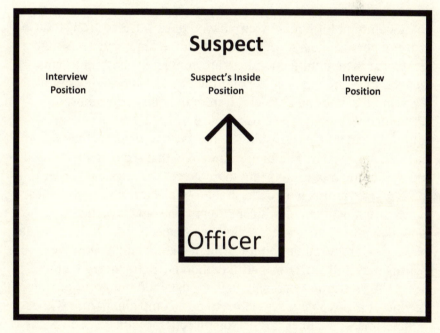

Figure 8. Field Interview position.

People are sources of information. There are several different types of individuals who provide information that may be used during court proceedings (Swanson et al., 2009). One source of information is the **complainant**. The complainant is the person who requests that legal action be taken. A complainant may request that a police report (e.g., crash report) be completed or the complainant may file a civil action lawsuit against a person. A **witness** is a person who saw something related to a crime. A witness may provide a written statement that provides first-hand information about the event. This may prove very valuable because a written statement may refresh the mind of a witness during court proceedings, which may be years later, or may prevent a witness from changing his or her story in court. For example, it is not uncommon for female victims who have suffered from spouse abuse to change their stories in court. Some female victims may feel that if their significant others are convicted and sent to jail, then their children may suffer significant hardships. For example, if a woman is poor and has children, it may be very important to her to receive income from her spouse. If her husband is sent to jail for a year, and, as a result, she receives no income, then her children may suffer. The mother may feel that the benefits of food and shelter are more important than the cost of physical abuse. In some cases, victims may be hesitant to make any claim of domestic violence against their significant others. In some jurisdictions, the state may prosecute domestic violence suspects in order to protect the victims from retaliation for filing the complaints. However, victims may still suffer if their livelihoods are impacted by the arrests. A **victim** is a person who has sustained injury as a result of a crime. It is possible for a victim to be a complainant or a witness to the crime. A **suspect** is a person directly or indirectly involved with violating the law. For example, if a man provided a woman with a gun, which she used to kill someone, the woman would be directly involved with the murder and the man would be indirectly involved with the murder. An **informant** provides information about a crime but is not the victim, witness, or suspect.

Police – Public Encounters (del Carmen, 2014)

Classification

- Consensual encounter
- Detention
- Arrest

Consensual Encounter

- Police officer does not need justification to initiate contact
- Police officer does not intend to restrain
- Officer may approach person in a public place
- Officer does not exert any authority over person
- Officer has no specific power to frisk or search person
- Officer should identify self as police officer
- Officer may ask for identification
- Officer may shine a spot light on the person
- Officer may develop probable cause to make arrest
- Officer may not demand person to answer questions
- Officer may ask questions while still maintaining a consensual status
- To make things clear, the officer should state to the suspects that they are not being detained and that they are free to leave, and then the officer should ask them if they are willing to answer a few questions
- Officer may ask individuals to take their hands out of their pockets
- Notion of consensual encounter extends to the police car
- Person is free to leave the scene at any time
- Person may ignore the officer
- Person does not have to cooperate with the officer

Detention

- Police officer needs reasonable suspicion to detain a person
- Police officer intends to restrain
- Officer can stop a person and can ask the person questions to investigate a crime
- Officer can frisk a person if safety is a concern
- Officer can hold a person for a reasonable amount of time to investigate a crime (only long enough to do job)
- Officer may ask for identification
- Person is not free to leave the scene
- Person may not ignore the officer
- Person does have to cooperate with the officer

Arrest

- Police officer needs probable cause to arrest a person
- Officer can arrest a person if 51% confident that the person committed a crime
- Police officer intends to arrest the person
- Officer can search a person after an arrest
- Person is not free to leave the scene
- Person may not ignore the officer
- Person does have to cooperate with the officer

REFERENCES

9-Code, 10-Code (n.d.). Dispatch magazine on-line. Retrieved from http://www.911dispatch.com/info/tencode.html

Davis, W.L. (2013). *Report writing for police officers* (2nd ed.). Bloomington, IN: Balboa.

Del Carmen, R.V. (2014). *Criminal procedures: Laws & practice* (9th ed.). Belmont, CA: Wadsworth.

Siddle, B.K. (2005). *PPCT Defensive Tactics.* Belleville, IL: PPCT Management Systems.

Sleewee (2013). *Police Signal Codes What Are Police Signal Codes?* Retrieved from http://www.sleewee.com/police-signal-codes.php

Swanson, C.R., Chamelin, N.C., Territo, L., & Taylor, R.W. (2009). *Criminal investigation* (10th ed.). Boston, MA: McGraw Hill.

CHAPTER 7. INTERVIEWING, QUESTIONS, AND THEIR USES

Interviews occur frequently throughout people's lives. According to Stewart and Cash (2008), individuals are often unaware that they are voluntarily or involuntarily participating in an interview. Individuals often give or receive information, interview or recruit for a job, or are engaged in the act of persuasion. Interviews are intermingled among interpersonal interactions and conversations and may occur in small group environments, in public presentations, and in structured interview settings. They may be structured or unstructured, sophisticated or simple, threatening or supportive, and they may take only a few minutes or last for several hours

This chapter will focus on the essential elements of interviewing, and it will describe how interviewing is distinguished from other forms of interpersonal communication. Interviewing is a relational form of communication and each type of interview has its pros and cons. Several types of interviews will be discussed and several examples will be presented.

Interviews are **interactional**. There is an exchange or sharing of roles, feelings, attitudes, beliefs, values, motives, and responsibilities in the sharing of information. The relationship and roles of the interviewer and interviewee may change from time to time during the interview process. It always takes at least two persons to make an interview successful. In addition, interviews frequently involve an element of risk.

Interviews are a complex and continuously changing **process.** This process is a dynamic interaction of variables that usually occur within a system or structure. No interview occurs in a vacuum, and communication and interactions are not static. While all interviews are unique, they all involve common elements of communication and interaction, which include motivation, perceptions, assumptions, expectations, verbal and non-verbal communication, levels of disclosure, listening, and feedback. Each participant brings his or her own unique personal history, values, beliefs, knowledge, strengths, and limitations to the interview process.

While interviews often involve more than two people, they never involve more than two **parties**, which are the interviewer and the interviewee. If more than two parties are participating, a group interaction is occurring – not an interview. Interviewing is a dyadic process that always involves two parties. One or both of the parties will bring an important goal to the interview process that will include a predetermined, serious **purpose**. The interview process includes a structured pre-planning of the selected topic, generating appropriate **questions**, and gathering information. The asking and answering of questions are critical to all interviews (e.g., public surveys, probing/informational/journalistic, recruiting, employment, performance assessments, persuasive, counseling, and health care applications).

Each type of interview serves a distinctly different purpose. The information-giving interviews involve orientation, instruction, training, coaching, and briefings. Information- gathering interviews include public surveys and polls, exit interviews, research and journalistic interviews, and medical and psychological interviews. Participant selection, screening, and placement are critical to the interviewing process. The interviewer must always be aware of potential interviewee problems and concerns as they relate to evaluations, appraisals, counseling, discipline, correction and reprimand, separation, and firing. The interviewer may experience difficulty in a) dealing with complaints and grievances, b) receiving suggestions, and c) discussing shared problems to achieve desirable solutions. Persuasion, therefore, is a major factor in changing the way each party thinks, acts, and feels.

Interviews are a relational form of communication between the two participating parties (the interviewer and the interviewee). Their relationship may be intimate, distant, casual, or formal and may depend on the interview situation, which may alter the interview relationship. Stewart and Cash (2008) describe an interview as "an interactional communication process between two parties, at least one of whom has a predetermined and serious purpose, which involves the asking and answering of questions" (p. 13). For an interview to be successful, one must understand the role of each party, the giving and receiving of information, the value of feedback, and the situational influence of outside factors.

The model of interpersonal communication contains many interactional variables, which include the interviewing parties, their roles, the perceptions they have of each other, the levels of communication (e.g., verbal and non-verbal, listening, and feedback), and the environment in which the interview takes place. One must develop the ability to detect empathy, to comprehend and evaluate information, to resolve problems, and to strategically utilize silence when evaluating non-verbal messages. Each party must understand the process of successful interviewing and must have an acute awareness of the interactional variables. These factors are a major determinant to the success of the interview process and whether the desired outcomes are realized.

The interviewer and interviewee need to be adaptable and flexible in deciding their interview method. The interview method may be directive (structured; the job interviewer maintains complete control), non-directive (unstructured; job interviewer allows the interviewee a lot of latitude in answering the questions), or a combination of both (University of North Carolina – Charlotte, 2014). Each individual is unique in his or her approach to the particular interview scenario because each individual is a product of his or her own past in terms of gender, age, race, ethnic background, culture, self-concept, self-esteem, language, verbal and non-verbal communication, and territoriality. In addition, knowledge of kinesics (i.e., the study of body language), and proxemics (i.e., the study of personal space) is important because individuals in different cultures communicate and relate to one another in different manners. In short, the behaviors and personalities of individuals are strong driving forces that impact the interviewing process, and, consequently, individual participation.

Being able to create effective questions is the cornerstone of any good interview. A person's ability to consciously ask the specific kinds of questions needed in order to obtain pertinent information is a skill that requires insight, awareness, and practice. Furthermore, there are multiple ways of designing questions for optimal results. Indeed, the wording and phrasing of questions will have a significant impact on the responses. If the goal of an interview is to obtain particular data, then it is crucial that the information seeker (i.e., the interviewer) align the design of the questions so that they generate the information sought.

Open-Ended Questions

The open-ended question is one of the most frequently used questions in interviews. The primary reason to use this type of question is to gain as much information as possible. These questions are not limited by only asking for specific bits of information. These questions provide the respondents with the freedom to answer in as much detail as they desire.

EXAMPLES:

1. What did you find when you entered the room?
2. What thoughts came to your mind when you discovered the he had disappeared?
3. What do you know about the tenants in the room above you?
4. At what point did you decide to investigate the noises next door?

The advantage of the open-ended question is that it encourages the respondent to elaborate on his or her answers or observations. In addition, more in-depth answers can often give the interviewer insight into the respondent's feelings, biases, and amount of understanding of the topic being discussed. The disadvantage of the open-ended question is it can give the respondent more time to engage in rambling replies, which could contain unrelated or irrelevant information that could hinder obtaining solid factual responses.

Close-Ended Questions

Close-ended questions are questions that are very narrow in detail. These questions limit the respondent's ability to decide how much information to provide in his or her answer.

EXAMPLES:

1. Where you the one driving the car?
2. Did you see someone leave the store?
3. Are you tired?
4. Are you willing to tell me the information?

Close-ended questions often result in gaining only a 'yes' or 'no' response.

Advantages of the close-ended questions include the ability to control the length of time of the interview, gaining very specific information, and answers that are easier to record and remember. Disadvantages of the close-ended question include not gaining enough information, less insight into the respondent's mindset and beliefs, and the respondent is not able to elaborate or explain answers in detail, which could result in frustration on the respondent's part.

EXERCISE: OPEN-ENDED AND CLOSE-ENDED QUESTIONS

Change these close-ended questions into open-ended questions

1. Did you see another woman outside?
2. Did you leave the location?
3. Are you going to discuss this problem?

Change these open-ended questions to close-ended questions

1. How often does he come by the house?
2. What were you thinking when the car drove away?
3. What motivated you to decide to enlist?

Presumptive Questions

Presumptive questions are questions that have a presupposition of fact that serves as a platform from which the question emerges. For example, if someone is asked if they are going to take out the trash before or after dinner the presupposition of the question is that the trash will be taken out either way.

EXAMPLES:

1. Did you take the car before or after you saw the man leave? (the presupposition is that the respondent took the car)
2. Did you use drugs last month or this month? (the presupposition is the respondent has used drugs)
3. Is he your friend or just someone with whom you hang around? (the presupposition is the respondent has some relationship with the other person)
4. Are you going to answer these questions now or after you have a drink of water? (the presupposition is the respondent will answer the question)

Probing Questions

Probing questions are frequently used as follow up questions to previous answers from respondents in order to obtain more in depth information. Reasons for asking these types of questions could be a desire to find the reason why the respondent answered a certain way previously, to look for inconsistencies in the previous response, or to assist the respondent in discussing a certain matter that he or she may have been hesitant in discussing.

Probing questions may also be used to rephrase the previous question so that the intent of the question is easier for the respondent to comprehend. Probing questions are also effective in gaining clarification, learning the reasoning behind the respondent's actions, and summarizing the information that has been given.

Pushing Probe

This type of probing question pushes the respondent to continue speaking or to supply an answer to the previous question. By pushing the respondent to continue speaking on the topic, one can gain more information and insight into the respondent's perspective.

EXAMPLES:

1. "Please continue."
2. "And?"
3. "Go on."

Information Gathering Probe

Information gathering probes are used to gain additional information from respondents. Sometimes a respondent may only give partial, vague, or evasive answers when being interviewed. In order to directly get to a specific answer, it may be useful to follow up with a probing question.

EXAMPLES:

1. Tell me more about that situation.
2. When you say the car was dark, what color might that be?
3. When you say you were upset, how upset were you when she began yelling?
4. What else can you tell me about the fight outside the hotel?

EXERCISE:

Provide effective probing questions to the following interview interactions. Make sure that the questions probe into the respondent's answers without starting a new subject.

Interviewer: Are you going to discuss this issue with your attorney?
Respondent: I guess it really depends.
Interviewer:

Interviewer: Tell me about the person you saw leaving the bank.
Respondent: He was tall.
Interviewer:

Interviewer: At what point do you think she knew the answer?
Respondent: Earlier.
Interviewer:

Interviewer: What motivated you to talk to the officer?
Respondent: I noticed something.
Interviewer:

PRACTICAL EXERCISE:

Read through the following interview and write what each type of question the officer is asking, whether it is an open-ended, close-ended, presumptive, or probing question.

Officer: Hi, did you see the man who just drove off?

Respondent: Yes.

Officer: Ok. Had you seen him previously?

Respondent: No.

Officer: So you never saw him previously?

Respondent: That's right.

Officer: How often do you come here?

Respondent: Most every day.

Officer: I see. So you come here every day but you are saying you have never seen that person previously?

Respondent: Well, I might have seen the car.

Officer: How often have you seen the car?

Respondent: A few times.

Officer: How many times is a few?

Respondent: I guess maybe four times.

Officer: Did you ever see the car before you started coming here?

Respondent: Maybe.

Officer: Where else did you see the car?

Respondent: I can't remember.

Officer: Ok. Did you notice the car today before or after you heard the loud noise?

Respondent: I guess it was after the noise.

Officer: Did you run out in the parking lot before or after the noise?

Respondent: After.

Officer: Do you know what the man who drove the car looks like?

Respondent: No.

Officer: You have seen this car at least four times previously and you never saw the man driving it?

Respondent: I don't know.

GROUP EXERCISE:

1. Get into a group of 3 – 5 people. Suppose there is a respondent. As a group, select a topic of interest and write down two questions for the respondent about the topic. After the group is finished, each person should take a moment and classify each question for its type. The group

should then compare notes to see how many in the group agree with each person's answer.
2. Stay in the same group. This time each group member will ask the respondent about a topic of interest using only open-ended questions.
3. Stay in the same group. This time each group member will ask the respondent about a topic of interest using only close-ended questions.

Neutral and Leading Questions

A neutral question is a question that permits the respondent to answer without any pressure or direction from the interviewer. When given an open, neural question the respondent will decide how much information and how much detail to give in his or her answers.

A leading question is a question in which the interviewer guides the respondent toward an already set answer.

EXAMPLE:

Are you aware of the rules? (Neutral question)
You are aware of the rules, aren't you? (Leading question)

How do you feel the prosecution is treating the witness? (Neutral question)
Do you feel that the prosecution is treating the witness unfairly? (Leading question)

What do you think about the policy that was just created? (Neutral question)
Don't you think there are some real problems with the policy that was just created? (Leading question)

Have you ever stolen in the past? (Neutral question)
What have you stolen in the past? (Leading question)

OUT OF CLASS EXERCISE

1. Watch an interview program on television (news, sports, or entertainment related). Note when neutral or leading questions are asked. Pay attention to which types of questions get the best responses from the person being interviewed. Which type of question is asked most frequently on the program?

The Structure of the Interview

Each interview has its own unique purpose and it is important to be aware of how the structure of an interview can facilitate or hinder the desired outcome of the interaction. It is essential to create a structure for the interview that works to the advantage of the interviewer. It is the responsibility of the interviewer to ensure that each interview's structure is appropriate to the specific setting and situation. This chapter will cover the three sections of the structure of an interview: the opening, the continuation, and the closing.

<u>Opening of the Interview</u>
The first minute of any interview is crucial. What the interviewer does or does not do during the opening can often influence how the respondent will judge the interviewer and the interview (Stewart & Cash, 2008). The opening of an interview usually determines how the overall interaction will play out. If the opening of an interview does not go well, it can lead to low quality information from the respondent or can create a defensive, unpleasant interaction between the respondent and interviewer. The respondent is not obligated to speak with the interviewer and, if the respondent feels uncomfortable, he or she can terminate the interview at any time.

The opening of the interview is when the primary background information about the topic of discussion is obtained. In the opening, the interviewer will need to restrict his or her questions to pertinent aspects of the topic being discussed. One of the main goals of the opening of the interview is to set a frame of open communication between both parties. If this has been achieved, it is much more likely that the respondent will engage fully in the interview process. When the respondent feels comfortable, he or she may be much more willing to disclose information.

Building rapport is the most crucial part of the entire interview. As previously stated, when the respondent feels comfortable, he or she may be more willing to be interviewed. According to Stewart and Cash (2008), rapport is "a process of establishing and sustaining a relationship between interviewer and interviewee by creating feelings of goodwill and trust" (p.77). Rapport does not mean sweet-talking or giving false praise to the respondent. It simply means giving the respondents interactions in a way that they feel comfortable in responding to the questions being asked. Giving the respondents polite smiles, making good eye contact, and making pleasant introductions can go a long way toward building and maintaining rapport.

Suppose you are an interviewer. To begin an interview, and to enhance rapport, you need to give an introduction (i.e., your name and title) and the reason for your presence. See the example below.

EXAMPLE:

"Hello sir. I'm Captain Dan Jenkins with the Sheriff's Department. I am here to talk with you about the incident that happened in your apartment complex last night."

From this point on, you explain to the respondent the purpose of your visit, how long the interview will last, how the information will be utilized, and why you decided to interview him or her.

EXAMPLE:

"As you may know, there was an assault last night in this complex and I have been directed to collect any information that may be useful in finding out what specifically happened. I only need to ask you a few questions that should take just a minute or two as I think you may be able to help me due to you living next door to where the incident happened."

EXERCISE:

In a group of three people, each person will practice giving an opening introduction and the reason for the interview for the following scenarios:

1. You are looking for a certain car that is often in a specific neighborhood. You decide to knock on a random door to ask the person inside if they have seen the car.
2. You are trying to find a lost child. You enter a video arcade to ask the staff if they have seen the child.
3. You need to talk to an employee of a certain company. You are calling the manager on duty to find out if that person is working today.

It is best to try and do these "off the cuff" to see what you need to work on in order to create an effective opening.

Continuation of the Interview
To continue the interview, one can use open-ended questions that are easy to understand and answer. Avoid using close-ended questions at this point because the goal of the interview is to get the respondent to open up and to divulge useful information.

EXAMPLE:

"What did you notice happening last night in the apartment complex?"
"What things did you hear or see happen last night?"

Once the respondent has started talking freely, it will be easier to use close-ended questions and probing questions to get more specific information from him or her. In this part of the interview, the information on the topic begins to move from a generalized view of the issue to more specific aspects of the topic.

EXAMPLE:

"You are telling me that there was a loud noise?"
"So when you said you heard a loud noise, from what direction did you hear it?"

The Closing of the Interview
The closing of the interview is an important part of the interview process. If the interview ends in haste or in an abrupt manner, the rapport that had been previously established could be dissolved (Milne & Bull, 1999). The closing is not something that just happens or is hurriedly paced. The main functions of the closing are to summarize the information gained and to end the interview without ending the interaction (e.g., there may be additional interviews in the future).

Closing techniques
1. Offering to answer any questions the respondent may have about the interview.

   EXAMPLE:
   "Do you have any questions for me about what we talked about today?"

2. Expressing Appreciation for the willingness to be interviewed.

   EXAMPLE:
   "I really appreciate you taking the time to discuss this matter with me today."

3. Summarizing the information gained in the interview.

   EXAMPLE:
   "Ok. You stated that you did not see anything in the complex last night but you did hear a loud noise across the hall at close to eleven o'clock. Other than that, you were unaware of anything else happening in the complex last night. I think that about does it."

4. Making sure there is no other information that was not discussed.

   EXAMPLE:
   "Are you sure there was nothing else you noticed last night that you have not already stated?" "Is there anything else I may need to know?"

5. Openly state the end of the interview.

   EXAMPLE:
   "I believe that covers everything I need to know."
   "Well, that's it for my questions."

Closing the interview non-verbally
Non-verbal actions can signal the end of the interview to the respondent. The following actions, along with verbal interview termination cues, can aid in closing the interview.

1. Closing your notebook and putting away the writing instrument
2. Offering to shake hands
3. Breaking eye contact
4. Standing up if you are already seated
5. Looking your watch

PRACTICAL EXERCISE

The following interview is between a police officer and a woman who lives in a neighborhood that had several burglaries over the past two nights. In this interview, note where the opening section, the continuation section and the closing section of the interview begin. In addition, name the types of questions (open-ended, close-ended, probing, etc.) that the police officer asks.

Officer: Good morning. I'm Officer Jackson with the City Police Department. I am working in the neighborhood today to find out any information I can about the burglaries that happened over the last two evenings. I would like to ask you a few questions that will only take a couple of minutes.

Woman: Ok.

Officer: Thank you. I appreciate you talking with me today. Did you see any vehicles ride through the neighborhood that were unfamiliar to you over the past week or so?

Woman: No. The only unfamiliar vehicle I saw that I can remember was a plumbing company van.

Officer: What did that van look like?

Woman: It was white and had a logo on it. I don't remember the logo or the name of the company but I do remember seeing the word "plumbing" on it.

Officer: Do you remember when you saw the van?

Woman: Sometime last week.

Officer: How many times have you seen it over the last week?

Woman: Just once.

Officer: Ok. Did you happen to see anyone in the neighborhood who was unfamiliar to you?

Woman: I did see a new couple walking down the street the other day but I think they just moved in three houses down.

Officer: So the people who live three houses down are new to the neighborhood?

Woman: Yes, I think so.

Officer: Ok. Other than those people, have you see anyone else who was unfamiliar to you?

Woman: I don't think so.

Officer: Ok. So other than the plumbing vehicle you saw only once, you have not seen any unfamiliar vehicles?

Woman: Right.

Officer: And you saw no one unfamiliar lately other than the couple you mentioned that may have moved in three houses down the street?

Woman: Correct.

Officer: I appreciate your willingness to talk with me today. If you happen to see or hear anything that you feel might be important for me to know, please feel free to contact me at the number on this card.

Woman: Ok.

Officer: Have a good day.

REFERENCES

Milne, R., & Bull, R. (1999). *Investigating interviewing: Psychology and practice*. Chichester: Wiley.

Stewart, C. J., & Cash, W.B. (2008). *Interviewing: Principles and practices*. New York, NY: McGraw-Hill.

University of North Carolina - Charlotte (2014). *Types of Interviews and Techniques*. Retrieved from http://career.uncc.edu/students/effective-interviewing/types-interviews-and-techniques

CHAPTER 8. BODY LANGUAGE

Humans communicate nonverbally via conscious and subconscious gestures, facial expressions, and body movements (Lambert, 2008). Although body language may be used to replace or reinforce speech, it may also betray a person's actual mood. Kinesics is the study of human communication when people talk with one another. Police officers may employ kinesics and should learn to read behaviors behind the words.

The Human Face

The lack of heavy facial hair distinguishes the human face from the faces of other mammals (Jackson, 2004). Humans exchange sophisticated facial expressions that are important for socialization. Thus, the lack of facial hair promotes human socialization.

Although there are about 6 billion human faces in the world, no two faces are exactly the same. Even the faces of identical twins differ slightly. Although the human face can display 100,000 different expressions, only seven facial expressions are biologically based and universally recognized: happiness, sadness, anger, surprise, disgust, contempt, and fear.

The human brain processes the human face as a whole and considers overall patterns. Patterns of light and dark and spacing among facial features allow viewers a three-dimensional view, which is necessary to distinguish among subtle facial details. Indeed, it is difficult for a human to recognize a person based solely on a two-dimensional drawing. In order to demonstrate this problem, caricaturists have learned to exaggerate distinctive facial features to help the brain recognize the subjects of the drawings.

Based on facial expressions, it has been found that police officers only have a 50/50 chance of detecting a liar (Jackson, 2004). Secret Service Agents, on the other hand, who have been trained to detect micro-expressions, consistently detect liars. Although micro-expressions are facial expressions that may only last one-fifth of a second, they reveal emotions that the suspects are trying to conceal.

Biometrics use biological or physical features to identify individuals (Jackson, 2004). Collecting information and using databases, authorities can identify people via fingerprints, eye retinas, voice patterns, and facial features. For example, although the human face has about 80 nodal points, biometric software only requires about 14 to 22 nodal points for recognition. Changes in facial expressions, hair style or color, skin tone, and lighting do not impact the software. Because the facial software focuses on the inner region of the face, growing a beard, growing older, and putting on weight have little impact on the success of the facial software. In addition, much like fingerprints, a person's ears display unique characteristics and allow for proper identification. Thus, when a police officer takes MUG photographs at the jail, the officer should include side view photographs of the suspect with a clear view of the suspect's ears.

Body Language and Deception

It is not uncommon for police officers to encounter individuals who are less than truthful. When police officers encounter individuals, they need to look for signs of deception. See Table 12. Although there are many clues that may be indicative of deception, police officers must always look at the totality of the circumstances. In other words, signs of deception are not absolute and must be considered within the context of the particular situation. Some people may be deceptive because they provide false information; other people may be deceptive by only providing partial information (i.e., by leaving important information out of their story).

Police officers often engage in critical thinking, which is using the available information to make best-practice decisions. It may not be uncommon for police officers to only receive partial information during an interview. For example, if the victims, witnesses, or suspects are located far from the officer, the officer may call the individuals on the telephone. Thus, the visual clues may be lacking. In addition, many individuals claim that truth is relative and perception of reality will depend on each person's perspective (Hatch, 2002).

Table 12
Body Language and Body Movements (Lambert, 2008; Lieberman, 1998; Meyer, 2010; Pease & Pease, 2004a; Starrett & Davis, 2006).

#	Body Language	Behavior Interpretation
1	Little or no eye contact; glances down and moves eyes from side to side	Sign of deception; guilty; does not like to make eye contact with interrogator; those who are falsely accused tend to make eye contact and to focus on false accusation
2	Little use of hands and arms to self-express	Sign of deception; when people try to cover the truth, they often cover their bodies with their hands and arms
3	Hands down; fists clenched	Sign of defensiveness
4	Palms up	Seeking information; has nothing to hide
5	Legs and arms close to body, may be crossed	Defending self; hiding information
6	Legs and arms stretched out	Secure, confident, comfortable
7	Arm movement stiff and mechanical	Attempting to portray passion about a subject; artificial emotions
8	Hand goes to mouth while speaking	Unconscious sign of deceit; trying to cover up spoken lies
9	Suspect touches face, nose, ears while listening	Suspect does not want to listen to the officer
10	Shoulder shrug	Suspect does not care or does not know; trying to be relaxed

Police officers need to be aware of a suspect's inconsistent actions (Lieberman, 1998). These may include words, gestures, and emotions in which there seems to be contradictory information. For example, a man may state affirmatively as he shakes his head from side to side. However, these expressions may be brief in appearance because the suspect may quickly cover them up. Any change in behavior should be suspicious. See Table 13.

Table 13
Body Language and Emotions (Lambert, 2008; Lieberman, 1998; Meyer, 2010; Pease & Pease, 2004a; Starrett & Davis, 2006)

#	Body Language	Behavior Interpretation
1	Punctuating a point after the fact, such as expressing anger after claiming to be angry	Suspect's emotions are not authentic; suspect talks before thinking and realizes he or she should have shown emotions earlier
2	Moves head on important syllables as speaks	Suspect is driving home a point; truthful
3	Incongruence between gestures and speech	Sign of deception; for example, someone saying that he or she feels sorry for you when you slipped on a banana peel and are laughing as he or she speaks
4	Delays emotions, prolongs emotions, and truncates emotions	Sign of deception; staged emotions seem out of alignment
5	Showing emotions while displaying movement in eyes and forehead	Sign of truthfulness; emotions displayed over wide area on face
6	Showing emotions while not displaying movement in eyes and forehead	Sign of deceit; forced smile; emotions confined to mouth area

Suspects who are guilty go on the defense (Lieberman, 1998). Suspects who are innocent go on the offense. Additional behaviors that an interrogator may observe are displayed in Table 14.

Table 14
Body Language (Lambert, 2008; Lieberman, 1998; Meyer, 2010; Pease & Pease, 2004a; Starrett & Davis, 2006).

#	Actions	Signs
1	Movement of head away from speaker; may be slow or abrupt (not a tilt of interest)	Signs of discomfort; suspect will distance himself from the threat or source of discomfort
2	Movement of head toward the speaker	Signs of comfort; closing the gap
3	Erect posture; shoulders back	Confident and secure
4	Hunched over; hands in pocket	Insecure
5	Face to face; squared off to accuser	Truthfulness; seeks to refute false accusations
6	Shifts or turns away from speaker	Signs of deceitfulness; does not want to confront truth
7	Movement toward exit; body angled toward door; may place back to wall	Signs of deceitfulness; trying to avoid ambush
8	Suspect has little or no physical contact with interrogator	Signs of deceitfulness; trying to minimize intimacy and psychological connection
9	Suspect fails to use index finger to either point at interrogator or up in air	Signs of deceitfulness; lack of conviction and authority
10	Suspect attempts to place physical barriers and obstacles between self and interrogator (e.g., cup of coffee)	Signs of deceitfulness; suspect trying to create a shield to protect self against interrogator

Police officers must also consider the content of the words provided by a suspect. See Table 15. Suspects may calculate with precision their choice of the words in order to convey a particular truth that they want the police officers to believe. In addition, suspects may throw out diversionary flares (what warplanes use to misdirect heat-tracking missiles) to see if the police take the bait. If the suspects can get the police to focus on their diversionary flares, then perhaps the suspects can prevent the police from detecting the truth.

Table 15
Content of Words (Inbau, Reid, Buckley; & Jayne, 2005; Lieberman, 1998)

#	Words	Interpretation
1	Suspect reflects/repeats the interrogator's words; repeats questions but changes a few words (e.g., Q: Did you ever…; A: I never…; Q: Was it you that…; A: It wasn't me that…, etc.)	Signs of deceitfulness; suspect does not spend much time thinking about answer and responds out of fear; repeats interrogator's words but makes a slight modification to change the meaning 180 degrees
2	Suspect uses bold words to immediately make his point (e.g., **No!**, I would never …); makes statements in absolute terms	Signs of deceitfulness; wants to make it crystal clear, to eliminate any doubt, and to stop further questioning; suspect's statements provide shield to self
3	Suspects make statements that are not absolute (e.g., perhaps, maybe, I cannot remember much more, etc.)	Honest suspects will make less specific statements and will clarify statements as needed; suspect's statements provide comfort to others
4	Suspect makes a "Freudian slip"	Police may catch a false statement; when a suspect is making a statement, the suspect will accidently change the intended sentence and say something that is on his mind
5	Suspect introduces a fictitious belief system to support his position; offers absolute assurance of innocence	Signs of deceitfulness; suspect feels evidence is unfavorable so depersonalizes and globalizes the question (e.g., suspect responds that it is a moral abomination, it is against my religious beliefs, etc.)
6	Suspects are uncomfortable with silence; suspect adds information without being further probed; speaks to fill gaps of silence; statements offered in piecemeal fashion	Signs of deceitfulness; suspect gets nervous if there is silence because he is not sure that his story has convinced interrogator; will speak until gets verbal confirmation to stop

7	Suspect implies answer but does not directly answer the question (e.g., Q: Do you love me? A: I have loved no one more. Q: Did you commit a felony? A: I have never been convicted of a crime.)	Signs of deceitfulness via omission; provides answers that attempt to satisfy interrogator without providing false information; suspect provides a diversionary flare

One sentence may have many meanings, depending on which words are emphasized. Suspects may try to emphasize a particular word in a sentence, which may provide an alternate message. For example, compare the following sentence. **Olga received a $500 fine for cutting down a state-owned tree**. If the word "**Olga**" is emphasized, then the sentence focuses on the importance of who cut down the tree (e.g., I never expected Olga to cut down a state-owned tree). If the word "**received**" is emphasized, then the sentence focuses on the fact that the punishment already happened (e.g., I expected the police to issue a warning for a first-time offense). If the words "**a $500 fine**" are emphasized, then the sentence focuses on the importance of the cost of the crime (e.g., I expected a $20 fine for the violation). If the words "**for cutting down**" are emphasized, then the importance of the sentence is how the tree was destroyed (e.g., burning down the tree may be okay, perhaps due to insect control). If the words "**state-owned**" are emphasized, then the importance of the sentence focuses on ownership of the trees (e.g., there may be no fine for cutting down county-owned trees). If the word "**tree**" is emphasized, then the importance of the sentence focuses on the object of the crime (e.g., there may be no fine for cutting down state-owned bushes). When the words of a suspect are written down in a police report, any emphasis and the actual meaning of the sentence may be lost. In short, it is not just the words that are spoken, but it is also how the words are spoken. See Table 16 for interpreting a suspect's response.

Table 16
Interpreting a Suspect's Response (Inbau et al., 2005; Lieberman, 1998; Zulawski & Wicklander, 2002)

#	Suspect's Response	Interpretation
1	Suspect provides a quick yes or no answer then takes a lengthy time to provide explanation; takes longer than usually to provide response to questions of personal beliefs	Signs of deceitfulness; suspect needs time to come up with an explanation after quick answer; suspect wants to provide the answer that he or she believes the interrogator wants to hear
2	Suspect repeats points already made; suspect's reaction is out of proportion; suspect appears outraged; tries to detach self from crime (e.g., instead of saying "my home" the suspect will say "the home").	Signs of deceitfulness; tries to convince interrogator through emotions because he or she cannot through evidence; suspect fails to acknowledge personal relationships and appears to be detached from items related to the crime
3	Suspect does not want to own his or her words; suspect is reluctant to use pronouns (e.g., *I*, *we*, and *us*); voice is higher; voice is flat; lack of inflection	Signs of deceitfulness; Q: Did you like it? Instead of saying, *Yes, I really liked it*, suspect will simply state *Yes*; truth teller is comfortable with personal position and will play with words (e.g., will elongate and vary the word *really* with voice inflection); liar's voice will be flat due to a lack of voice inflection; liar under stress will have vocal cords tighten up, which lead to a higher voice.
4	Suspect mumbles and speaks very softly; words not clear; misspoken words; poor sentence structure; out of fear, suspect may speak loudly and quickly	Signs of deceitfulness; suspect not passionate about words; suspect may simply reply by repeating the interrogator's words; words seem forced

5	Suspect makes statements that sound like questions (speaking style for question is different than speaking style for statement); head, voice, and eyes lift at end of statement; suspect lacks conviction	Signs of deceitfulness; suspect looks up at end of statement and widens his eyes, which indicate that suspect is unsure of his statement and is seeking confirmation from the interrogator
6	Suspect constantly questions someone else's motives and behaviors; suspect continually states that other people are corrupt; if the suspect cannot determine the interrogator's thoughts, the suspect will continually ask if the interrogator believes him (truthful people expect to be believed)	Signs of deceitfulness; reflection of how the suspect sees himself; suspect projects self onto others; it takes one to know one
7	Suspect focuses on internal factors rather than on external factors; suspect more interested in how he appears to the interrogator rather than making his point clear; suspect plays defense instead of offense (instead of focusing on winning, suspect focuses on not losing)	Signs of deceitfulness; suspect has little self-confidence (e.g., high confidence = man focuses on how attractive a woman looks; low confidence = man focuses on how he looks to attractive woman); suspect focuses on how he or she sounds as he or she makes statements; suspect puts on act in order to manipulate the interrogator's perception
8	Suspect provides information without including a third person's point of view; a third person's perspective requires the liar to be more clever	Signs of deceitfulness; suspect may mention a third person but not his or her opinion; For example, *I came home and told my wife that I joined the military* (lie) versus *I came home and told my wife that I joined the military and she was outraged* (truth)

9	Suspect fails to include negative details in statement, unless the negatives are used as a defense; statements are one-dimensional, which focus on the positive details; only positive thoughts are primary emotions	Signs of deceitfulness; true events often include good and bad; a suspect making up a falsehood will focus on positive details (unless the negative details are essential to the statement)
10	Suspect willingly answers questions but fails to ask relevant questions; suspect not interested in learning anything (e.g., suspect fails to ask about the well-being of others); focused on self-interests	Signs of deceitfulness; suspect is only concerned about convincing interrogator that he or she is truthful; fails to consider other perspectives, which may be very important to everyone else
11	Suspect appears more relaxed or happier when subject changes; suspect smiles or laughs nervously when subject changes; suspect appears less defensive when subject changes	Signs of deceitfulness; the truthful resent false accusations and insist that they be further explored; guilty suspects want to quickly change the subject because they feel discomfort
12	Suspect is more concerned about how to respond to an accusation rather than about being accused; suspect is not angered that his reputation has been tarnished and that his integrity has been questioned	Signs of deceitfulness; the truthful will be caught off guard and surprised that their integrity has been questioned; the liar will remain fairly expressionless when he or she is accused of a crime
13	Suspect starts sentences with *"To tell the truth"*, *"To be perfectly honest"*, etc.; suspect asks, *Would I lie to you?"* ; suspect states, *"I never lie."*	Signs of deceitfulness; honest people do not feel that they have to start their statements by claiming that their statements are true; criminals have good reasons to lie; unless it is part of a particular person's everyday language, stating something like *"To tell the truth"* means that everything before the statement were lies and everything after the statement will be a lie; suspect has to declare his or her virtuous nature because he or she cannot prove it otherwise

14	Suspect has agenda; suspect may head off in own direction and provide irrelevant information; suspect's statements sound rehearsed; rehearsed statements provide information that was not asked for by the interrogator; suspects recite facts and details that should not be easily recalled	Signs of deceitfulness; providing too much specific information on a particular date may indicate that the suspect tried to record information on the date of the crime in order to provide an alibi
15	Suspect tries to buy time by having the interrogator repeat the question; suspect wants to think about question and to prepare response; suspect may ask a question to buy time	Signs of deceitfulness; suspect delays response; suspect may ask, "What do you mean?" "Why would you ask me that?" "What do you think?"
16	Suspect says something that sounds too good to be true (e.g., I have never lied in my life)	Signs of deceitfulness; if statement is found to be false, suspect will lose all credibility; it is better to admit an infraction and to explain it rather than to deny an infraction if it is true
17	Suspect implies something is true by saying the opposite; suspect implies something is true without actually saying it; suspect implies something is true through denial	Signs of deceitfulness; suspect may say, *"I do not want you to blame her for the crash because she has a problem and is an alcoholic"*; suspect may say, *"I do not want you to think that I dislike you, but I am too busy for the rest of my life to see you"*; suspect may say, *"Kris was at Alcoholics Anonymous, but she was probably just attending the meeting as a criminal justice student."*

18	Suspect uses humor and sarcasm to answer a serious question; suspect wants to make interrogator look foolish about probing further; interrogator must obtain a serious answer	Signs of deceitfulness; interrogator may ask, *"Did you cheat on you wife with your secretary?"* The suspect may answer, *"Yes, every time I go to work, we sleep together. In fact, we plan to have enough kids to rule the country. In fact, with hundreds of dependents for tax deductions, I am doing my wife a service."*
19	Suspect may state that he does not have what the interrogator is exactly looking for but that he does have something similar	Signs of deceitfulness; before believing the suspect, interrogator needs to confirm that the suspect does not have the originally requested item
20	Suspect provides numbers that are multiples of one another	Signs of deceitfulness; because a liar may have a hard time coming up with a variety of numbers quickly, a liar may provide numbers that can be easily calculated (e.g., I have 2 computers, 4 jobs, 8 friends, and I make $32,000 per year)
21	Suspect's face may become flush; suspect may display signs of rapid breathing and increased perspiration; suspect may tremble; suspect's voice may crack; suspect may have a hard time swallowing; suspect's voice may increase in pitch; suspect may have a hard time focusing on the questions; suspect may whistle	Signs of deceitfulness; suspect may become flush due to fear; suspect may attempt to control breathing by taking deep, audible breaths; suspect may hide hands if they are trembling; suspect's vocal cords may tighten up, causing a change in pitch; anxiety causes mucus buildup in the throat, causing suspect to clear throat; stress may cause the suspect to lose concentration; suspect may whistle to relax and to build confidence

22	Suspect agrees with interrogator and uses the interrogator's own words to support his or her cause; suspect deflects the interrogator's strengths; suspect does not confront or resist the interrogator; suspect attempts to turn a negative factor into a positive factor	Signs of deceitfulness; the interrogator may state, *"I know every road officer in the department but I do not know you."* The suspect may reply, *"That's right, I am an undercover officer with top clearance and you are not supposed to know who I am."* Suppose a particular food makes people sick and gives them diarrhea. A suspect may claim that the food helps eliminate toxins from the body and helps people lose weight through a natural process.
23	Suspect attempts to eliminate the interrogator's suspicions of a crime by opposing a less significant infraction	Signs of deceitfulness; the suspect may claim that a wife would be a fool to keep a no-good husband who flirted with another woman, when in fact the suspect is currently cheating on his wife
24	Suspect will try to direct attention away from real issue; suspect downplays change or extraordinary event; suspect tries to slip information in without bringing attention to it	Signs of deceitfulness; a change in the suspect's normal activities is suspicious; interrogator should question extraordinary event; like a magician, a suspect will attempt to direct the interrogator's attention to where the suspect wants it to go
25	Interrogator makes a false statement and tests the suspect's truthfulness; interrogator sees if the suspect will agree with a statement that the interrogator knows is false	Signs of deceitfulness; if a suspect lies about one thing, the suspect will lose credibility and all of the suspect's statements will be questionable; the interrogator may state, *"I know that you did not commit the crime because you were out of town that night."* The suspect may reply, *"That's right, I was nowhere near the crime scene."* However, the interrogator has a police car video recording that places the suspect at the crime scene at the time of interest.

26	Suspect makes a story that is hard to believe and argues that it must be true because common sense indicates that a lie would not be so far-fetched	Signs of deceitfulness; suspect embellishes the story; suspect argues that if the story were a lie, the suspect would have made the story more believable

Police officers can employ a variety of verbal abstract techniques in order to find the truth. Sometimes, it is not exactly what the interrogator says that gets a confession but it is the manner in which it is said. See Table 17.

Table 17
Verbal Abstract Techniques (Inbau et al., 2005; Lieberman, 1998; Zulawski & Wicklander, 2002)

#	Verbal Abstract Technique	Signs/Interpretation/Trick
1	Interrogator should allude to the suspect's deviant behavior without accusing the suspect of deviant behavior	Signs of deceitfulness if suspect gets defensive or inquires about the interrogator's questions; if an interrogator believes that the suspect robbed the liquor store the night before, the interrogator may ask the suspect if he or she went out drinking the night before
2	Interrogator should offer the suspect a similar story with very specific behavior that involves someone else; interrogator implies that he or she already knows the answer	Signs of deceitfulness if suspect gets uncomfortable and defensive by claiming that he would never do such a thing; signs of truthfulness if suspect offers good advice and is thankful for the chance to offer helpful advice; if an interrogator believes that a police officer has destroyed evidence, the interrogator will inform the officer that some police evidence has been destroyed and he will ask the officer for his advice in dealing with the destruction of evidence problem; signs of truthfulness if suspect does not ask the reason why the interrogator brought the issue up but simply attempts to help interrogator solve the problem

3	Interrogator should offer the suspect a story of similar behavior but in a general manner; interrogator implies that he or she already knows the answer	Signs of deceitfulness if suspect gets uncomfortable and defensive and asks about the question or if he or she attempts to change the subject; if an interrogator believes that a police officer has destroyed evidence, the interrogator will indicate that an officer would be silly to steal evidence due to all of the video cameras in the area; if the police officer denies the claim but asks about the video evidence, this would be a sign of deceitfulness; signs of truthfulness if suspect opens up about the surveillance cameras and discusses how to effectively use the evidence to make a prosecution
4	Interrogator asks the suspect direct questions about the crime; technique is more effective if suspect is caught off guard and is unable to prepare for the questions; if given advanced notice, suspect may rehearse responses, may convince himself that his actions were justified, and may practice relaxing during responses	Interrogator should not: give advance warning, reveal what he or she knows, or interrupt the suspect when he or she is talking; interrogator should build a rapport (e.g., by matching the suspect's gestures, speech rate, and word choice), build a baseline to use as reference (e.g., ask questions for which the interrogator already knows the answers, and see how the suspect responds), have a relaxed posture, square off with the suspect, provide moments of silence, ask "really?", and ask if there is anything else.

5	Interrogator asks the suspect leading questions about the crime; interrogator confines the suspect's responses to the crime; interrogator seems disappointed with response; interrogator makes the suspect comfortable with admitting the violation via pride	Interrogator seeks admission to crime, not confession to crime; if the interrogator believes that the suspect cheated on his wife last night with Lisa, the interrogator may ask the suspect what time he got back from Lisa's last night (if the suspect provides a time, this places the suspect with Lisa last night); interrogator may lead the suspect into confession by appearing to understand that a little deviance is expected in life.
6	Interrogator uses time (i.e., the crime is old news) as a tool to get suspect's confession; two important factors are when the crime occurred and when others become aware of crime; interrogator makes suspect believe that the crime is no big deal; interrogator makes suspect believe that he knew about the crime all along, which gets the suspect to believe all is okay	Suspect will perceive the crime as insignificant if the crime happened a long time ago; suspect will perceive the crime as insignificant if others became aware of the crime a long time ago
7	Interrogator has no evidence but has gut feeling suspect is guilty; interrogator appears to have big concern and acts surprised or hurt about something	Interrogator may state to the suspect that he or she may try to lie, but the interrogator knows the truth; interrogator may state that everyone knows about it; interrogator may state to the suspect that they both know why they are now talking together

8	Interrogator believes suspect is guilty but cannot prove it; interrogator provides misleading information and sets the seed of doubt	Suspect will provide excuses to explain possible evidence; if interrogator claims that a crime occurred and fingerprints have been collected, suspect may try to explain why his or her prints were at the scene; if interrogator claims that there was a witness, the suspect may claim that there are many other people who like him or her
9	Interrogator maximizes the crime; interrogator gets suspect to admit to a minor infraction, which the interrogator makes the suspect believe is no big deal	Interrogator accuses the suspect of major crimes, and many of them; interrogator claims that if it were just the minor infraction, it would be no problem (e.g., interrogator accuses the suspect of attempted murder but claims that if the suspect simply attempted to smacked his wife around a little bit, that is understandable and perhaps even expected)
10	Interrogator may stare at suspect and encroach upon the suspect's personal space, causing mental claustrophobia; interrogator asks the suspect about related information in an attempt to investigate the real concern	Signs of deceitfulness if suspect attempts to make story fit the interrogator's facts; if a suspect claims that he or she was at home during a crime, the interrogator may claim that the police was at his or her neighbor's home for a report at the time of the crime and they noticed that his or her car was not there.

11	Interrogator uses a third party to plant the seed of doubt in the suspect's mind; using a third party maximizes the interrogator's credibility; innocent persons will not be interested in fixing problems that do not exist	A third party will approach suspect and state that another person is getting tired of his misconduct; third party will tell the suspect that the suspect's activities are common knowledge, but the third party knows how the suspect can fix the problem; third party appears to agree with the suspect's actions but asks the suspect if he or she is sure that he or she will not get into trouble (a guilty person will hesitate and think about it)
12	Interrogator praises past crime; interrogator assumes that the suspect has already committed the crime; suspect must admit old crime in order to take advantage of new opportunities; suspect assumes the interrogator has evidence that the suspect has committed crime	Interrogator makes suspect believe that his or her past crime is a valuable skill and is needed for a new job (e.g., the suspect's criminal skills may be used to make anti-crime policies); interrogator makes the suspect believe that it is an open discussion and that upper management needs the best person for the job (if the suspect hesitates, this is a sign of guilt because he or she is thinking about his options)
13	Interrogator provides partial information, which is true; interrogator sets seed of doubt about the rest of the story, which is unknown	Interrogator may claim that the suspect has been in jail for drugs before, which is true; the interrogator then claims that he or she knows all about the suspect's manufacturing of drugs the night before, which is unknown; the interrogator then states that he or she is upset and does not want to talk about it right now (if the suspect is innocent, he or she will want to address the false accusation now; if the suspect is guilty, he or she will honor the interrogator's request and not want to escalate the hostile situation)

14	Interrogator informs the suspect but does not accuse the suspect; interrogator evaluates the suspect's response to the information; a guilty person becomes defensive and tries to not be blamed; an innocent person attempts to find out who is responsible and does not realize he or she is being accused	Signs of guilt if the suspect is defensive, very focused on his or her response, focuses on being accused, and does not show concern about the obvious, such as being a victim; an innocent person would be concerned about all aspects of the problem, which may include being the victim
15	Interrogator presents the positives of telling the whole story, the negatives of failing to resolve the matter, and then forces the suspect to make a choice; the positives and negatives must be realistic and believable; interrogator tells the suspect to tell the whole story (this does not imply that the suspect is lying but it does give the suspect credit for being partially truthful)	Interrogator tells the suspect that management has big plans for him, such as a promotion, a vacation home, an expense account, and a company vehicle; interrogator tells the suspect that everyone makes mistakes and that until the matter is resolved, the suspect will receive nothing; interrogator also states if he finds out that the suspect is guilty from another source, the suspect, who will be labeled a liar, will be fired and will have a hard time finding another job; interrogator then asks suspect to make a choice
16	Interrogator gets suspect to think emotionally; interrogator makes suspect feel that he is not alone	Interrogator admits to suspect that he or she has also committed some deviant acts; interrogator asks the suspect to provide details before the interrogator will provide details; suspect will believe there is an exchange of information
17	Interrogator focuses on the suspect's intentions, not the suspect's actions; interrogator gets suspect to admit that he or she committed the crime, but that it was an accident	Interrogator tells the suspect that sometimes things get out of control and accidents are understandable; interrogator tells the suspect that if the actions were intentional, then that is not okay

18	Interrogator praises suspect and seeks partnership; interrogator praises suspect's behaviors as creative and innovative	Interrogator tells the suspect that being secretive is silly and that he or she wants a part of the action; interrogator tells suspect that being deviant is creative and wants the suspect to elaborate on his or her creativity
19	Interrogator tells suspect that he or she will gain nothing if he or she fails to cooperate; interrogator tells suspect that what he has done can be overlooked, but lying about it cannot be overlooked	If the suspect fails to cooperate with the interrogator and nothing is resolved, then both will lose (interrogator will not get confession and suspect will surely be penalized, such as by losing his or her job)
20	Interrogator tells the suspect that there is a deadline for talking and that the cost will go up if the deadline is not met	Interrogator tells the suspect that once the interrogator leaves the room, nothing the suspect says will matter after that point; interrogator tells the suspect that he or she wants to give the suspect one last chance to tell his or her side of the story before the interrogator decides what to do
21	Interrogator tells the suspect that he or she takes full responsibility for the suspect's actions; interrogator states that he or she understands why the suspect committed the act; interrogator focuses on the suspect's grievances	Interrogator tells the suspect that there were good reasons for his or her acts; interrogator asks the suspect what he or she can do for the suspect to help him or her from doing this again (interrogator assumes that the suspect is guilty)
22	Interrogator tells the suspect that if he or she lies, there will be greater penalties; interrogator relies on the suspect's imagination to determine penalties; interrogator assesses the suspect's reaction to the possibility of a higher penalty	Interrogator tells the suspect that he or she hates to do it, but based on the available information, he or she must do what one has got to do (interrogator will not expand on what he must do)

23	Interrogator attacks the suspect's ego; this technique is very effective for those who have large egos	Interrogator tells the suspect that he or she knows the suspect cannot talk because the suspect is the puppet of the local drug dealer, who is pulling his strings (the suspect will confess to prove that he or she is no one's puppet)
24	Interrogator convinces the suspect that the interrogator is on his side; interrogator may provide an excuse for suspect's actions and will provide a solution to eliminate any concerns	Interrogator praises the suspect and indicates that there may be slight exaggerations and that by correcting the exaggerations, the suspect will be in a better position; interrogator asks the suspect what exaggerations need to be modified
25	Interrogator emphasizes to the suspect that the time and impact of the penalty is unknown; there is no indication of exactly when the penalty will occur; the interrogator stresses that the cost of the penalty is not isolated to this event and will impact other parts of the suspect's life	Suspect will have a hard time enjoying life if, at any time, the penalty may be enforced; suspect will have no comfort if he believes his life will never be normal again; interrogator tells the suspect to come clean, take his or her slap on the hand, and move on with his or her life
26	Interrogator makes the suspect believe that the suspect has no value; interrogator's apathy toward the suspect will make the suspect nervous	If the interrogator makes the suspect believe that he or she does not care that the suspect is lying, then the suspect will confess just to get the interest of the interrogator
27	Interrogator asks the suspect a direct question; question must be objective and specific; once the suspect provides an answer, interrogator will follow up and ask additional details; interrogator relentlessly attempts to trip suspect up by comparing the many specific answers provided by the suspect	If the suspect is truthful, he or she will answer right away; if the suspect takes a while to respond, he or she may be contriving story; a made up story usually lacks details and the suspect will trip up when too many specific questions are asked; a liar seeks to change the topic

28	Interrogator asks the suspect a question, but adds false information in the question; question has to sound reasonable to be believable; suspect must have first-hand knowledge about the topic	Sign of deceit if suspect answers the question incorrectly (e.g., suspect stated that his knows Jim really well and that he stayed with him last week - interrogator asks the suspect if Jim's sister is still ill, even though interrogator knows that Jim has no sister
29	Interrogator asks the suspect in a nonthreatening way to support his or her statements	If the suspect states that he or she checks books out of the library all of the time, ask to see the suspect's library card; sign of deceit if suspect provides excuses why he or she cannot produce the evidence
30	Interrogator adds presumptuous information to suspect's statement; suspect hears false information and agrees via adoptive admission	Sign of deceit if suspect fails to correct presumptuous information (e.g., if suspect states that he failed to go to work, interrogator may state that it is understandable because the bridge was closed – even though the bridge was not closed – and suspect does not correct statement)
31	Interrogator wants to find out about suspect's acquaintance; interrogator appeals to suspect's ego; instead of asking the suspect about what the acquaintance did wrong, the interrogator will ask the suspect what he or she would have done; suspect believes that he or she is providing positive information instead of negative information	Due to loyalty, police officer A may not want to admit that police officer B did a poor job; instead of directly asking about the poor behavior of officer B, the interrogator will ask officer A what he or she would have done

32	Interrogator wants to find out the true motives from someone of power; interrogator places the suspect in a situation where the suspect feels obligated to respond truthfully	If suspect of power makes a questionable decision, the interrogator will ask the suspect to state what is required to make a different decision (which the interrogator believes is better) that achieves the same outcome; if the suspect's answer is realized, then the suspect will feel obligated to change his position
33	Suspect lies to interrogator to protect the interrogator's feelings, so interrogator makes the suspect feel guilty about lying	Interrogator tells the suspect that he or she has faith in the suspect and that he or she believes the suspect would not intentionally hurt him or her by being dishonest (if the suspect seeks the approval of the interrogator, the suspect will change his story)
34	Interrogator asks the suspect questions that make it clear there is an opportunity to improve the statement; interrogator makes the suspect feel comfortable in changing his statement	Interrogator may ask the suspect if the suspect likes his supervisor's management style. If the states yes, then the interrogator will ask the suspect what it would take to love his supervisor's management style
35	Interrogator takes proactive measures to eliminate *"I don't know"* responses; interrogator does not want to make the suspect feel foolish about his or her behavior; interrogator reduces the pressure on the suspect by seeming to ask about something else; interrogator makes suspect believe that there was no intent involved with the suspect's actions	Interrogator may state to the suspect that he or she understands that the suspect does not know the answer but he or she wants the suspect to take his or her best guess; interrogator may ask the suspect to describe his or her feelings and how he or she can feel that way; interrogator may ask the suspect for any subconscious motivations (eliminates intent); interrogator may ask suspect about past similar situations that generated the same reaction; interrogator may ask the suspect to describe just one reason for his or her actions (this will open the door for further probing)

36	Victim does not want to talk because is too embarrassed; interrogator tries to minimize the embarrassment of the victim; interrogator tells the victim that he or she does not have to talk about it (this takes the pressure off of the victim); interrogator confides in the suspect by telling the suspect a story in which the interrogator messed up (this demonstrates that the interrogator trusts the suspect and the suspect will feel obligated to and comfortable with sharing information)	Interrogator may simply ask *yes* or *no* questions (this will not require the victim to elaborate); interrogator may tell the victim that he or she experienced the same thing and the interrogator may ask the victim if he or she wants to hear what happened; interrogator may ask the victim where he or she fits in on a scale of 1-10 (interrogator should not say *fall on the scale* because *fall* has a negative connotation and should not let 1 be nothing because this will allow the victim to select an easy out)
37	Interrogator seeks a confession when there are multiple suspects; interrogator speaks with one suspect at a time; when suspects do not feel personally responsible, they may not confess; when there are many suspects, there is a diffusion of responsibility and there is no motivation for suspects to cooperate with the interrogator	Interrogator tells suspect that he or she trusts the suspect and that he or she is not like the other suspects; interrogator tells the suspect that he or she can trust the interrogator; interrogator tells the suspect that what was done is not that important, but telling the truth is most important (the interrogator can count on the suspect); if this fails, the interrogator will try this tactic on the other suspects, one at a time

38	Interrogator questions experts with advanced knowledge; interrogator does not have the expertise in the field; there is a change in personnel and the second person was supposed to carry out an order from the first person; the interrogator will ask the second person a question to see if the second person confirms a false statement (e.g., interrogator ordered coke from person A, person B brings pop, and interrogator asks person B if the pop is root beer)	Interrogator states the opposite of what he or she really wants, and sees if the suspect agrees with it (e.g., an interrogator is looking for a drug that will make a person wired, so the interrogator asks the doctor if the medication's side effects will make him or her drowsy); if the suspect disagrees with the interrogator's statement, then the doctor is likely truthful; if the suspect agrees with the interrogator's statement, then the doctor may simply be pushing the product
39	Interrogator is dealing with a person who has nothing to lose and who does not care to cooperate; interrogator needs to raise the stakes	Police officer has a search warrant to take blood from a marital art expert; martial art expect states that he or she will refuse and will fight officer; officer states that if the suspect fights the officer, the officer will file assault charges against the suspect and will also sue the suspect for any damages
40	Interrogator attempts to get second-hand information from an individual who has talked with the suspect; interrogator makes the individual believe that he already knows the truth and overshadows it by showing emotions; interrogator should use the appropriate emotion (e.g., humor, concern, sympathy, surprise, etc.)	Interrogator may state that he or she just found out what happened and will ask the person how he or she is holding up or if there is anything that the interrogator can do

41	Interrogator directs the conversation and elicits the needed information; interrogator responds first and sets the mode of information exchange (e.g., smiles, nods, etc.); interrogator sets the pace of the conversation (i.e., fast, slow, etc.); interrogator uses certain words that require the suspect to provide additional information	After the suspect makes his or her statement, the interrogator will get additional information by responding with one of the following words: *meaning, and,* or *so.* Each of these words added to the end of a suspect's statement will require an explanation and additional information.
42	Interrogator turns vague responses into more direct responses; interrogator asks suspect for details	If the suspect states that the police officer used excessive force, the interrogator will ask the suspect to articulate the facts (e.g., what exactly did the office do?); if an officer stated that the person looked suspicious, the defense attorney will ask the officer to explain what lead to that conclusion (e.g., the officer needs to state that the suspect would not make eye contact, had shaking hands, was sweating, etc.)
43	Interrogator needs to stop the suspect from talking or from continually interrupting the interrogator; interrogator plays on the suspects ego and curiosity	Interrogator may say to the suspect: *Please do not let the facts interfere with your opinion*; *I have some very upsetting news for you*; *I hate to insult your intelligence so this is the last time I am going to say this*; *I am sorry that the middle of my statement ran into the beginning of your sentence*; etc.

44	Interrogator assumes that his or her suspicions are fact; interrogator states two facts that the suspect knows are true; interrogator focuses on a reasonable request and not on a threat, which will put the suspect at ease and will open up the discussion	**Bad technique:** Interrogator states, *Have you been smoking marijuana? Because if I find out that you have, I will lock you up and throw away the key* (focuses on the punishment). **Okay technique:** Interrogator states, *You have been smoking marijuana, haven't you* (indicates that the interrogator may know something)? **Good technique:** Interrogator states, *Let's talk about your marijuana usage* (focuses on the discussion). **Best technique**: Interrogator states, *I know that you have recently possessed and smoked marijuana, but just promise me that you use it at home and that you do not to go to work high* (has credibility because interrogator stated two facts and there is no mention of threat or punishment).
45	Suspect attempts to deceive the interrogator by telling the interrogator what the suspect believes the interrogator wants to hear; interrogator does not let the suspect know what the interrogator wants to hear, which will neutralize the suspect's deception	**Allows suspect to know interrogator's thought:** Interrogator states, *I like Joe. Is Joe trustworthy?* **Does not allow suspect to know interrogator's thought:** Interrogator states, *What do you think about Joe?*

46	Interrogator asks the suspect questions that are very likely true for most people; interrogator seeks to determine if suspect is currently honest by asking about past infractions; interrogator asks a question that the suspect cannot answer in absolute terms but if the suspect does answer in absolute terms, then the interrogator knows that suspect is being deceitful	Interrogator asks the suspect if he or she has ever stolen anything in his or her life (which is most likely "yes"); interrogator asks a kleptomaniac if he or she will stop stealing cold turkey (a "yes" will indicate deceit because intervention will most likely be required and a truthful suspect needs to mention it)
47	Interrogator uses embedded commands in sentences to implant suggestions in the suspect's mind; interrogator uses hand gestures during the commands to distract the conscious mind, uses short pauses before and after the commands, and changes the volume of the words during the commands; interrogator will embed commands like *tell the truth, say it, it is the right decision, clear the air now, get on with your life, tell me what happened, go straight, take care of your family*, etc.	When the human brain perceives initial information as truthful, it will perceive supplemental information as truthful; $n + p = 5$ statements, where $n = 4$ truthful statements and $p =$ embedded command *"I know that you have never been in trouble before* (true), *that you are scared* (true), *and that you want to minimize your trouble* (true). *Because you want to put this behind you* (true), **you need to tell the truth** (embedded command)."
48	Interrogator uses embedded commands in sentences to implant suggestions in the suspect's mind; interrogator embeds commands that illicit actions, which can be readily observed	Interrogator may tell the suspect that he or she is not sure if the suspect is lying, unless the suspect wants to admit it by blinking his or her eyes really fast (this may lead an untruthful suspect to blink his or her eyes really fast).

49	Interrogator alleviates the suspect's guilt via the process of disassociation; interrogator wears down the suspect's defenses by continually repeating phrases that distinguish the "old suspect" from the "new suspect"	Interrogator may state to the suspect, *"Perhaps the old you was capable of doing this, but I know that you would never do it today and it is only important who you are today."*
50	Interrogator watches the eyes of the suspect when the suspect is thinking; interrogator evaluates whether suspect is recalling information or creating information; interrogator should start by asking questions that develop a reference	Recalling information is a sign of truthfulness; creating information is a sign of deceitfulness; for recalling visual memories, the eyes of right-handed individuals will go up and to the left and the eyes of left-handed individuals will go up and to the right; for creating visual memories, the eyes of right-handed individuals will go up and to the right and the eyes of left-handed individuals will go up and to the left
51	Interrogator creates a conditioned response in the suspect	Interrogator chooses a behavior and performs that behavior when he asks the suspect questions that the interrogator knows will be answered truthfully; when the interrogator asks the suspect questions and wants to find the truth, the interrogator will perform the behavior, which will generate a conditioned truthful response from the suspect
52	Interrogator develops a rapport with the suspect and then leads the suspect's thinking; interrogator explains to the suspect why having an honest conversation is important	Interrogator may state to the suspect, *"I went to your high school and I was in the same situation. I understand the pressure that friends can put on you. You talking about it is the right thing to do. Let's put this behind us so we can both move on. It is the smart thing to do"*

53	Interrogator uses mild trance inducers; used to gain control of the conversation; used to gain time or to disrupt the suspect's train of thought	Interrogator may state to the suspect, *"You didn't eat yet and you're still hungry. Are you never going on vacation sometimes? If you are expecting me to give you a break, you wouldn't have asked for it."* The variety of non-related subjects in the sentence disrupts the suspect's train of thought.
54	Interrogator implants an artificial suggestion in the mind of the suspect, which changes the suspect's perception of reality; interrogator plants the seed of concern in the mind of the suspect and lets it grow	Interrogator may state to the suspect, *"Everyone knows that you cheated on your wife. Have you noticed how all of your friends look at you funny?"*

Table 18
Human Behavior (Lieberman, 1998; Pease & Pease, 2004b; Pollock, 2004; Thompson & Jenkins, 2004)

Human Behavior
Many decisions are emotionally based. An argument based solely on logic is marginally persuasive. To be effectively persuasive, arguments based on logic need to be transformed into arguments with emotions. For example, an interrogator may state to the suspect, *"Your deceitfulness hurts me. If you are honest, I won't say a word to your spouse about your indiscretions"*.
Interrogator may dramatically increase the suspect's anxiety level by making a problem seem permanent, by making it seem more significant than it truly is, and by making it seem like it will affect other parts of the suspect's life.
Because the human mind and body are linked, changing the body will change the mind. If a suspect is in a state of denial and refuses to budge on his claim, change his physical state (for example, if he is sitting, have him stand or move around).
Suspects do not want to change their position due to ego; it is an admission of failure. However, the interrogator may introduce new information and ask the suspects to reconsider their position (this is effective if the new information is relatively recent; otherwise, suspects may feel foolish for not knowing it).

Human Behavior
When an interrogator cannot sway the suspect, the interrogator reverses his or her own direction and exaggerates the suspect's position. For example, if a suspect states that because he is angry he will not leave his home, which will cause him to miss his court date, the interrogator will tell the suspect that if he misses the court date, he will not have to worry about leaving his cell for next 20 years.
Interrogator takes control of the situation and speaks directly and softly; interrogator expects suspect to listen and does not ask for opinions. The suspect perceives the topic to be of great importance if the interrogator makes a big deal about it. If the interrogator compliments the suspect, the suspect will be more receptive; if the interrogator criticizes the suspect, the suspect will be less receptive.
Interrogator breaks suspect down by making him tired, hungry, and thirsty. Suspect will not think clearly under these conditions and will confess to end stress and to achieve comfort.
Interrogator must have plans and backup plans; when the interrogator's options are limited, the suspect will have the advantage; when the interrogator has several options, he gains leverage; for example, if the interrogator has several suspects, he or she does not need the first one to confess because there are other suspects who may confess – this decreases the first suspect's power.
If the interrogator wants to encourage a behavior, such as a confession, he or she must get the suspect to see it as something simple and as a single task event (individuals spend time on the things that they like); if the interrogator wants to discourage a behavior, he or she must get the suspect to see it as something difficult and as a multitask event (individuals think of the many things that bother them when they do an activity that they do not enjoy).
Human behavior may be motivated via pleasure and/or pain; the suspect will act when the benefits outweigh the costs; the interrogator must get the suspect to believe that by confessing, the topic will be behind him or her and that the subject will not be brought up again (benefit); if the suspect believes that a lengthy interrogation will follow the confession (a high cost), he or she has no incentive to confess.
Individuals see what they choose to see; wishful thinking blinds individuals from seeing clues and from seeing reality; a interrogator who seeks compliments, confirmation, or confrontation will miss the true meaning of the suspect's message.

Human Behavior
Individuals see how they have learned to see; interrogators must consider truth from different perspectives; morals determine appropriate behavior; there are many different ethical systems (e.g., cultural relativism, situational ethics, ethics of care, religious, natural law, ethical formalism, egoism, ethics of virtue, etc.)
Emotions impair judgment; interrogator plays on emotions to manipulate behavior; for example, an interrogator may tell a feminist that her place is in the kitchen, a religious person that God expects a confession, and a vain person that no one likes her.
Suspect will attempt to deceive interrogator by creating trust via a bond; suspect may attempt to flatter interrogator, or may claim that they are alike.
A suspect may offer the interrogator a gift, which may make the interrogator feel obligated to the suspect; gratuities should not be accepted by a police officer if they affect a police decision.
An individual may attempt to deceive a person by making the original offer excessively high and then by lowering the cost a little bit (the savings seem like a good deal); doubling the price and then lowering the cost by 20% seems like a good deal for the consumer; the total value must be compared to the final cost, irrelevant of any savings, when making the best-practice decision.
People resist change; people with low self-esteem resist admitting they are wrong; people of low self-worth behave in ways to make past actions right; people can be manipulated by getting them to commit to something small and by increasing the demands over time; once individuals have developed a sense of obligation, their actions can be manipulated (e.g., this is how cults operate)
An individual may be influenced by other people's desires; a man may go a year without a date, then when one woman wants him, many women suddenly do (supply and demand); an objective person must not let other people's interests dictate his or her actions
Just because someone dresses as an expert does not make that person an expert; individuals will try to enhance their credibility via superficial means; a police officer may wear a campaign hat for image, respect, authority, and professionalism
People want what they cannot have; rare items are often valuable (supply and demand); wise individuals must realize that just because something is rare does not make it valuable
Wise individuals will always challenge the data; statistics can be manipulated and there are always limitations (variables, data collection, methodology, data analysis, interpretation, etc.); wise individuals do not accept arguments as true without confirmation

Human Behavior
Suspect will gain trust and credibility by offering some information that benefits the victim; once the suspect's credibility has been established, he or she will influence the victim to make less than optimal decisions.
Suspect will request a large favor from the victim, expecting the favor to be declined; once declined, the suspect will ask the victim for a smaller favor; the victim feels bad for refusing the second favor because it is relatively small, compared to the original request.
Suspect will try to manipulate the victim by attacking his or her ego; the victim will act and make a poor decision in order to protect his or her pride. For example, a suspect may state to a victim, *"I used to have a sweater like the one you are wearing, then my dad got a job." "Perhaps these sweaters are too expensive for you." "You should take a look at the clearance rack."* This tactic may motivate a victim to purchase an expensive sweater to make a point.

Assessing Truth & Body Language

(BodyLanguageCards.com, n.d.; Erskine, 2001; Inbau et al., 2005; Lambert, 2008; Lieberman, 1998; Meyer, 2010; Pease & Pease, 2004a; Starrett & Davis, 2006; Zulawski & Wicklander, 2002)

Body Language
• > 7,000 different facial expressions
• > 700,000 forms of body language
• 65% of social meanings transmitted non-verbally
• Head (e.g., nodding)
• Face (e.g., blushing)
• Eyes (e.g., winking)
• Nose (e.g., flaring nostrils)
• Lips & mouth (e.g., smiling)
• Arms (e.g., crossing)
• Hands (e.g., thumbs up)
• Handshaking (e.g., strength of squeeze)
• Legs & feet (e.g., crossing)

Truth

- Same meaning for words? (e.g., dinner ≠ supper)
- Same meaning for gestures? (e.g., eye contact = respect or deceit)
- Deception (incorrect assumptions; magic)
- Two individuals can say exactly same thing but have different meanings (e.g., *Who's on First?*)
- Officer should separate witnesses as soon as possible so that they do not contrive a common story (consensus)

Deception

- State of being deceived or misled
- Intrinsic part of interrogation because criminals are dishonest
- Interrogator must be able to recognize and manage deception
- Interrogator must be able to recognize verbal and nonverbal signs
- Reading a person's reactions can provide indications of deception

Signs of Deception

- Verbal and nonverbal signs are incongruent
- For example, suspect denies that he did something then he starts to sweat profusely
- As suspect's fear of crime detection increases, so will the incongruence between his verbal and nonverbal signs (e.g., sweat more)
- Suspect is usually unaware of the incongruence

Clustered Behavior

- Truthful behaviors come in clusters
- Deceptive behaviors come in clusters
- Five different deceptive responses to any one question or issue is a sign of deception; fewer than 5 is not enough

10 Verbal Ways to Assess Truth

1. Suspect's verbal signs
2. Suspect's moods
3. Information offered by the suspect
4. Suspect is overly polite
5. Suspect uses delay tactics
6. Suspect throws interrogator a bone
7. Suspect points out truthful or cooperative behavior
8. Suspect makes moral or honest exclamations
9. Suspect's method of recollection
10. Suspect gives in

Suspect's Verbal Signs

How a suspect says "no" may indicate deception. Below are signs of deception.

1. Too friendly when saying "no"
2. Shifting body when answering
3. Crossing legs
4. Looking away
5. Shutting eyes (blinking a lot)
6. Shaking head
7. Biting lips
8. Appearance of insincerity
9. Hesitates before answering
10. A breathless "no"
11. Appearing thoughtful or too casual
12. Eyes directed somewhere else
13. Blank stare while answering
14. Saying "no" many times in rapid succession

Suspect's Moods

- Moods indicate deception when they change after a specific question is asked.
- Lying creates stress, changes in mood may indicate an increase in stress, therefore, changes in mood may indicate deception
- There are 6 states that indicate changes in mood

1. Anger
2. Swearing, attacking the interrogator, victim, or case facts
3. Depression
4. Comments about emotional problems, depression, or insomnia; any statement about personal life problems (e.g., family, health); statement about the punishment that the suspect may receive as a result of the investigation; suicidal comments
5. Denial
6. Using rationalization words ("almost, sort of, possibility"); saying that there are memory lapses (I don't remember); stalling (laughing, asking the question to be repeated); shifting blame (discussing other's culpability); irrelevant details or evading incriminating details by discussing overall issues; avoiding a question or only answering a portion of it; statements that lack emotion (refusing to discuss something hurtful or appearing to be unaffected)

Information Offered by Suspect

- If a suspect offers additional information to support his denial, this may be a sign of deception
- Honest people will respond and simply say that they did not do it
- Untruthful people tend to elaborate their responses

Suspect is Overly Polite

- Being overly polite or too helpful is a red flag for deception
- Suspect uses these tactics to get the interrogator to like him
- Suspect trying to find out what the interrogator knows and what direction the interrogator is headed
- Suspect tries to direct the interrogator away from something and toward someone or something else

Suspect uses Delay Tactics

- There are several different types of delay tactics a suspect may use to buy time
- Repeat question so can have time to think of answer
- Answer the question with a question (does not actually answer the question)
- Says does not understand question
- Says "Are you accusing me of this?" This breaks the flow of the interrogation
- Tries to shift blame to someone else

Suspect Throws Interrogator a Bone

- It is rare that a suspect initially admits completely to the crime
- Throwing a bone means that the suspect admits to a lesser crime
- Suspect does this to give the impression that he is truthful
- This is a sense of compromise and is close to a confession

Suspect Points Out Truthful or Cooperative Behavior

- Suspect points out how truthful or cooperative he is in order to delay answering the question
- Often a sign of deception

Suspect makes Moral or Honest Exclamations

- If a suspect begins making exclamations about his morals or honesty, it may be a sign of deception
- "I swear to God"
- My father is a police officer/priest
- Honestly, truthfully

Suspect's Method of Recollection

- How a suspect recalls the details of the event
- A truthful person will tell a story with only minor changes
- An untruthful person needs to have an excellent memory to maintain a series of lies
- Interrogator needs to get very specific about minor details
- Have suspect reaffirm details and ask raid questions so the suspect has no time to think about his answers

Suspect Gives In

- The suspect admits to the crime
- "If I pay for the stuff, will you let me go?"
- "I'll confess if it makes you happy"
- The innocent do not generally admit guilt or offer to pay for the crime

Nonverbal Signs

- Based on the fight or flight response of humans
- Primitive physiological response to the perception of threat (e.g., perpetrator's loss of freedom)
- Sympathetic nervous system initiates physiological changes, such as increased heart rate

Important Note

- Guilty person may perceive that the interrogator believes him or her, may become comfortable, and may display little stress
- Innocent person may perceive that the interrogator does not believes him or her, may become uncomfortable, and may display much stress

Altered Behavior

- Nonverbal clues are harder to conceal than verbal clues
- If interrogator points out nervous behavior, suspect may try to alter behavior
- There is no single behavior that indicates absolute guilt

5 Factors for Nonverbal Behaviors

1. Proxemics
2. Psychological aspects
3. Memory
4. Eye movement
5. Specific body parts

Proxemics

- Examination of personal space based on cultural, behavioral, and sociological aspects
- Interrogator uses comfort space to increase or decrease intensity of interaction
- Suspect may also use comfort zone to manipulate interrogator
- For example, suspect may move away from interrogator in order to reduce stress
- There should be nothing between the suspect and interrogator
- Interrogator should never get closer than two feet from suspect
- Purpose is not to threaten suspect, but rather to control the suspect's attempt to cushion the stress level

Psychological aspects

- Automatic nervous system is primarily subconscious and, as such, is beyond the control of the conscious mind
- It controls the heart, smooth muscles (such as blood vessels), and internal glands and organs
- Suspect may not know that he is exhibiting signs
- Sympathetic nervous system is of particular interest

Sympathetic nervous

- Inhibits certain functions while preparing the body for a stressful situation
- Peripheral blood flow is constricted, causing blood flow to the skin to decrease and overall blood flow to the heart and muscles to increase to help prepare the body for "flight or fight"
- Adrenaline is released and blood-sugar level is increased
- Heart rate and breathing increase

Memory

- Deceptive persons experience more memory lapses than persons telling the truth
- May be due to repression, where the suspect has hidden the event from conscious thought
- May be because person is too emotional to discuss event
- Very often due to intentional memory loss, so suspect does not have to lie
- If ask about a specific event, suspect will most likely remember
- Once suspect remembers a specific fact, other facts will fall into place and this makes memory lapse more unbelievable

Eye Movement

- Relates to where a person looks after being asked a question while he is thinking about the answer
- By observing eye movements, the interrogator may tell whether the suspect is telling the truth or is lying
- A baseline is established during the baseline assessment phase of the interrogation
- Positions are accurate about 90% of the time
- The other 10% may be left handed people who look in the opposite direction
- There are exceptions to the rule; therefore, a baseline is needed
- Ask questions to get the suspect to recall things with imagine

From the interrogator's point of view when facing a suspect, the suspect's eyes:

- Up and to right – person is recalling something visual that was actually experienced (truth)
- To the side and right - person is recalling sounds actually experienced (truth)
- Down and to right – person is getting in touch with his or her inner feelings or internal dialogue; talking to self
- Up and to left – the person is creating visually, probably not something actually experienced (lie)
- To the side and to the left – person is creating an auditory thought (lie)
- Down and to the left – person is thinking about his or her feelings

Specific Body Parts – Head

- Tilted – listening
- Straight – listening, may be angry
- Chin hits chest – depression, resignation
- Head in hands – thinking about what was said and may be an indication of internal dialogue
- Pyramid with hands – suspect feels superior
- Thinking pose (elbow on knee, fists on forehead) – suspect probably faking paying attention and trying to think around the topic
- Untruthful persons roll head in an effort to stretch tense neck muscles – movements quick and jerky
- Tilt head down – submissive attitude
- Tilt head back – arrogance; elevate self above the act in question

Specific Body Parts – Facial Expression

- Includes mouth, eyes, nose, and complexion
- A person who smiles and uses the whole mouth is likely truthful
- If show only upper teeth, then suspect feels in control of the situation
- Overly concerned pleasant look on face is a sign of false interest or disguised concern of fear
- Flushing in face is an indication of fear – blood flow to large muscles due to stress response
- Redness is a sign of anger – due to increased blood pressure
- Eyes and lips become darker – lack of oxygen due to stress
- Suspect freezes face – attempting to hide what is going on inside
- Facial twitching – 1/4 to 1/2 second in duration is sign of stress
- During stress, blood pressure in nose changes, causing the nose to become irritated and to itch. Thus, deceptive persons touch nose more often
- Muscles around mouth are controlled involuntarily by genuine emotions
- Hard to fake a smile that appears sincere
- Suspect may attempt to deceive interrogator by, for example, crying for the victim when the suspect is actually crying because he is close to getting caught
- Quick, surprised sounding laughs or inappropriate smirks are a sign of being insincere or deceptive
- Carotid artery often pulses visibly and shakes Adam's Apple when suspect is stressed

Specific Body Parts – Eye Blinking

- A change in amount of eye blinking is a sign of deception – use baseline for reference
- If eyelids stay closed longer than normal during interrogation, it may be a sign of stress and that suspect does not want to look at the interrogator
- Decrease in amount of blinking can be a sign of intense internal dialogue and that the suspect is considering whether to confess; it may indicate an increased interest in what the interrogator is talking about
- Squint - nervous
- Glance up and stare at the interrogator more than usual – nervous
- Persons who wears glasses may push them up on the nose to hide their eyes
- Glasses may slide down due to sweat

Specific Body Parts – Eye Contact

- Average person maintains eye contact 40-60% of the time during conversations
- Too much or too little eye contact may be a sign of deception
- May be influenced by culture or other social norms
- Too much eye contact may be an attempt to show truthfulness or interest or to see how the interrogator is reacting
- Too little eye contact may be the attempt to avoid looking at the interrogator so that behaviors are not identified through the eyes

Specific Body Parts – Mouth

- Yawning – may indicate need for oxygen due to emotional demands of interrogation
- Yawning – may be used to feign disinterest or to buy time
- Yawning – suspect may actually be tired or bored with the interrogation
- Keep time of day and duration of interrogation in mind when evaluating yawning
- Breathing more rapidly – signs of deception
- An untruthful person will breathe about 18-22 times more per minute than a truthful person
- Breathing will be shallow, causing the suspect to gasp and sigh occasionally
- Attempting to hide mouth may indicate trying to stop mouth from what it is saying
- Biting lips – sign of stress
- Dry mouth – stress causes mouth to produce less saliva so will produce clicking sound
- Untruthful suspect will try to wet lips and swallow more often
- Untruthful suspect will ask for water more often

Specific Body Parts – Arms

- Shrug from shoulder – denial
- Dropping or hunching shoulders – depression or acceptance
- Pulling shoulders back while tightening the neck – anger
- Protect vital areas – stressed, threatened
- Hugs self – self reliance
- Elbows and hands loose to side - relaxed
- Excessive hand usage – nervousness (depends on culture) or poor verbal skills
- Jerky movements – untruthful
- Excessive rubbing – deception
- Changes in motor skills (e.g., when writing statement) – deceptive behavior

Specific Body Parts – Legs

- Wiggling, shaking, or bouncing feet is a sign of stress
- Slides feet under chair, especially if cross legs while doing this – stress
- Turns and crosses legs so that they are facing away from interrogator - rejection
- If legs are open and facing interrogator – acceptance
- If suspect puts one leg out in front, maintaining distance between him and interrogator
- If suspect points one leg toward door – ready to leave
- Feet flat one floor, toes pointed inward – sign of introverted person
- Feet flat one floor, toes pointed outward – person may feel uncomfortable or superior
- Crosses legs higher up on the knee compared to ankle – defensive posture
- Women may cross legs according to culture norms
- Truthful persons may display these signs if they become uncomfortable during interrogation

Specific Body Parts – Sitting Position

- Sitting as though ready to run, leaning to one side with feet under weight of body (may also be facing door) – stress and wants to leave
- Slouched back with legs kicked out, hands draped over side of chair, or hands tucked in pants – trying to appear macho or overtly bored
- Turning chair backwards – trying to distance self from interrogator (barrier)
- Relaxed person will move around and change positions while sitting in a chair
- Deceptive person may freeze his body into one position for long periods of time, clenching fists, maintaining rigid posture, and sitting on hands
- Deceptive person will move chair before sits down and at angle away from interrogator; may move chair away from interrogator or sit in it sideways to protect abdominal area (i.e., vulnerable area)

REFERENCES

BodyLanguageCards.com (n.d.). Retrieved from http://www.bodylanguagecards.com/

Erskine, J. (Producer/Director), & Cleese, J. (Writer). (2001). *The human face* [Motion picture]. (Available from the British Broadcasting Corporation via AOL Time Warner Company at 4000 Warner Blvd. Burbank, CA 91522)

Hatch, J. (2002). *Doing qualitative research in education settings.* Albany, NY: State University of New York Press.

Inbau, F.E., Reid, J.E., Buckley, J.P., & Jayne, B.C. (2005*). Essentials of the Reid technique: Criminal interrogation and confessions.* Boston, MA: Jones and Bartlett.

Jackson, D.M. (2004). *In your face: The facts about your features.* New York, NY: Viking.

Lambert, D. (2008). *Body language 101: The ultimate guide to knowing when people are lying, how they are feeling, what they are thinking, and more.* New York, NY: Skyhorse.

Lieberman, D.J. (1998). *Never be lied to again: How to get the truth in 5 minutes or less in any conversation or situation.* New York, NY: St. Martin's Press.

Meyer, P. (2010). *Lie spotting: Proven techniques to detect deception.* New York, NY: St. Martin's.

Pease, A., & Pease B. (2004a). *The definitive book of body language.* New York, NY: Bantam.

Pease, B., & Pease A. (2004b). *Why men don't have a clue and women always need more shoes: The ultimate guide to the opposite sex.* New York, NY: Broadway.

Pollock, J.M. (2004). *Ethics in crime and justice: Dilemmas & decisions.* Belmont, CA: Thomas-Wadsworth.

Starrett, P., & Davis, J.N. (2006). *Interview & interrogation with eyewitness evidence* (2nd ed.) (2006). San Clemente, CA: LawTech.

Thompson, G.J., & Jenkins, J.B. (2004). *Verbal judo: The gentle art of persuasion.* New York, NY: Harper.

Zulawski, D.E., & Wicklander, D.E. (2002). *Practical aspects of interview and interrogation* (2nd ed.). New York, NY: CRC.

CHAPTER 9. INTERROGATION

Unlike an interview, which is a free-flowing, non-accusatory meeting used to collect information, an interrogation is an accusational interaction between the government and suspect, which is conducted in a controlled environment with the goal of persuading the suspect to tell the truth (Inbau et al., 2005). The interrogator's goal is to obtain useful information that may be used against the suspect in court. Thus, to get the suspect to talk, it is important to develop a rapport or comfort level with the suspect.

Before the interrogator asks the suspect any questions directly related to the crime under investigation, the interrogator should spend a few minutes to develop a relationship of common ground with the suspect (Inbau et al., 2005). The interrogator may discuss sports, hobbies, or something else in which they both can relate. Another way to develop a rapport with the suspect is to mirror the suspect's behavior. For example, if the suspect has a habit of flicking her hair back, then the interrogator may flick her hair back (Barth, 2004). The interrogator can start the process with the spelling of the suspect's last name (Inbau). Then the interrogator may ask the suspect about her social security number, phone number, and current employment. The information may help guide the rest of the interview.

In order to become better informed and to determine if the suspect is the likely perpetrator, the interrogator should conduct an interview with the suspect prior to conducting the interrogation (Inbau et al., 2005). The interviewer should, if possible, become thoroughly familiar with the facts of the case before beginning the interview. Because the officer needs to determine if a crime has actually been committed, the alleged victim should be interviewed first. Following the victim, the investigator should interview suspects who are least likely to be guilty of the crime and work toward the more likely suspect. By doing this, the officer will have more intelligence when interrogating the actual perpetrator. When interviewing a suspect, the officer should ask the suspect what he believes happened, who he believes is the suspect, and why he believes the person committed the crime (i.e., the motive).

Once the interrogation starts, the interrogator should generally make an introductory statement (Inbau et al., 2005). The introductory statement has three purposes: to clearly identify the crime being discussed, to establish the interrogator's objectivity, and to persuade the suspect that his lies will be detected. It has been shown that an introductory statement increases both the suspect's truthful and deceptive behavior symptoms. Below is an example of an introductory statement.

Victor, during the interview today, we will be discussing the allegation made against you. I want you to understand my role, which is to establish the truth. When I interview a person, it does not matter to me, one way or another, what the person did, as long as he tells the truth. Sometimes a person may be afraid to acknowledge certain statements because he may be afraid of how others may perceive it. However, if a person lies about something small, then there is a natural tendency to believe that the person might be lying about something big. Therefore, it is very important for you to tell the complete truth today.

After the introductory statement, the interrogator should begin the interrogation with an initial open-ended question (Inbau et al., 2005). The open-ended question allows the suspect to provide a narrative response. The interrogator may remain silent during the process to encourage the suspect to keep talking. Forced silence by the interrogator may create an ambience that encourages the suspect to provide a full response to the open-ended question. Following is an example of an initial open-ended question. *"Please tell me everything you know about the mascot prank at your school last Friday night."*

Table 19
Signs of Truthfulness (Inbau et al., 2005)

Similar level of detail throughout the statement	Although one individual may provide a different level of detail from another individual, each person interrogated should provide similar amounts of detail throughout his or her own statement.
Information out-of-sequence	People have primary and secondary memories. The primary memories, which are the most important facts, may stimulate secondary memories, which are less important facts. Secondary memories may be stimulated out of time sequence.
Personal thoughts and feelings expressed	Because emotional states are psychologically linked to behaviors, a truthful statement often includes what the person felt or thought at the time of the incident.

Table 20
Signs of Deception (Inbau et al., 2005)

Detail Level Varies	If a suspect is very detailed for most of the statement, then all of a sudden becomes quite vague, the change in behavior is suspicious.
Perfect chronological order	Although a person who has retold the account many times over may remember things in chronological order, an account that fails to make out-of-sequence statements may indicate rehearsal and the account is suspicious.
Missing personal thoughts and feelings	Individuals' emotions are intertwined with their behaviors. Thus, when a person is deceitful, they only say the facts and nothing but the facts. They fail to mention emotions that should be attached to their actions. *"When I heard it, I was afraid..."*

Gap-in-time statements	When a person makes a statement that skips some time, the statement is suspicious. It may be because the suspect did something during the time that he is trying to conceal. *"I arrived at 3:00 pm. Before I knew it..."*
Implied-action statements	Incomplete statements that require the interrogator to make assumptions are suspicious. The statement, *"He started to hit me..."* does not claim that the action was completed.

Interrogation questions need to be asked so that they provide the information sought. In other words, the questions need to be valid. First, the interrogator's questions should not bias the responses. Second, the questions need to elicit responses that cannot be interpreted in more than one way. Finally, the questions should be asked in a way that does not trigger defensive mechanisms, which may prevent the suspect from providing complete information.

Table 21
Techniques for Interrogation Questions (Inbau et al., 2005)

Rule	Example
Whenever practical, ask open-ended questions because they allow for more complete information without influence by the interrogator.	Closed-ended: Were you at the school on Saturday? Open-ended: Why were you at the school on Saturday?
Do not use aggressive language that triggers defensive reactions.	Incorrect: Did you steal the item? Correct: Did you take the item?
Do not use compound questions.	Incorrect: Did you see the item and did you take the item? Correct: Did you see the item? Did you take the item?

Direct questions should be short and to the point.	Did you talk to Jim on Saturday?
Do not provide memory qualifiers in the question.	Incorrect: Do you remember if Jim called you? Correct: Did Jim ever call you?
Do not ask negative questions.	Incorrect: You did not do it, did you?

Table 22
Handling less than Complete/Truthful Responses (Inbau et al., 2005)

Less than Complete/Truthful Responses	Response
Responses that do not offer a definite answer (*I was at the school last month...*)	Rephrase the same question (*Were you at the school yesterday?*)
Responses that contain words that decrease the suspect's confidence or personal commitment (*To the best of my knowledge...*)	Ask a hypothetical question (*Is it possible...*)
Responses that omit information (*I did commit a crime when I was 12...*)	Ask a follow-up question (*Besides that time...*)

Police officers conduct interrogations for the purpose of collecting information, which is needed in an investigation (Swanson et al., 2009). The four main objectives of an interrogation are to obtain important facts, to eliminate innocent individuals, to identify the perpetrators, and to obtain a confession. The interrogator governs the interrogation process and setting. The interrogator must ensure privacy and control the interruptions, planned or otherwise, because privacy may be the psychological tool needed to get the perpetrator to confess. Perpetrators may be more willing to talk to a single person in a private setting.

Before police officers can effectively conduct interviews or interrogations, they must familiarize themselves with the case (Swanson, et al., 2009). An officer must become familiar with the offense, the victims, and the suspect. By analyzing crime scene evidence and by theorizing about the motives, the interrogator may develop a suspect profile, which may suggest a plan of attack. See Table 23 for a pre-interrogation checklist.

Table 23
Pre-interrogation Checklist (Swanson, et al., 2009)

Number	Information Important to Interrogator
1	Law book description of the crime; elements of the crime
2	Perpetrator's motive and method of operation
3	Tools or weapons used by perpetrator
4	Time, date, and location of offense
5	Nature and value of damage
6	Physical evidence collected, including witness statements
7	Names of individuals who have information about crime
8	Entrance and exit points of perpetrator
9	Entrance and exit routes of perpetrator
10	Weather conditions at time of crime
11	Method of perpetrator's travel to and from crime scene
12	Details for other cases that have the same modi operandi

False Confessions

Although false confessions are rare, individuals in the past have been known to provide false confessions (Inbau et al., 2005). In some cases, after the individuals were convicted, DNA testing had identified other individuals as the perpetrators. There are four factors that appear to be consistently related to false confessions, which are a) the suspect is a juvenile, b) the suspect has a mental or psychological impairment, c) the suspect was interrogated for an inordinate amount of time, and d) the suspect was coerced with threats or promises.

Suspect is a Juvenile and/or has a Mental or Psychological Impairment

Juveniles and the mentally or psychologically impaired do commit serious crimes. Interrogators must use caution when interrogating juveniles or individuals who have mentally or psychologically impairments (Inbau, et al., 2005). If a juvenile is less than 15 years of age and has never been interrogated in the past, the officer should carefully discuss each point of the *Miranda* rights to ensure that the child understands them. If the child does not understand his or her rights, the interrogator should not conduct an interrogation.

When a juvenile or mentally or psychologically impaired person confesses, the interrogator must corroborate the information (Inbau, et al., 2005). This can be achieved if the interrogator withholds specific details from the suspect so that the interrogator may verify the confession's authenticity. When an interrogator corroborates a confession, the confession becomes more credible.

Suspect was Coerced or Interrogated for an Inordinate Amount of Time

A suspect's rights must be respected at all times. A police officer who uses illegal tactics and techniques during an interrogation may be personally sanctioned. Although there is no absolute rule about the length of an interrogation, a typically interrogation usually lasts about one to two hours (Starrett & Davis, 2006). Using improper interrogation techniques and tactics may disqualify a suspect's confession from being admitted in court. Therefore, an interrogator should not make any threats or promises of leniency, or should not use physically abusive tactics to gain a confession. See Table 24 for examples of improper threats and/or promises (Inbau, et al., 2005).

Table 24
Examples of Improper Threats and/or Promises (Inbau, et al., 2005)

Examples of Improper Interrogation Techniques
You will face the death penalty unless you confess.
The police will hound you every day for the rest of your life if you do not confess.
If you do not confess, we will lock up all of your family members.
If you confess, we will release you and you will be free to sleep in your own bed tonight.
The police do not let the suspect sleep for three days until he confesses.
The police slap the suspect on his hands with a ruler until he confesses.

Credibility of Confession

The interrogator should assess the credibility of a confession (Inbau, et al., 2005). After all, the judge or jury needs to be convinced that the suspect is guilty beyond a reasonable doubt of the filed charge. If the suspect changes his story in court and the available evidence does not support the suspect's guilt, then the case may fall apart (this does not mean that other charges will not be filed against the suspect). See Table 25 for factors that may impact the credibility of a suspect's confession.

Table 25
Factors that May Impact the Credibility of a Suspect's Statement (Inbau, et al., 2005)

#	Factors that Impact the Credibility of a Confession
1	Suspect's age (e.g., may be too young to understand what is happening)
2	Suspect's prior experience with the *Miranda* warning
3	Suspect's culture and understanding of the language
4	Suspect's behavior during the interrogation (e.g., body language)
5	Addressing suspect's physical needs (e.g., refusing to let suspect use restroom)
6	Presence of witnesses during interrogation (e.g., suspect may refuse to confess if family members are present)

7	Suspect's physical, mental, and psychological condition
8	Length of interrogation (e.g., continuously questioning a suspect for 2 straight days)
9	The degree of detail that the suspect provides (e.g., information that only someone at the scene would know)
10	The interrogator's corroboration of the suspect's confession
11	The use of illegal interrogation techniques (e.g., use of pain to gain confession)

People like to talk in order to reduce the psychological and physiological pressures that build internally (Swanson, et al., 2009). It has been estimated that about 80% of all individuals will confess to a crime. Of the 80% confessions, some of these individuals are actually guilty and some are actually not guilty. Thus, convictions cannot be based on confessions alone. In other words, police officers need to corroborate each confession.

Most guilty suspects look for an opportunity during an interrogation to confess (Swanson, 2009). A good interrogator will provide the suspect an opportunity to confess, which will reduce the perpetrator's internal psychological and physiological pressures. In short, the interrogator's job is to make the confession easy for the perpetrator.

There are many different interrogation techniques. The following tables are an overview of various interrogation techniques (Inbau et al., 2005; *Interrogation*, 1991; Starrett & Davis, 2006; Zulawski & Wicklander, 2002). Techniques may also be combined to get the best results.

Appeal to Authority

- Interrogator must make authentic statement
- Interrogator must be flexible
- Interrogator must be able to think of words and phrases on the spot
- Interrogator should never use words that indicate his or her true feelings about the crime under investigation
- Interrogator should avoid facial expressions that give feelings away

Example - Buggery

"I have heard that some world famous psychiatrists say that all people are inclined to be homosexual. However, most of us learn to control our sex drives. For one reason or another, some of us experience a natural condition that prevents us from controlling our sex drives. It is a known fact that Greek soldiers have been sleeping with men since ancient times. When you think about it, this has been going on in Europe for centuries. Maybe Americans just haven't risen to that level of cultural sophistication yet."

Everybody's Doing it

- Interrogator needs to play down the seriousness of the crime
- Interrogator must assure the suspect that everyone in the world is doing it too

Example – Sex Crime

- "Son, do you think you are the only red-blooded male who has ever touched a girl? Guys think about it all the time However, most of us don't have the guts to do anything about it. Girls feel the same way. Sex is just human nature; it's natural. People would think that you are strange if you didn't think about it. The way they dress and act, the broad was probably asking for it"

Blame Someone Else Technique

- Interrogator needs to size up suspect (physically)
- Short and fat physique - humor them
- Tall and slender - appeal to intellect

For Example - Theft

"I don't blame you for stealing a car radio from Ford Motor Company. They won't miss it with all of their millions of dollars. With how little they pay you, they owe it to you. I probably would have taken a lot more. I don't blame you at all for what you did."

Appeal to Intellect

- Interrogator needs to close the gap between the interrogator's communication level and the suspect's superior communication level
- This technique is effective when dealing with a person with superior education or intellect and the interrogator cannot challenge the suspect in his field
- Interrogator brings the suspect closer to his own level of education
- The interrogator plays upon the suspect's intellect
- The interrogator will not attach any blame to the suspect
- The interrogator will not mention the criminal act
- The interrogator seeks to elicit a rationalization for the act

Example- Sexual Deviance

"Doctor, by community standards, you are the most respected man in society. I just can't comprehend how a man of your intellect could be involved in something like this. Please help me understand the reason for this."

Respect for Position in Society Technique

- The interrogator may be required to interrogate someone who is beyond reproach (e.g., priest)
- Interrogator must be flexible and able to ad lib
- Interrogator must have and use a repertoire of words and phrases
- The interrogator must keep referring to the fact that the suspect is well respected in society

Example – Sexual Misconduct

"Father, most everyone respects you. I respect you. Your parishioners respect you. Since this incident happened, I have no doubt that you prayed and asked for forgiveness. Don't let us down; we respect and love you. I know in the end that this whole situation will come out right".

Publicity Technique

- Interrogator needs to refer to the amount of publicity that may result if the public ever finds out that the suspect was involved in this criminal act
- Interrogator should never condemn the suspect
- Interrogator should always provide the suspect a way out

Example

"Sir, this matter is going to break the hearts of a lot of the people who know and love you. I just hope that there are not a lot of media people in the court room; maybe I can get you into court during the lunch hour, when few people will be around to see. The very last thing we want to do is to have to bring your family down to police headquarters to interview them about this situation. If we both just think really hard, maybe we can get figure something out. There must be some kind of a reason for what happened here. Our main goal is to keep this matter out of the press because we do not need all of that attention. Can you arrange to take a vacation after this situation blows over?"

Face-Saving Technique

- The interrogator supplies a justification for the incident so that the suspect may save face
- Interrogator blames someone else
- The interrogator supplies the suspect with an excuse so that the subject may rationalize the crime
- The interrogator only seeks a confession and does not care the reason that the suspect gives for committing the crime

Example – Sexual Misconduct

"I just don't know what gets into these kids these days. They want to try these things out and then they complain. You know those 14 year old girls look like 20 year old women with those short miniskirts and makeup. I have no doubt that these girls nowadays may even ask for it. You know, 9 out of 10 times these girls are to blame."

Oedipus Technique

- The interrogator breaks down suspects who are charged with incest
- This is a face saving technique; blames human nature
- Children are attracted to opposite sex parent and jealous of same sex parent
- The interrogator should tell the story of Oedipus; Oedipus was separated from parents, killed his father, married his mother, and once the mother realized that Oedipus was her son, she committed suicide
- In addition, a sense of inferiority during childhood (e.g., small stature) may cause individuals to overcompensate their disadvantage via violence; give examples such as Hitler, Napoleon, and Mussolini
- Interrogators should research the family tree to see if the suspect had siblings and two parent households, whether the father or mother was liked better, and if the suspect felt he had to continually prove himself

Example - Incest

- Interrogator will tell the suspect that the Oedipus complex exists in everyone, especially during child development
- Sometimes the repressed desire for the opposite sex parent shows through the superego, resulting in incest – this is not the suspect's fault
- If a male child did not have a father figure, he will learn feminine traits from his mother, which may lead to homosexuality
- If a female child did not have a mother figure, she will learn masculine traits from her father, which may lead to homosexuality
- Interrogator should go along with the suspect and suggest that larger and more powerful people are always picking on him or her

Control Gimmick

- The interrogator makes a point to let the suspect know that the interrogator is in complete control; the interrogator demonstrates authority over the suspect
- The interrogator tells the suspect where to sit, to refrain from smoking, etc.
- The interrogator should not use a threatening voice
- The interrogator may let the suspect ramble
- The interrogator may use suggestive questioning to steer the interview back on course
- The interrogator must never let the suspect control the interrogation

Suggestibility Technique

- The interrogator appeals to the suspect's subconscious attitudes via direct suggestion
- The interrogator sets the stage for a confession; similar to face saving technique but blames self-circumstances
- The interrogator may suggest a reduced power of recall (e.g., intoxication) and suggest to the suspect that he may not have realized what he was doing
- The interrogator may suggest a necessity for the crime (e.g., sickness in family)
- The interrogator suggests possible justifications to persuade the suspect to accept a justification for committing the crime

Example - Breaking & Entering

The interrogator may suggest that a suspect committed breaking and entering because of family financial problems (needed money to feed kids), family sickness (needed money for kid's medicine), peer pressure, jealously caused by someone else's actions, or overindulgence in alcoholic beverages

File Gimmick

- The interrogator will use a black marker to print the suspect's name in large block letters on the outside of the file so that the suspect can see his name
- Interrogator will sit in a chair, pretend to scan the contents of the file, and have an indifferent attitude

Example

- The interrogator will occasionally nod his head, as if confirming what was found in the file, and the interrogator will make an odd look at the suspect
- The interrogator will continue to nod and give odd looks at the suspect, which will make the suspect believe that the interrogator has conclusive evidence on file

Heaven & Hell Technique (Hot & Cold)

- This technique has been used in religion and brainwashing
- The interrogator lets the subject see "hell" and then offers the suspect a piece of "heaven" as an alternative
- The interrogator keeps repeating glimpses of hell and then offers some comfort
- The interrogator will isolate the suspect and dress the suspect sloppily; the suspect will lose his dignity, identity, and will feel forsaken
- Near the beginning of interrogation, the interrogator will offer the suspect a reward, such as a drink; the interrogator may indicate that the suspect may be removed from isolation
- The suspect starts to regain his identity and starts to believe that by cooperating with those individuals in power, the damage may be minimized

Example

- The interrogator will hint at loss of job, loss of children's respect, loss of wife, loss of preferred sexual activity
- The interrogator will hint about what the suspect's young wife will do while he is in prison because she is beautiful and others will want her
- The interrogator will ask about what the neighbor's will think
- The interrogator will imply there will be no publicity, the neighbor's will not find out, and there might be a way to save his job and social status

Accident Technique

- The interrogator will blame the victim, but claim that the situation was the result of an accident or misunderstanding
- For example, the interrogator will claim that the sexual encounter was consensual up to a point, that the victim fell on the knife during the event, or that the gun accidentally fired
- The interrogator will provide the suspect with a ready-made excuse for whatever happened during the crime; this will allow the suspect to rationalize the event
- **Goal:** to get an admission; it does not matter what the excuse is

Appeal to Intelligence or Conscience Technique

- Interrogator will stay away from the actual crime committed and will focus on the weapon or drug
- The interrogator will state that an innocent child may get hurt due to the abandoned drugs or weapons
- The interrogator only needs the suspect to confirm that the weapon or drugs is not a danger to anyone

Example – Crime with Gun

Interrogator: "You have a child, and you know how kids have a tendency to find things in strange places. I hope you stashed that gun of yours very well. I wouldn't want your kid to accidently find that gun and to hurt or kill himself or another child. Did you hide the gun so that your kid, or any kid, won't find it?"

Double stick (Agent Provocateur) Technique

- The interrogator will place agent provocateur #1 in cell next to suspect
- The interrogator will place agent provocateur #2 in another cell next to the suspect so that he can overhear the conversation between the suspect and provocateur #1
- Only provocateur #1 will interact with the suspect
- Provocateur #1 will pretend to show empathy for the suspect and will attempt to get the suspect to talk about the crime

Example – Drug Arrest

- People demand drugs
- Cannot get job due to recession
- Need to feed kids
- Not hurting anyone
- There are more important crimes for police to enforce

Lawyer Gimmick

- The interrogator will imply, but will not say, that the suspect will waste money by hiring a lawyer
- The interrogator should tell the suspect that if he is guilty, he will need to hire a very good lawyer; however, no one, including the lawyer, will be able to help the suspect
- Only the suspect can help himself by admitting what he has done so that he can get help; this is the first big step on the road to recovery
- The longer the interrogator talks without interruption, the more likely the suspect is guilty

Example

The interrogator will ask the suspect why he would waste good money on an expensive lawyer if he were innocent. If the suspect is guilty, however, he should hire a good lawyer because he will need it. The interrogator will tell the suspect that only he can help himself. Not his parents, his priest, his lawyer, or even his doctor will be able to help him until he helps himself by telling the truth and by admitting that he made a mistake. Once the suspect takes that first big step toward recovery, he will be able to receive the proper treatment.

Mistake Technique

- This technique is most effective with first offenders or juveniles
- The interrogator will suggest that the suspect took the item by mistake and afterwards was too afraid to return it for fear of being blamed for theft
- The interrogator will imply that the suspect is just a victim of the circumstances, which could happen to anyone
- The interrogator will imply that the situation was created only because the suspect was trying to do the right thing
- The interrogator will state that most people would admire such a person

Exaggeration Technique

- The interrogator will enlarge the seriousness of the crime, increase the number of charges, or inflate the dollar value of the crime
- The suspect may confess to one crime in order to deny the other charges
- The interrogator should keep referring to the more serious charges when discussion the crimes
- This creates an imbalance in the suspect's mind
- The suspect does not know for sure if he will be convicted; therefore, he may confess to prevent from getting a harsher punishment

Example – Simple Theft

Interrogator: "So we finally got the person who has broken into at least 25 homes. Your trademark has been found all over town. Being convicted of 25 charges will surely rack up a great many years in prison."

Objective: to get suspect to say "I only broke into one home, not 25."

Relative Technique

- Interrogator will attempt to establish rapport with the suspect
- The interrogator will keep insinuating that the suspect is a distant relative (i.e., the suspect resembles the interrogator's relative)
- The interrogator will intentionally make a mistake and call the suspect by the relative's name
- Again, the interrogator will refer to the resemblance
- The interrogator will state that the relative had the same concern but that he received the needed help in time
- The interrogator will suggest that his relative admitted the problem to himself, which was first step, before his relative was able to get professional help
- The interrogator will state that his relative has a good job now, is married, and is doing well
- The interrogator will state that his relative's first step was to admit the mistake

Flattery Technique

- The interrogator will inflate the suspect's ego
- This technique works best on individuals who like flattery
- This technique works on most people
- This technique may not work for crimes of violence
- This technique works well with crimes that involve employing a skill (e.g., safe cracking)

Example - Flattery Technique

- That was a very clean job
- I have never seen a job pulled off with such precision
- That job required a lot of planning and complex reasoning
- That job could only have been successfully accomplished by an expert
- That job required a lot of guts
- That job must have taken a very a long time to execute
- There's no way in the world that the average guy could have done it
- This is one for the history books

Secretary Technique

- This technique is used when there are two suspects
- The interrogator will separate the two suspects
- The interrogator will place Suspect 1 in an interrogation room
- The interrogator will have Suspect 2 close by so that he can hear the voice of the interrogator but cannot understand what is being said
- After a little while, the interrogator will lean out of the interrogation room door and will yell for his secretary to bring her notepad; the interrogator will yell loud enough to ensure that Suspect 2 can hear what is going on
- The secretary brings her notepad into the interrogation room and remains long enough to give the perception of a confession
- **Goal:** to get Suspect 2 to believe that Suspect 1 provided evidence against him; Suspect 2 may then feel compelled to provide evidence against Suspect 1

White Collar Technique

- White collar crime may consist of employee theft or embezzlement
- Individuals who commit white collar crime are often subjected to office management discipline
- Individuals who commit white collar crime are not the typical criminal types that police officers see in the field
- The use of emotions is very effective against white collar criminals
- The interrogator may only need to pat the suspect on the shoulder or to give him a handshake to start the conversation
- The interrogator should obtain background information on the suspect and should seek details
- The interrogator will use sentiments against the suspect

Example

- The interrogator should look at contents of the suspect's wallet; photographs may prove valuable
- The interrogator should question the suspect about individuals in his photographs (kids, wife, etc.); the interrogator should ask the suspect about his thoughts related to his wife or son

Behavioral Symptom Technique

- Most individuals are nervous when being interrogated
- A guilty suspect will display definite behavioral symptoms (i.e., body language) when asked about the crime
- The interrogator will bring attention to suspect's body language
- For example, some signs include blushing, fidgeting in the chair, evading the answers, sweating, movement of Adam's apple, avoiding eye contact, and dry mouth
- The interrogator will claim that innocent individuals would not display such symptoms
- The interrogator will imply that the suspect is falling apart, that his body is giving every indication of guilt, and that his body is killing itself by him attempting to withhold information
- The interrogator must train to look for clues, which may be subtle

Good Cop, Bad Cop Technique

- The interrogator must have information about the crime and background information on the suspect
- This technique involves two officers – one bad cop and one good cop
- During this technique, the bad cop gets the suspect mentally off balanced, which makes him susceptible to the advice of the good cop
- The bigger police officer will assume the role of bad cop
- The bigger police officer will become impatient, start to bang on the table, yell, and make his face become flush (to appear angry)
- The bad cop will call the suspect a liar, state that they should throw the book at him, and leave the room
- The good cop will state that the bad cop keeps getting them into trouble because of his anger issues, that he has been trying to get a new partner, that the bad cop is his boss, and that once the bad cop returns the interview is over
- The good cop will act as though there is a conspiracy and will move closer to the suspect and lower his voice; the interrogator will state that if the suspect committed the crime, he better admit it before the bad cop comes back. Good cop will say, "Once my partner comes back, it will be too late for you because he won't let me talk to you anymore." The good cop will state that he will write the report, which is better than the bad cop writing it up

Example

"This sack of crap is a lying fool. He hasn't shown a shred of honesty. I don't know why you're willing to spend so much time with him. Why don't we just lock him up? I'm not going to stand here and listen to lie after lie! We don't need to talk to him anyway. I'm done. You do as you please, but I'm out of here. I can't stand this guy!"

When the hard-nose cop leaves, the good cop uses a soft approach.

Split Pair Bluff Technique

- This technique is used when there are two suspects
- The interrogator will separate the two suspects and will place them in the same corridor with 3 or 4 cells between them so that they cannot talk with one another
- The interrogator will wait a while
- The interrogator will then take Suspect 1 out of cell and they will walk past the cell of Suspect 2
- The interrogator will let Suspect 1 sit in a room for about 30 minutes
- The interrogator will not speak to Suspect 1; the interrogator will let Suspect 1 sit by himself
- The interrogator will then take Suspect 1 back to his cell
- As they pass Suspect 2, the interrogator will state in a loud voice, "Thanks, I think that has cleared things up, and I'll see what we can do for you."
- The interrogator will then place Suspect 1 back into his cell and the interrogator will leave the area
- After about 5-10 minutes, the interrogator will get Suspect 2 and tell him that it is his turn now
- **Goal:** to get Suspect 2 to believe that Suspect 1 turned evidence on him, which may cause Suspect 2 to turn evidence on Suspect 1

Can You Take it Back Technique

- This technique is effective when there is the possibility of recovering the stolen merchandise
- The interrogator will tell to the suspect that if he returns the item, or part of it, perhaps the victim may decide not to prosecute
- The interrogator must not promise the suspect that he will not be prosecuted
- For cases of theft from an employer, the interrogator may tell the suspect that the boss probably steals from the company on a regular basis, and cheats on his taxes, but just hasn't been caught yet
- The interrogator will tell the suspect that it is the employer's own fault by leaving money around, entrapping employees via temptation
- The interrogator will tell the suspect that if the employer gets some of the money back, perhaps he will understand and decide not to prosecute

Extension Technique

- The interrogator will ask the suspect questions about his background before focusing on the topic at hand
- The interrogator will get the suspect to admit that he had thought about committing the crime in the past and how easy it would be not to get caught
- Then, through subtle questioning, the interrogator will get the suspect to admit that at one time or another he had taken a small article from the company
- Once the suspect admits to taking something at a particular point in time, the interrogator will extend this to a period of time, asking suspect how much he has taken over a two month period
- The interrogator will keep extending the time period to the current case
- The interrogator will tell the suspect that he has already admitted to stealing from company so the current case is no different
- **Goal:** to get the suspect to admit that he thought about taking an item, get the suspect to admit that he took an item at a single point in time, and then extend the time period to the current case

Hot Confession Technique

- This technique is effective when catching the criminal in the act because, at the time of arrest, the perpetrator will be in state of mental imbalance
- After the suspect is placed under arrest, the officer will tell the suspect that they finally caught him, the perpetrator who is responsible for more than 20 similar crimes in that area
- By increasing the number of charges against the suspect, the suspect may attempt to defend himself by confessing to only a few of the crimes
- **Goal:** to exert pressure by accusing the suspect of many crimes so that suspect will chose to minimize the damage by confessing to fewer crimes

Logical approach

- This technique is effective with suspects who have prior criminal records
- A perpetrator will attempt to make the best deal possible when he or she feels that the case is strong against him or her
- Because conspiracy is linked to a habitual charge, suspects with prior criminal records may be willing to make a deal to avoid a possible conspiracy charge
- If suspects are at risk of being habitual violators, they may jump at the chance to plead guilty to lesser charges
- If the police mention that they may file many charges against the suspect, the suspect may choose to plead guilty to fewer charges

Example

- You didn't talk last time either, and you got 7 years.
- Don't talk again and see what you'll get. Perhaps 10 years this time.
- Don't talk and maybe you'll get 10 years… maybe 12 or 14.
- I thought you were smarter than that.
- You didn't hurt anyone.
- Did the broad even see the gun?
- If she didn't see the gun, then it's simple theft.
- We'll only charge you with 2 counts, even though you committed more.
- Perhaps we will charge you with conspiracy, which will make you a habitual violator.

Drunk Technique

- A person under the influence of an intoxicant may not be afraid of authority
- An intoxicated person may become belligerent
- The interrogator may need to humor or flatter the suspect to get a confession
- The interrogator should not berate an intoxicated suspect, which may only aggravate the situation

Ego Deflation

- The interrogator will purposely attempt to deflate the suspect's ego
- The interrogator must size the suspect up
- The suspect may be insecure and clumsy or smart and prideful

Example

- Who helps you put your pants when you get up, your mom?
- I bet your mom has to wipe your butt when you use the toilet.
- You're not smart enough to commit a crime like this.
- You should be out on the street corner asking to clean the windshields of passing cars.
- You're nothing but a worn out record; an 8-track tape player; a has-been.
- Cut the crap. Who's your boss? What did you get for your efforts? You probable got two bucks for cleaning the guy's windshield.

Yes or No Technique (Last Chance Appeal)

- The interrogator will create an imbalance in the suspect's mind
- The interrogator will tell the suspect that once the interrogator leaves room, the suspect will not have another opportunity to talk with anyone from the police department
- The interrogator will tell the suspect that this is his last chance to tell his side of the story so he better act while he still has time

Example

- I got things to do. Don't waste my time.
- I don't have time to mess around with a minor-leaguer like you.
- I'm only going to give you one more chance to talk.
- Speak to me when I tell you to speak or I'll put you in your cell and let you rot.
- Lie to me and I'll leave and that's it.
- This is your last chance

Conspiracy Technique

- The interrogator will keep his voice down as he talks; the interrogator will act as if there is a conspiracy
- The interrogator will tell the suspect that the place may be bugged and that other officers may be trying to listen through the door
- The interrogator will get close to the suspect and will tell the suspect to keep his voice down
- The interrogator will tell the suspect that what is done is done
- The interrogator will tell the suspect to admit to what he has done so that they can put the situation behind them
- The interrogator will tell the suspect that if it were an accident, he should just say so. Perhaps the interrogator could write up the report so that it does not sound so bad.
- The interrogator will tell the suspect that he may be able to ask for less time; maybe they can make a deal
- The interrogator will tell the suspect to use his head, and perhaps the suspect can get off the hook
- The interrogator will remind the suspect not to talk too loud, so no one else can hear him

What would you do? Technique

- The interrogator will reverse roles with suspect; very effective technique
- The interrogator will ask the suspect what he would do if he were the police officer
- When the suspect assumes the role of the interrogator, the suspect will many times make a deal for himself

Example

- Look, I wasn't born yesterday.
- We both know why I am here.
- What would you do if you were in my shoes?
- What do you expect me to do?
- Just give me something to work with.
- I'll work with you but you got to give me a break.
- You've got to give me something to work with.

Pyramid of Lies Technique

- When a suspect tells a lie, he or she opens a can of worms and must tell additional lies to support old lies; the suspect will create a pyramid of lies
- Once the interrogator can demonstrate that the suspect has produced one lie, the pyramid of lies will collapse
- The interrogator will provide the suspect with false information to see if the suspect agrees with it.
- If the suspect agrees with the false statement, then the officer knows that the suspect is being less than truthful.

Example

- **Interrogator:** "You say you were at Michigan Ave and Wayne Rd at about 9:00 pm last night, right? That must be true because Officer Davis stated that he saw you near that location when he was towing a car last night. He stated that you yelled his name as you passed by."
- **Suspect:** "That's right. I did see Officer Davis last night."
- **Interrogator:** "Impossible, because Officer Davis is on vacation and did not work last night" (the interrogator now knows that the suspect is lying)

Someone Always Talks Technique

- The interrogator will tell the suspect that the first person to talk is the one the police will believe
- The interrogator will tell the suspect that there are many people who could talk about the crime; there are witnesses and accomplices. Eventually, someone will talk about it.
- The interrogator will tell the suspect that once someone talks about it, it will be too late for the suspect and he will take the fall
- The interrogator will tell the suspect that if the suspect's accomplice talks first, the police will believe the accomplice; this means that the suspect will take the fall, which will cause the suspect to face an uphill legal battle
- Therefore, the suspect needs to get his story in first

Other Guy technique

- This technique is effective when there are two suspects
- The interrogator will tell the suspect that it's not him that they want; the interrogator wants the suspect's partner
- The interrogator will tell the suspect that his partner carried a weapon, which makes the crime more serious; in addition, his partner has committed similar crimes in the past
- The interrogator will continually reinforce the idea that his partner is the one who carried the weapon and is the bad apple
- **Goal:** to get the suspect to admit that he did not realize his partner was carrying a weapon

Example

- Look, we are not concerned about you; you're not the one we're after.
- Did you know your partner was carrying a weapon?
- He's the one that we want.
- He pulled a similar crime last month and stabbed a guy.
- Did you know he was carrying a weapon when you were with him?

Compulsion to Confess Approach

- This technique is based on the human need to confess
- The interrogator will tell the suspect that there are physical and psychological manifestations of guilt, which include sweating and breathing rates
- The interrogator will tell the suspect that he knows that the suspect wants to tell the truth, but there is just one little thing stopping him
- The interrogator will tell the suspect that if they can overcome this barrier, then the suspect will be able to relieve the physical and psychological pressures that have built up inside the suspect and are displaying themselves via behavioral symptoms
- The interrogator will tell the suspect that confession is a human compulsion
- If the suspect is Catholic, the interrogator may use the Church's prayer of confession

Service Club or Society Technique

- This technique is effective when suspects belong to a service club or fraternity (e.g., Masons, Knights of Columbus, etc.)
- The interrogator should examine the suspect's contents (rings, pins, membership cards, photographs, etc.) to establish that he or she belongs to a service club or fraternity/sorority
- The interrogator should use that information against the suspect
- The interrogator should use the ideals of the service club against the suspect's conscience

Example

"Hey, I see you're wearing a Masonic ring. Everyone knows that Masons support truth. Does being a Mason mean anything to you? By the standards of your club, you are required to right what is wrong. You're supposed to be truthful. Do you understand what I mean? You know what you have to do. Your wife, your kids, and the Masons will all respect you for doing the right thing. People accept that everyone is human and people make mistakes. But they will all shun you if you violate your oath to your club."

Conscience Technique

- The interrogator must not use this technique on an individual who is psychotic (i.e., a person who has no conscience)
- This technique is effective on people who have sound minds and who are religious

Example

Interrogator: "If you win this case, you will only be beating yourself. As long as you live, you will see that little girl that you killed. Her blood screams out to God for justice. You will wake up in the middle of the night and wonder when her justice will be carried out. Who knows, perhaps her justice is served by you hearing her screams in your dreams for the rest of your life. You must also wonder if you will be able to live with your own children. Perhaps the urge to kill will overcome you again and you might kill your own children. It is not too late to ask God to forgive you."

I want you to talk Technique

- The interrogator will tell the suspect that the next question is very important and that the suspect needs to answer it very carefully, because he is going to be stuck with the first answer that he gives
- The interrogator will imply that he already knows the answer to the question and that he is simply testing the suspect's truthfulness
- This techniques implies that the interrogator expects the suspect to lie; knowing this, the suspect often tells the truth without the interrogator ever asking the question

Example

"The next question that I am going to ask is very important and you need to take your time and think before you answer. You will be stuck with your first response. I am going to tell you something, I found something out recently and I have a very good reason for asking this next question. Be aware, I am not asking this question for my own health, but it may impact your own health."

- **Goal:** to get the suspect to tell the truth upon hearing this.

Special Needs Technique

- When the interrogator questions individuals with mental impairments, the interrogator must keep it simple
- The interrogator may have to explain each question at a fourth grade level
- The interrogator must be sure that the suspect understands each question and that the suspect understands the answer that he is providing
- The interrogator must explain things in easy to understand terms

Blame Society Technique

- Interrogator will blame society for the root cause of the crime
- Interrogator will need to listen to the suspect's statements of self-pity (e.g., never got a break in life), which may provide clues of actual abuse
- Interrogator may find something in the background that influenced the suspect to do wrong
- Interrogator will supply the suspect with a ready-made excuse for the commission of the crime
- Interrogator will tell the suspect that it is not his fault, but society's fault or the fault of someone who led him down the wrong path

Example

- You have a hard life
- Your parents are divorced and you never knew your father
- You were bullied at school
- Your mom kept getting evicted every few months
- You never had the chance to attend church
- You never had a chance to play team sports at school
- The one time you commit a crime, you get caught
- The cards have always been stacked against you

Technique for Juveniles

- The interrogator must not be belligerent to juvenile suspects
- The interrogator must try to understand suspect's perspective
- The interrogator must listen to the juvenile suspect
- The interrogator may provide a ready-made excuse for the suspect's actions, which may include a) blaming parents, society, or the school, b) jealousy issues, c) the need to be recognized, or d) ignorance of the law
- Interrogator should ask the child what he or she thinks is going to happen to him or her if found guilty
- Most juveniles believe that they will immediately go to jail if they confess
- Interrogator should explain to them that they will not go to jail but that they will have to appear before a juvenile judge or be spoken to by a social worker
- They will be relieved
- Provide an example of what happened to a child in a prior case (e.g., youth was spoken to by a social worker)

Interrogation of Females

- A male interrogator must use caution when interrogating a female suspect, who may file a sexual complaint against the officer
- An interrogator should video tape an interrogation whenever possible or have a police officer of the same sex as the suspect to witness the interrogation
- Because female suspects may be emotional, the interrogator may use their emotions against them
- The interrogator will appeal to her love of her children and will stress how she will not be a part of her children's lives while she is in jail
- The interrogator will appeal to her jealousy of her husband or boyfriend, stressing that they will enjoy themselves while she rots in jail
- The interrogator will appeal to her self-worth, telling her that she will be just a number and no longer an individual; she will be owned by the state
- The interrogator should find out whether the female suspect has children; if she does have children, the interrogator needs to praise her children, telling her how good looking her children are
- The interrogator will stress the value of family relationships and her love for her family

Car Thief Technique

- This technique is used for car thief investigations
- The officer should ask the suspect what the mileage is on the odometer, who the suspect purchased the vehicle from, what is in the glove box and trunk, the last time and place of service, what type of oil is in the vehicle, and other questions only the owner would know
- The interrogator must be calm, which has a settling effect on the suspect and may get the suspect to talk
- The interrogator may use rapid-fire questions, which provide little time for suspects to think about their answers before they respond
- The interrogator should not ask the suspect to confess; the interrogator should simply ask the suspect to tell the truth

Fetish Technique

- This technique is effective for sex crimes that involve fetishes
- Odd trademarks (e.g., bite marks, removal of underclothing, etc.) discovered at crime scenes may be used to questions suspects
- In order to determine a particular fetish, the interrogator must investigate the background of the suspect
- The interrogator may ask the suspect about his childhood, the best and worst things that have happened to him, the ways that he was disciplined by parents or teachers, the ways that he was treated by other children, and his relationships with parents, siblings, and other people in society
- The interrogator will attempt to link the fetish at crime scene to a fetish displayed by the suspect
- The suspect may mention something about the crime scene that no one outside of law enforcement knows

Before an interrogation can take place, the suspect must waive his rights to remain silent and to have a lawyer present (Inbau et al., 2005). The interview should be conducted in a controlled area free from distractions. A suspect is more likely to reveal secrets to an interrogator in the privacy of a room than in the presence of additional people. Because a suspect may lie in order to avoid the consequences of his crime, the interrogator should not mention the consequences of the crime if conviction is realized. A suspect may decide not to talk if he believes that not talking to the interrogator will prevent a conviction and minimize any consequence. In other words, clues must be eliminated that may remind the suspect that if he talks he will be prosecuted. Thus, the police department should not have police emblems on the wall, the interrogator should be in plain clothes, and the interrogator should not display handcuffs or a badge. In addition, the interrogator should not be armed for safety reasons.

Americans do not like their personal space encroached upon. For the white American middle-class male, 27 inches is about the right proximity for an interrogation. Closer than 27 inches makes the suspect uncomfortable and more than 27 inches makes the suspect's facial signals hard to read (Swanson et al., 2009). See *Figure 9* for personal space distances. Because individuals do not want interrogators to get too close to them, officers may use this proximity factor to their advantage during an interrogation. There should be no barriers between the interrogator and suspect, including the table. Indeed, some experts believe that interrogators should be knee to knee with the suspects with the capability of expanding and shrinking the proximity as needed.

Public	Impersonal	Casual	Personal
(> 12′)	(5′-12′)	(1.5′ - 5′)	(< 20″)

Figure 9. Personal space (Starrett & Davis, 2006)

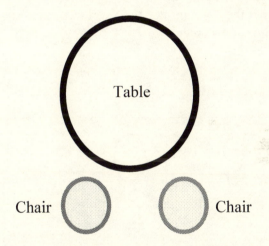

Figure 10. Interrogation proximity (Swanson et al., 2009)

Generally, the interrogator should be seated about 4 feet directly in front of the suspect (Inbau et al., 2005). If the chairs are offset, this may negatively impact the direction of the suspect's gaze. The chairs in the room should be straight-back chairs and should place the interrogator and suspect at eye level. A straight back chair will help prevent the suspect from becoming too relaxed and from slouching, which may prevent the suspect from giving his full attention. Chairs should place the interrogator and suspect at eye level because the suspect may be less cooperative if he is made to feel inferior by being required to look upward toward the interrogator.

There are several requirements inside an interrogation room. First, there should be ample lighting so that the interrogator can clearly see the suspect's face (Inbau et al., 2005). Second, there should be a table, a microphone, and a video recording device inside the room. Third, if the suspect is of the opposite sex as the interrogator, then department policy may dictate that an observer, who is of the same sex as the suspect, be in the room whenever the interrogator is inside the room. Finally, if the suspect and the interrogator cannot communicate due to a language barrier, an interpreter may need to be in the room. Following is a room layout of an interrogation room. Eliminate the chairs for the observer and/or interpreter if they are not needed. Nothing should be between the interrogator and suspect.

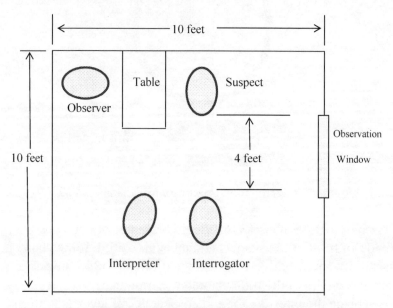

Figure 11. Interrogation room (Inbau et al., 2005).

REFERENCES

Barth, J. (2004). *International spy museum: Handbook of practical spying.* Washington, DC: National Geographic.

Inbau, F.E., Reid, J.E., Buckley, J.P., & Jayne, B.C. (2005). *Essentials of the Reid technique: Criminal interrogations and confessions.* Boston, MA: Jones and Bartlett.

Interrogation: techniques and tricks to secure evidence (1991). Boulder, CO: Paladin.

Starrett, P., & Davis, J.N. (2006). *Interview & interrogation with eyewitness evidence* (2nd ed.). San Clemente, CA: LawTech.

Swanson, C.R., Chamelin, N.C., Territo, L., & Taylor, R.W. (2009). *Criminal investigation* (10th ed.). Boston, MA: McGraw Hill.

Zulawski, D.E., & Wicklander, D.E. (2002). *Practical aspects of interview and interrogation* (2nd ed.). New York, NY: CRC.

CHAPTER 10. BUILDING AN EFFECTIVE RESUME

In order to best prepare a resume for maximum success, it is best to begin thinking from the potential employer's perspective about what qualities he or she is looking for in a future employee. The resume is the information that the potential employer will use to decide who has the skills and qualities that are best suited for the job description. If the resume is less than stellar, the likelihood of being asked in for an interview is very low. A good resume is the first step in obtaining an interview.

The following two steps are a simplified method in putting together a resume that is professional and attention getting (Kursmark, 2003).

Step 1

Identify the kind of job you desire. The more specific you are about what type of job you are looking for, the more you will be able to write a resume that fits that particular job description. If your resume is too generic, it might not catch the attention of the employer who will be going through the many different resumes.

Start by writing the specific type of work that you are interested in performing. Using non-specific words like "law enforcement" is not going to give your resume a clear-cut edge over other non-specific resumes that your employer will have to read. Instead of simply stating "law enforcement", one could write "crash scene reconstructionist" or "computer crime investigations" to get a more specific goal in mind.

Step 2

Identity the main qualifications and duties of the position desired. Make sure that you thoroughly investigate what the job you want entails in terms of experience desired and work performed. The job description may carry much of this information. If not, then an internet search of similar jobs may give you some good ideas about what will be expected from you as an employee.

Begin to target the specific skills set, experience, and education that you have, which will make you a good candidate for the job. Then, write out the qualities that you have that will make you a good candidate for the position (e.g., communication skills, critical thinking skills, interpersonal skills). Depending on the job, these qualities are sometimes just as important (if not more so) than your employment history or education.

You will want to give quality information for the following sections.

Education – List any degrees or certifications that you have earned. When listing these, make sure to list the title of the degree or certification, where it was obtained, and the date you obtained it. You could also list your grade point average and any awards or honors that you have earned.

Skills Section – The skills section of the resume will include any relevant skills that you possess pertaining to the job that you are seeking (e.g., proficient in Microsoft Word, Excel, and PowerPoint). Make sure that you describe the level of your ability. There is a big difference between someone who is "proficient" and someone who is merely "familiar with" a certain skill set.

Other qualities – In this section, you can include anything that you believe will show that you have more to offer than just the minimum requirements (e.g., bi-lingual, good public speaker, effective multi-tasker).

Experience - The experience section of the resume will include your work history and any other experiences related to work in the field you are seeking (e.g., law enforcement internships). It is important to include all relevant information about your previous experience. This will include the title of your job, your personal title or position, the name of the company that you worked for, the dates of your employment, your job responsibilities, and any awards or significant accomplishments that you obtained while working at the company.

Following are examples two types of resumes: the reverse chronological resume and the functional resume (Fortune Personnel Consultants, 2014; "*The job hunter's checklist*," 1994). Generally, the reverse chronological resume is preferred. See Table 26 for the pros and cons of the reverse chronological and functional resumes.

Table 26
Pros and Cons of the Reverse Chronological and Functional Resumes

Resume Type	Pros	Cons
Reverse Chronological Resume	Preferred by hiring professionals Good if no large gaps in employment Focuses on dates of employment Indicates seamless employment Highlights well-respected employers Shows consistent growth and advancement Easy to review and to obtain particular information	Highlights employers who have bad reputations Advertises large gaps in employment, too many changes in jobs, or too little experience

Functional Resume	Focuses on jobs skills accumulated Groups job skills by type of experience Conceals large gaps in employment, too many changes in jobs, and too little experience	Difficult to review May be discarded because it takes too much effort to review Suspicious because may be trying to cover up large gaps in employment, too many changes in jobs, or too little experience

Reverse Chronological Resume

Olga E. Hernandez, Ph.D.

ph: 313-555-0472; email: ohernandez@anywebaddress.com

WORK EXPERIENCE

Wayne Technical College – Department Chair for Criminal Justice: 2010 – Present

My responsibilities have included changing a philosophy-based criminal justice program into an application-based criminal justice program that employs critical thinking. I have a) designed a new curriculum, b) developed program objectives, goals, syllabi, and addendums, c) collaborated with local law enforcement departments to ensure that the program is in alignment with community needs, d) developed the content for each course ensuring that the content adheres to state standards, e) developed student learning outcomes and program assessment standards, f) determined needed resources for the program and completed purchase orders in order to obtain the resources, g) participated in the development of divisional and departmental strategic plans, h) created and developed a new capstone course in the state approved curriculum, i) selected textbooks, j) taught a variety of law enforcement courses, k) developed the college's first online courses in criminal justice, l) chaired advisory committee meetings, m) recruited adjunct professors, n) advised students, and o) managed the criminal justice program budget.

U.S. Dept. of Homeland Security - U.S. Customs & Border Protection: 2000 – 2007

I was responsible for protecting the American public against terrorists and instruments of terror while facilitating the timely movement of legitimate cargo and travelers. This required enforcing laws related to revenue and trade, seizing contraband, examining agricultural items for pests and diseases, and inspecting persons in determining their admissibility into the United States.

Responsibilities also included enforcing the laws of numerous Federal agencies, checking criminal records, conducting searches, writing reports, making arrests, collecting duties, and resolving radioactive anomalies. This included using a variety of tools, including numerous computer databases and many non-intrusive detection devices.

Indiana State Police – Master Trooper: 1990-2000

My job responsibilities included public service, traffic enforcement, and criminal investigations. Some of my responsibilities included collecting, preserving and documenting evidence, writing reports, administering field sobriety and preliminary breath tests, investigating and protecting crash scenes, administering emergency first-aid to crash victims, enforcing traffic laws, making criminal arrests, testifying in court, providing assistance to the general public, speaking to school children about drug concerns and traffic safety issues, and training new police officers. Some major cases that I have investigated and resolved involved attempted murder, forgery, counterfeiting, intimidation, battery, theft, criminal recklessness, and a variety of drug violations. I was post commander for the district and incident commander at many hazardous scenes. I was the lead investigator, and usually the sole investigator, of any case that I initiated.

Ford Motor Company - Program Manager/ Design Engineer: 1985-1990

I was a product design engineer and program manager. I was responsible for a variety of programs. I was the engineer to first implement the electronic control module into the pleasure boat industry. This included meeting design requirements, writing product specifications, performing test-to-failure statistical research, negotiating the sales and warranty agreements, and working with the manufacturing plant to ensure production quality. Others programs that I was responsible for included audio systems, power train systems, passive restraint systems, warranty claims analysis, and cost analysis forecasting.

EDUCATION

Wayne State University, Detroit, MI
Doctorate Degree: Criminal Justice

Eastern Michigan University, Ypsilanti, MI
Master's Degree: Accounting

University of Michigan, Ann Arbor, MI
Bachelor's Degree: Electrical Engineering

Federal Law Enforcement Training Center, Glynco, GA
U.S. Department of Homeland Security/U.S. Customs & Border Protection

Indiana Law Enforcement Academy, Plainfield, IN
Trooper - Indiana State Police

Additional Training/Certifications
FAA: Helicopter Pilot License
PADI: Advanced Open Water Scuba Diver
FCC: Technician Plus Amateur Radio License
State of Michigan: Basic Emergency Medical Technician

Technical Skills
Excel, Lotus, Word, Word Perfect, PowerPoint, SPSS

Important Writings
1) Terrorism and Homeland Security (ABC Publishing)
2) Police-Community Relations (ABC Publishing)
3) Emotional Intelligence and Criminal Justice (XYZ Publishing)
4) Cybercrime and Hacker Techniques (XYZ Publishing)
5) Criminology and Crime Prevention (LoGiudice Publishing)

Awards/Honors
1) U.S. Department of Homeland Security Commissioner's Award
2) U.S. Department of Homeland Security Scholastic Award
3) Nominated for the Ford Motor Company's Worldwide Leadership Excellence Award
4) University of Michigan Upperclassman Engineering Departmental Award
5) President of the National Electrical Engineering Honor Society
6) Graduated with Distinction (Wayne State University)

Functional Resume

Estenia O. Hernandez
ph: 734-555-8432; email: ehernandez@anywebaddress.com

SUMMARY OF QUALIFICATIONS

Experienced leader with a management style that empowers and motivates others to achieve a common set of goals. Demonstrated ability to recruit, hire, coach, and develop staff in the areas of customer service, sales, operations and accounting.

SKILLS AND ACCOMPLISHMENTS

Management
- Streamlined 6 Customer Service Departments to 1 central location.
- Streamlined Accounting procedures, which eliminated the need for 2nd shift and 2nd location.
- Implemented company-wide cross training, which saved the company $120,000 annually.
- Reduced overtime by 90%, which saved the company over $75,000 annually.
- Established company policies and procedures for Customer Service, Sales, Distribution, and Accounting Departments in multiple locations.
- Responsible and accountable for departmental budget.

Sales
- Managed and trained outside sales staff of 300.
- Started up a Merchandising Department, which increased sales by 50%.
- Coordinated with national suppliers, introduced new products, and marketed plans and strategies.
- Managed entire Nestle blue box freezer program for the state of Ohio.
- Achieved Gold level status with St. Johns Pharmaceuticals for sales accomplishments.

- Visited customers and accounts to check sales, service levels, and product placement.
- Directed all business-to-business sales activities on a daily basis for key accounts.

Customer Service / Call Center
- Managed 450 customer service representatives in a local call center.
- Introduced and implemented new marketing programs to call centers.
- Monitored agents on phones and provided feedback for quality control.
- Researched and proposed solutions to improve email performance, to reduce cost, and to streamline processes for improved overall efficiency operation.
- Created scripting and rebuttals for customer service representatives on various procedures.
- Analyzed reports to determine and gage metrics, conversion rates, trends, potential issues, and forecasts.

Human Resources
- Conducted two-week interval training classes for new hires in two national locations.
- Updated training manual and classroom exercises for training classes.
- Created and updated job descriptions.
- Participated in company sponsored job fairs.
- Recruited, interviewed, and tested new applicants.
- Trained and coached new supervisors and managers in all aspects of management and operations.
- Trained hourly employees in accounting, customer service, and sales.
- Implemented and initiated various employee motivational events.
- Received Certificates of Recognition for High School Co-op Programs.

Accounting and Finance
- Monitored, balanced, and analyzed a $83 million advertising budget for 54 brands.
- Saved $3,000,000 annually by ensuring discounts were taken on payments to vendors.
- Reduced late payments to vendors by 72%.

Technical Skills
- Excel, Lotus, Word, Word Perfect, PowerPoint, SPSS
- Licensed Realtor since 1985

EMPLOYMENT HISTORY 02/2002-Present

<u>Mayflower Corporation</u> Atlanta, Michigan
Customer Service Manager

<u>Blue Bird Real Estate Services</u> Romulus, Michigan
Managing Partner / Realtor

<u>Hawkeye Publications</u> Belleville, Michigan
Customer Service Program Manager

<u>Otrompke Farms, LLC</u> Mackinac, Michigan
3 Positions based on promotions.

- Department Head of Customer Service, Sales and Merchandising
- Business Operations Manager
- Route Accounting Supervisor

<u>LoGiudice Brewery Corporate Headquarters</u> Wayne, Michigan
3 Positions based on promotions

- Direct Marketing Expense Coordinator
- Accounts Receivable / Credit
- Accounts Payable

EDUCATION

Wayne State University, Detroit, MI 2002
Master's Degree: Marketing

Ferris State University, Big Rapids, MI 1998
Bachelor's Degree: Accounting

REFERENCES

Fortune Personnel Consultants (2014). *Wrong Resume Format Can Hurt You.* Retrieved from http://www.fpcnational.com/career-tips/resume-writing/9-resume-writing/55-wrong-resume-format-can-hurt-you

Kursmark, L.M. (2003). *Best Resumes for College Students and New Grads.* Indianapolis, IN: JIST Works

The job hunter's checklist: All the essential steps of a successful job search (1994). Holbrook, MA: Bob Adams.

CHAPTER 11. CODE COMMUNICATION

Consequence of Wrong Assumptions

Magic shows are successful because they challenge the viewers' assumptions. The viewers are led to believe that something is true when it is not true (Stoddard, 1954). The next time that you watch a magic trick, try to determine what assumptions you are making. For example, the picture below on the left indicates that the box should be 3 inches deep. However, the ruler seems to disappear. The photograph below on the right uses the same box and seems to make the legs of a four inch figure disappear.

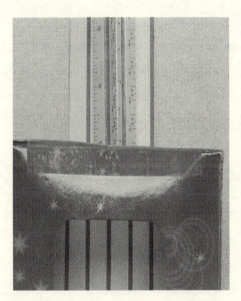 

Figure 12. Magic box.

Table 27
Magic Definitions (Evans & Keable-Elliot, 1989)

Deception Technique	Example
Illusion	Intellectually misleading the viewer via imagery
Sleight of Hand	Skilled movements of the hand to mislead the viewer
Misdirection	Hides information
Distraction	Draws attention away from the information

Misdirection and distraction are tools used to conceal information (Evans & Keable-Elliot, 1989). Misdirection hides information while distractions draw attention away from information. Distractions only work a few times before the information seeker becomes aware of what is happening. Misdirection, on the other hand, is more effective because it exploits flawed assumptions made by the information seeker. Until the flawed assumptions are corrected, the information seeker will continued to be fooled.

Table 28
Misdirection (Evans & Keable-Elliot, 1989)

Misdirection Technique	Example
Fool the eyes	People believe what they think they have seen; perform a move realistically and people will believe it.
Attract Attention	Draw attention to one hand while the other hand goes unnoticed; this can be extremely dangerous to a police officer in the field.
Psychological moment	Strike when a break is expected in the action because this is the time the viewer is less attentive.
Cover-up	If something cannot be hidden, such as an incriminating noise, cover it up with a louder unrelated noise.
Repetition	If actions are continually repeated, the viewer will come to expect them and will fail to notice anything out of the ordinary.
Time Lapse	People have a short memory and, if a lot of things are happening, people will forget to focus on something that may have initially caught their attention.

Assumptions are important in law enforcement because a solution that is based on the wrong assumptions may be less than optimal. For example, the effectiveness of the sex offender community notification process relies on the assumptions of the labeling and deterrence theories. Authorities rely on labeling and deterrence in order to get sex predators to **rationally** decide not to commit additional sex crimes due to the high cost. First, people learn to identify other individuals in the way that they are labeled (Vold, Bernard, & Snipes, 2002). Thus, the labeling theory indicates that sex offenders will be easily recognized by local community members if sex offenders are publically labeled and if their crimes are advertised. In regards to Megan's law, it is assumed that all sex offenders are alike and, consequently, they are all labeled as a homogenous group of sex predators (Corrigan, 2006). However, different types of sex offenders are not all motivated by the same reasons. Hence, a single program designed to modify their various behaviors will not work. Second, Megan's law relies on the idea that most sex offenders are strangers to their victims and that offenders are **mentally disturbed** predators who attack without warning or reason. In other words, mentally disturbed predators are expected to make rational decisions. In addition, most sex crimes against children are committed by friends or family members and not by strangers. Thus, community notification efforts are ineffective because they are not in alignment with the problem. Because the research findings do not support the argument that community notification deters stigmatized sex offenders from committing repeat sex offenses, then perhaps programs that rely on theories that support the argument that sex offenders are mentally disturbed need to be investigated (Langevin et al., 2004; Zevitz, 2006). In other words, limited resources may be better spent on programs that address mental illnesses instead of labeling and rational choice. As stated earlier, the solution to the problem must be in alignment with the theory used to explain the crime. See *Table 8* for various criminal theories and their limitations.

Sport Codes

Baseball players, football players, and coaches use codes to communicate. In baseball, the third-base coach will give signals to the batter, indicating what the batter should do. For example, the rule may be that the first signal after the coach touches his hat is the required action by the batter.

Table 29.
Baseball Secret Codes

Key = Touch Hat	Required Action
Elbow	Bunt
Knee	Swing away
Shoulder	Take a pitch
Hit and run	Make contact with ball (man on first base is running)

In football, the quarterback may use an audible signal at the line of scrimmage. After the play has been called in the huddle, the quarterback will assess the defensive formation at the line of scrimmage. The quarterback may realize that the play called in the huddle will not work. Because there is no time for a re-huddle, the quarterback needs a way to change the play at the line of scrimmage. The quarterback can change the play via an audible signal. For example, the code may be to run the play immediately called after the word **BLUE**. If the play called in the huddle was "*31 dive*" and the quarterback wants to change it to "*48 sweep*", the quarterback may yell out along the line of scrimmage in each direction, "***Blue 48, Blue 48.***" Thus, the play has been changed from a *31* dive (carried out by the fullback) to a *48* **sweep** (carried out by the tailback). See *Figure 13* for an example of codes as they relate to players and holes. The first digit of the play number represents the particular back who will receive the ball and the second digit represents the hole in which the back shall run. For example, looking at the designations listed below, a 21 is a quarterback sneak to the left of the center and a 48 is a tailback sweep to the outside right. Notice that the even numbered holes are to the right of the center and the odd numbered holes are to the left of the center. In addition, because BLUE is the agreed upon code word for a play change, if the quarterback yells, *"RED 48"*, then the original play will be carried out. To prevent the defense from figuring out what plays will be executed, the code word may be changed at any time.

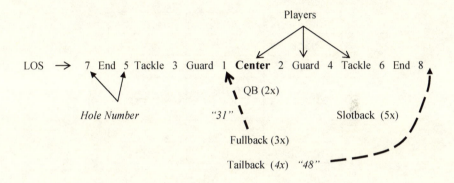

LOS = Line of Scrimmage; QB = Quarterback

Figure 13. Football secret codes for offense.

Marked Deck of Playing Cards

Below is a key that may be used to read each playing card. Dots may be placed in particular boxes to indicate the card's suit and value. Of course, the box will appear on every card but the dots' positions will vary on each card.

Diamonds	Queen	Hearts
Jack		1
10		2
9	King	3
8		4
7		5
Spades	6	Clubs

Figure 14. Key for marked card deck.

If the dots below were indicated on the back of a playing card, what is the card?

•		
		•

The above card is the 4 of diamonds.

If the dots below were indicated on the back of a playing card, what is the card?

		•
	•	•
	•	

The above card is the ace of hearts.

Secret Codes

Secret codes have been used since ancient times (Brook, 2014). For example, the ancient Greeks would write a message on a spy's shaven head. Once the hair grew back, the spy would deliver the message. This technique was effective because the interrogators seldom thought to shave the head of a captured spy.

Modern spies use the available technology to communicate information (Brook, 2014). For example, modern computers use thousands of pixels to create images. Spies can hide secret messages within the pixels. Unless a person knows exactly where to look in an image, it will be extremely difficult to recognize the message.

Secret codes may be used by police officers and prisoners. Police departments may use secret codes to protect officers in the field. For example, suppose a crash victim is sitting next to an officer in the field and the officer has requested a computer check on the person. Then suppose the police dispatcher obtains information that the person is a wanted murderer who has killed police officers. The dispatcher may not want to provide that information to the officer until the dispatcher is sure that the suspect cannot overhear the information. If the suspect is a murderer, he may know the common police codes. Thus, the dispatcher should provide a secret code to the officer to warn the officer that something is wrong and privacy is needed.

Inmates may use secret codes so that they can conduct business within correctional facilities without corrections officers interfering with their business. For example, inmates may want to import drugs into the correctional facility, they may want to plan an escape, or they may want to put a contract killing (i.e., hit) out on someone. Thus, it is important for law enforcers to recognize secret codes.

Computer Translation Codes

With modern technology, a person can write a text message and have the computer immediately translate it to other languages. Below are examples of a text message that has been written in English and translated to other languages. The translated message can be sent to a receiver but the receiver will need to know the language used to translated it back it English, which can be accomplished via the computer. This is a simple task if the message is electronic and the cut-and-paste option is available.

Computer language translations

English: Ciphering and deciphering codes is sometimes difficult but always fun.

Arabic: الشفرات وفك كرموز يتم في بعض الأحيان صعبة ولكن ممتعة دائماً.

Russian: Шифрование и расшифровка кодов иногда трудно, но всегда весело.

Hungarian: Titkosítás és kód megfejtése, néha nehéz, de mindig szórakoztató.

The following are techniques that are used to cipher and decipher information (Brook, 2014; Janeczko, 2004; Peterson, 1966; Wrixon, 1998)

Reverse the words

Read each word backwards. Do not change the order of the words in the message.

Example: study hard.
Code = yduts drah.

Read every second letter

This is a test.
Code TIHSIUSOIASHALTNEDSGT.

Code stick

Wrap a strip of paper around a tube. Write the message on the paper. Remove the paper. In order to read the message, a tube with the proper diameter must be used.

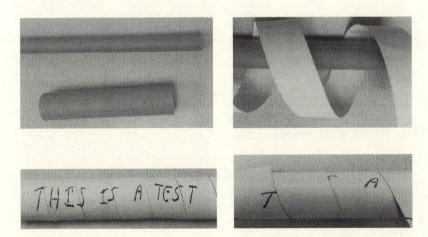

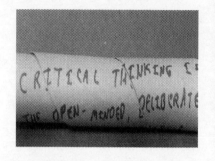
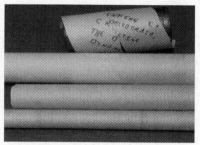

Numbers Stand for Letters

A	B	C	D	E	F	G	H	I	J	K	L	M	N	O	P	Q	R	S	T	U	V	W	X	Y	Z
1	2	3	4	5	6	7	8	9	10	11	12	13	14	15	16	17	18	19	20	21	22	23	24	25	26

Example: Help = 8 5 12 16 or 8.5.12.16

Reverse the Alphabet

A	B	C	D	E	F	G	H	I	J	K	L	M	N	O	P	Q	R	S	T	U	V	W	X	Y	Z
Z	Y	X	W	V	U	T	S	R	Q	P	O	N	M	L	K	J	I	H	G	F	E	D	C	B	A

Example:
JUSTICE = QFHGRXV

Half-Reverse Alphabet

A	B	C	D	E	F	G	H	I	J	K	L	M
N	O	P	Q	R	S	T	U	V	W	X	Y	Z

Example:
JUSTICE = WHFGVPR

Pigpen

If the first letter in the pair is to be used, then no dot will be present in the symbol. If second letter is to be used, then a dot will appear in the symbol.

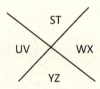

AB	CD	EF
GH	IJ	KL
MN	OP	QR

```
       ST
 UV   ><   WX
       YZ
```

For example:

⌋ = A   ⌴ = C   □ = I

⌐• = P   ⩔• = T   ⟨ = W

Rosicrucian Cipher

ABC	DEF	GHI
JKL	MNO	PQR
STU	VWX	YZ

Every letter has a dot. Align the dot with appropriate letter.

For example:

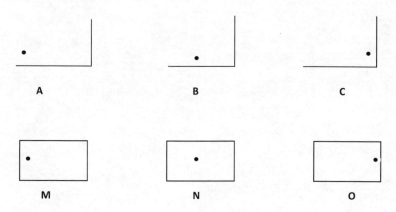

Block cipher

To cipher, sentences are broken down into an equal number of letters in each row. To decipher, all rows are linked. Words need to be discovered by adding spaces in appropriate places.

THIS IS VERY EASY!

THISI
SVERY
EASY!

Keyboard Cipher

Use the keyboard and shift to the left or right the predetermined number of places. When the end of the row on the keyboard is reached, the user will cycle to the far end of the same row and will continue to travel in the same direction.

Example Keyboard shift 2R (shift to the right 2 places)

QWERTYUIOP = ERTYUIOPQW
ASDFGHJKL = DFGHJKLAS
ZXCVBNM = CVBNMZX

Date Shift Cipher

Use the Date June 4, 2012

Write it as 0 6 0 4 2 0 1 2

The date will continue to repeat until the code is complete. When the end of the alphabet is reached, the alphabet will cycle around and will continue in the same direction. The direction of travel along the alphabet may be forward or backward.

Cipher the following message (+ direction): This is a lot of fun.

T + 0 =	T
H + 6 =	N
I + 0 =	I
S + 4 =	W
I + 2 =	K
S + 0 =	S
A + 1 =	B
L + 2 =	N
O + 0 =	O
T + 6 =	Z
O + 0 =	O
F + 4 =	J
F + 2 =	H
U + 0 =	U
N + 1 =	O

Decipher the following message using the data Feb 14, 2014 (+ direction): I JNRC MZPH.

(Date = 02142014)

I + 0 =	I
J + 2 =	L
N + 1 =	O
R + 4 =	V
C + 2 =	E
M + 0 =	M
Z + 1 =	A
P + 4 =	T
H + 0 =	H

Answer = I LOVE MATH.

Page-Paragraph-line-word-letter

23.2.3.15.3
Means page 23, paragraph 2, line 3, word 15, third letter

7.5.11.8
Means page 7, paragraph 5, line 11, eighth word

Dot Code; Line Code; Zig Zag Code

Cipher: Report

Dot Code Key

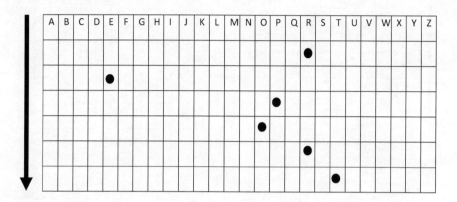

Dot Code

Line Code Key

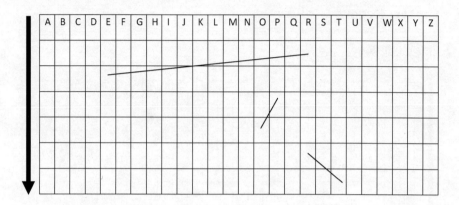

Line Code

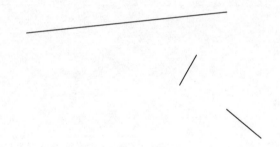

Zig Zag Key

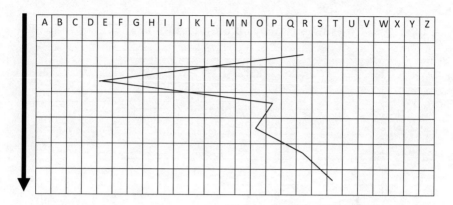

Zig Zag Code

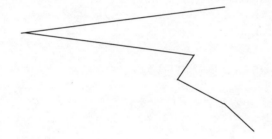

Greek Square Cipher

Cipher text by using a row by column technique.

	1	2	3	4	5
1	A	B	C	D	E
2	F	G	H	IJ	K
3	L	M	N	O	P
4	Q	R	S	T	U
5	V	W	X	Y	Z

Ciper TEXT = 32.11.44.42.24.53
Decipher = MATRIX

Rail Fence Cipher

TEXT = DO NOT DELAY THIS IS NOT AN EXERCISE

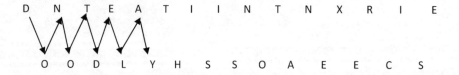

Semaphore Cipher

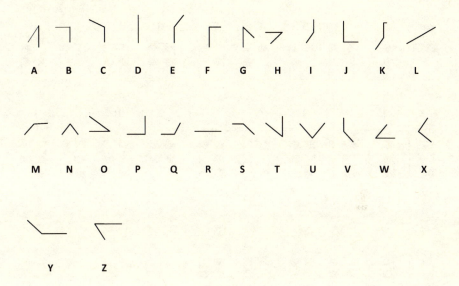

Braille

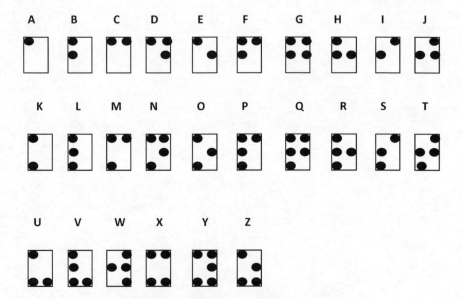

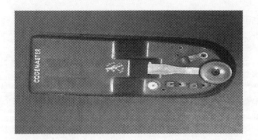

Figure 15. Morse code keyer.

Morse Code

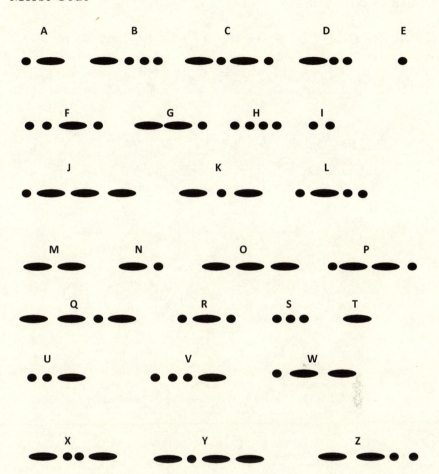

Moon's Code

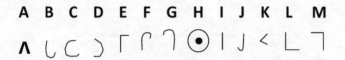

Circle Code

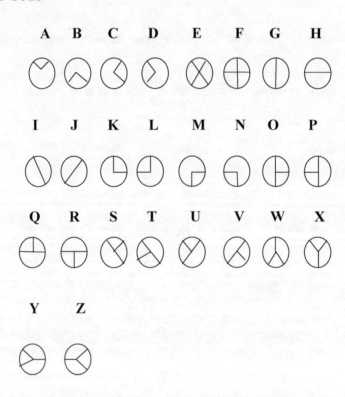

Word Grille

A grille is a cover that has holes cut out on the cover in select places. Inside the holes words are recorded. After the final message is recorded, random words are added to the document. The message can be read if the viewer has a grille that matches the one used to make the message.

Sebald Code

The message starts with the first word after the word **RING**, uses every 11th word until the word **RING** appears again.

I **ring we** do we were this test have fun store buy car **cried** a start movie hunch probable his she her yes let **much** her school **ring** alive police.

Message = We cried much.

Space Code

The words are in the correct order but the spaces are not in the correct places. Rearrange the spaces to make the appropriate words.

Ilo vet ogotos choo land tost udyh ard.

Message = I love to go to school and to study hard.

Problems Section

Determine the code being used and decipher the message.

1) rednu eht egdirb
2) VWLOOOAL BSZWIEFAYTSEVRU
3) FI SH OU TO FW AT ER
4) 42.23.34.32.12.45.43
5) Rocket ring starry frolicking too quail banshee bismuth zoo rose can doodle rooter night painting kazoo ring close.
6) FNAO HCPHSEAAITJS
7) deppils no eci
8) 20.8.21.14.4.5.18 19.20.15.18.13
9) CUBOVN
10) Y KB JKEQ
11) kool kcab
12) I tsol ym niahcyek
13) MSUTAUPRXDLY CCOHGAUIKRMS
14) DGYRAIOZLZRLEY NBAERAPRS
15) 19.16.15.9.12.5.4 13.9.12.11
16) 9.14.6.12.21.5.14.26.1
17) 3.15.18.18.15.19.9.22.5
18) KOZGBKFH
19) NZTTLG
20) IVELOFGRLM
21) B EO NTI ME
22) CUNAGBZ
23) FCNEXYR
24) 13.34.33.22.42.45.15.33.44
25) FRZNAGVPF
26) FOO TBA LLO RSO CCE RTO DAY
27) WO OD EN CH OP PI NG BL OC KS
28) FLYI NGTR APEZ EART ISTS
29) UPZUTG
30) GVIIVHGIRZO

31) Fools ring this is not piglets game knife bell nacho guitar flour yarn is irritated owl two cramp rump longer guzzling gizzard lobe nova wrong importance notice point door wing republic talking scouts ring football college.
32) ZOGGTI
33) HXIFPEZL
34) 32.11.44.42.24.13.15
35) PI GSMA YFL Y EVEN TUA LLY
36) Jittery rain bug ring paper hit glass icicle clay cake wishing assassin novel xenophobia lock or too foot guard third revolution gang crime did crash car plastic curb street cab ring troll responsible.
37) 42.11.24.33.12.34.52
38) Popcorn dancing ring smile rock pry crying lying fellow long ostrich ember nope salad often sun hot young fun fool old cruel good bad okay please ring boy man lady luck.
39) HAV EAN I CED AY
40) HI TTI NGCON CR ETE HUR TS
41)

42) (Catalan language): Vull trobar la traducció d'aquest missatge.

Use the required technique and cipher the message.

1) Reverse the Words: They went outside.
2) Reverse the Words: The fish swam away.
3) Reverse the Words: The leaf fell from the tree.
4) Reverse the Words: It was a beautiful day.
5) Numbers Stand for Letters: I run fast. Provide code.
6) Numbers Stand for Letters: Do not go. Provide code.
7) Numbers Stand for Letters: It will be dark. Provide code.
8) Numbers Stand for Letters: The smoke dissipated. Provide code.
9) Reverse the Alphabet: Backward and forward.
10) Reverse the Alphabet: Straight across.
11) Reverse the Alphabet: The glass cracked.
12) Reverse the Alphabet: A baby cried.
13) Half-Reverse Alphabet: He is blond.
14) Half-Reverse Alphabet: The house collapsed.
15) Half-Reverse Alphabet: We played cards.
16) Half-Reverse the Alphabet: The sun shone.
17) Keyboard Cipher: Turkeys gobble. (-4)
18) Keyboard Cipher: The windmill turned. (-2)
19) Keyboard Cipher: Some plants wilted. (+2)
20) Keyboard Cipher: Thank you. (+2)
21) Greek Square Cipher: Horses eat hay.
22) Greek Square Cipher: I heard a noise.
23) Greek Square Cipher: Crickets chirped.
24) Greek Square Cipher: He said no.
25) Rail fence cipher: Totality of Circumstances.
26) Semaphore cipher: Crime.
27) Braille cipher: Proof.
28) Morse code cipher: Hot zone.
29) Circle code cipher: Report.
30) Pigpen cipher: Mug Shot.
31) Date Code Cipher: Criminalistics. Use November 22, 1963 (+ direction).

Answers to Sample Problems Section

Answers - Determine the code being used and decipher the message.

1) under the bridge –Reverse the Words
2) WOOL SWEATER -Read Every Second Letter
3) FISH OUT OF WATER -Block Cipher
4) RHOMBUS - Greek Square Cipher
5) Starry night. - Sebald Code
6) NO CHEATS –Read Every Second Letter
7) slipped on ice - Reverse the Words
8) THUNDERSTORM -Numbers Stand For Letters
9) PHOBIA – Half-Reverse Alphabet
10) I AM LATE -Keyboard Cipher (+ 2 to decipher)
11) look back – Reverse the Words
12) I lost my keychain – Reverse the Words
13) STURDY CHAIRS -Read Every Second Letter
14) GRIZZLY BEAR -Read Every Second Letter
15) SPOILED MILK -Numbers Stand For Letters
16) INFLUENZA -Numbers Stand For Letters
17) CORROSIVE -Numbers Stand For Letters
18) PLATYPUS -Reverse the Alphabet
19) MAGGOT -Reverse the Alphabet
20) REVOLUTION - Reverse the Alphabet
21) BE ON TIME - Space Code
22) PHANTOM – Half-Reverse Alphabet
23) SPARKLE – Half-Reverse Alphabet
24) CONGRUENT -Greek Square Cipher
25) SEMANTICS – Half-Reverse Alphabet
26) FOOTBALL OR SOCCER TODAY -Block Cipher
27) WOODEN CHOPPING BLOCKS -Block Cipher
28) FLYING TRAPEZE ARTISTS -Block Cipher
29) TINTED -Keyboard Cipher (- 2)
30) TERRESTRIAL -Reverse the Alphabet
31) This is wrong. - Sebald Code
32) BELLOW -Keyboard Cipher (+ 4)
33) SMELTING -Keyboard Cipher (+ 5)

34) MATRICE -Greek Square Cipher
35) PIGS MAY FLY EVENTUALLY -Space Code
36) Paper or plastic. -Sebald Code
37) RAINBOW -Greek Square Cipher
38) Smile often please. - Sebald Code
39) HAVE A NICE DAY -Space Code
40) HITTING CONCRETE HURTS -Space Code
41) Kong - Braille
42) I want to find the translation of this message. - Computer translator

Answers - Use the required technique and cipher the message.

1) yeht tnew edistuo.
2) eht hsif maws yawa.
3) eht fael llef morf eht eert.
4) ti saw a lufituaeb yad.
5) 9. 18.21.14. 6.1.19.20
6) 4.15. 14.15.20. 7.15
7) 9.20. 23.9.12.12. 2.5. 4.1.18.11
8) 20.8.5. 19.13.15.11.5. 4.9.19.19.9.16.1.20.5.4
9) Yzxpdziw zmw ulidziw.
10) Hgizrtsg zxilhh.
11) Gsv tozhh xizxpvw.
12) Z yzyb xirvw.
13) Ur vf oybaq.
14) Gur ubhfr pbyyncfrq.
15) Jr cynlrq pneqf.
16) Gur fha fubar.
17) qepfowj atzzgo
18) efq pyvabyjj etwvqa
19) Fqxt wsdzuf rpsutg
20) ukdza iqo
21) 23.34.42.43.15.43. 15.11.44. 23.11.54
22) 24. 23.15.11.42.14. 11. 33.34.24.43.15
23) 13.42.24.13.25.15.44.43. 13.23.24.42.35.15.14
24) 23.15. 43.1.24.14. 33.34
25)
    T t l t o c r u s a c s

    o a i y f l c m t n e

26)

┐ — ┘ ⌐ ⌠

INTERVIEWING, INTERROGATION & COMMUNICATION for LAW ENFORCEMENT

27)

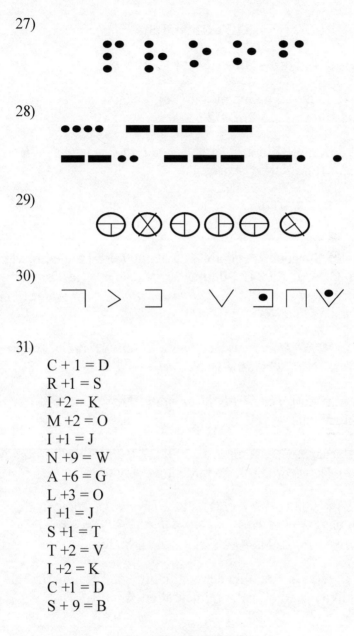

28)

29)

30)

31)
    C + 1 = D
    R +1 = S
    I +2 = K
    M +2 = O
    I +1 = J
    N +9 = W
    A +6 = G
    L +3 = O
    I +1 = J
    S +1 = T
    T +2 = V
    I +2 = K
    C +1 = D
    S + 9 = B

Answer = DSKOJWGOJTVKDB

REFERENCES

Brook, H. (2014). *Spying*. Tulsa, OK: Usborne.

Corrigan, R. (2006). Making meaning of Megan's law. *Law & Social Inquiry, 31*(2), 267-312.

Evans, C., & Keable-Elliott, I. (1989). *The Usborne complete book of magic*. Tulsa, OK: Usborne.

Janeczko, P.B. (2004). *Top secret: A handbook of codes, ciphers, and secret writing*. Cambridge, MA: Candlewick.

Langevin, R., Curnoe, S., Federoff, P., Bennett, R., Langevin, M., Peever, C., et al. (2004). Lifetime sex offender recidivism: A 25-year follow-up study. *Canadian Journal of Criminology and Criminal Justice, 46*(5), 531-552.

Peterson, J. (1966). *How to write codes and send secret messages*. New York, NY: Scholastic Book.

Stoddard, E. (1954). *The first book of magic*. New York, NY: Franklin Watts.

Vold, G., Bernard, T., & Snipes, J. (2002). *Theoretical criminology* (5th ed.). New York, NY: Oxford University Press.

Wrixon, F.B. (1998). *Codes, ciphers & other clandestine communication: Making and breaking secret messages from hieroglyphs to the Internet*. New York, NY: Tess.

Zevitz, R.G. (2006). Sex offender community notification: Its role in recidivism and offender reintegration. *Criminal Justice Studies, 19*(2), 193-208.

CHAPTER 12. JOB INTERVIEW & ORAL PRESENTATIONS

Many law enforcement agencies require an oral interview as part of the hiring process. These interviews provide law enforcement agencies with first-hand observation of whether or not the applicants meet specific criteria and whether they are in alignment with the particular department's philosophy. The purpose of the oral board interview is to assess skills that cannot be assessed by written examinations alone, such as motivation, attitudes, oral communication skills, problem-solving skills, and an understanding of police work (Denton, 2009).

Typically, a law enforcement interview will be conducted by a board panel, which many times is comprised on three board members. The board members are trained to assess the responses to the questions at the oral interview (Denton, 2009). The questions themselves are created by experts in the subject matter. This allows the panel to ask questions that are relevant to the job. To standardized the oral interview, and to reduce complaints (and lawsuits) of being unfair, the same set of predetermined questions are asked of all applicants. In addition, the applicants are only allowed a predetermined amount of time to complete the entire interview. For example, the board may indicate to the applicant that he or she has 25 minutes to answer 13 questions. The applicant may spend as much time as necessary on each particular response. However, once 25 minutes have passed, the interview is complete. Questions may be repeated, but the questions will not be rephrased or paraphrased.

A very important point to make is that the oral board will only assess the information that the applicant provides. Therefore, the applicants need to articulate their responses and to provide the best possible answers. Even if a particular response does not directly apply to the question, the applicant must provide some information that can be assessed. For example, if the oral board asks if you were in the military, and if you were not in the military, you would not simply respond by saying, "No." This provides little information to assess and will result in a failing score. The applicant should respond by mentioning any experiences related to teamwork, discipline, obtaining constructive objectives, physical fitness, following orders, giving orders, meeting timelines, training, and any other information similar to what the military provides. For example, if the applicant played sports, this can be used to describe some of the factors that military experience can provide. The applicant should respond by saying that although he or she has no military experience, he or she has played sports, which promoted teamwork, discipline, physical fitness, and so on.

When applying for police work, applicants must understand that law enforcement can be broken down into three general categories, which are criminal investigation, public safety, and traffic enforcement. Each response should be directed toward one or more of these categories. For example, an applicant with a college degree may indicate that he or she can properly process a crime scene, can effectively serve the public because he or she understands the community, and can effectively budget time and resources.

Prior to the Job Interview

An applicant should prepare for a law enforcement interview. An applicant will appear to be less than serious if the oral board asks the applicant general questions about the department and the applicant cannot respond. An applicant should review information about the department, the essential job functions, the salary, the department's philosophy, and the local community before the date of his or her interview.

At the Job Interview

Applicants need to be professional. Applicants need to dress and speak professionally. In addition, applicants should sit up straight, make eye contact with the board members, and show body language that indicates interest. This means that applicants should not continually look at their watches during the interview, which may indicate that the applicant is worried about wasting valuable time at the interview. The oral board will observe body language, just as interrogators evaluate body language during an interrogation. Near the conclusion of the interview, the board members may ask the applicant for any last comments. The applicant should take this opportunity to thank the oral board for their time and consideration. In addition, the applicant should use this time to provide an overview of personal qualifications, to indicate excitement for the position, and to indicate that he or she will do what it takes to be successful.

Commonly Asked Questions at Police Job Interviews

1) What have you done to prepare yourself for police work?
2) What was a major problem that you experienced and what did you do to resolve it?
3) Why do you want to be a police officer?
4) Where do you plan to be in 10 years?
5) Explain what police officers do.
6) If a traffic violator screams in your face, what will you do about it?
7) If your partner does something that is inappropriate, what will you do about it?
8) If you stop an officer and the officer is intoxicated, what will you do about it?
9) Provide three words that best describe you.
10) If you are the first officer who arrives at a house that is on fire and a person near the home suddenly flees as you approach, what will you do?
11) What is your biggest weakness?
12) What do you do to relieve stress?

Appropriate Answers for Job Interview Questions

1) What have you done to prepare yourself for police work? Discuss the following.
   - Education and training. Address what you know about criminal investigation, public safety, and traffic enforcement.
   - Sport participation, teamwork, discipline, physically fit
   - Leadership roles
   - Work experience and responsibilities
   - Military
   - Deal with people on continual basis; resolve customer concerns
   - Understand community concerns

2) What was a major problem that you experienced and what did you do to resolve it?
   - Articulate the use of critical thinking (making best-practice decision based on available information)
   - Discuss the variables, who were impacted, and why it was a tough issue
   - Discuss something that had a positive outcome based on your decisions

3) Why do you want to be a police officer?
   - To serve the community
   - Provides a significant purpose in life, which is to help other people
   - Exciting and challenging work; always something different
   - It is a way of life, not just a job
   - Enjoy that type of work; if enjoy work, will be good; if good, will get promoted

4) Where do you plan to be in 10 years?
   - Indicate that you plan to be with the same department; otherwise, they will not be interested in spending the resources to train you for another department
   - Indicate that because you like law enforcement, you will be good at you job; because you are good at your job, you will be promoted; when promoted, you be at a position where you can help other police officers to better serve the public

5) If a traffic violator screams in your face, what will you do about it?
   - As long as the violator obeys your lawful orders, continue to do your job
   - Let the violator vent his anger, as long as there are no safety concerns
   - The violator has a right to protest the government

6) Explain what police officers do.
   - **Criminal Investigation**
     - Set perimeters
     - Search crime scenes
     - Sketch crime scenes
     - Collect evidence and complete property record and receipt forms
     - Collect latent fingerprints
     - Roll fingerprints
     - Radio communications
     - Case reports, intelligence reports, firearms reports, probable cause affidavits, charging forms, use of force reports, search warrants, fingerprint cards, etc.
   - **Public Service**
     - Create and present anti-crime brochures
     - Change car tires; provide transportation to persons in distress
     - Conduct safety and anti-drug presentations at the local schools

- **Traffic Enforcement**
  - Complete DUI investigation including probable cause affidavits and charging forms
  - Use RADAR, VASCAR, and LASER
  - Write citations and warnings for traffic violations to enhance public safety
  - Complete crash investigations, use software to draw electronic diagrams, and photograph crash scenes

7) If your partner does something that is inappropriate, what will you do about it?
   - Applicant must distinguish between minor policy violation and law
   - For minor policy violation, the applicant should approach the officer and discuss the rule violation. If the officer corrects his behavior, then it was handled.
   - For minor policy violation where the officer fails to correct his behavior, the applicant should proceed up the chain of command and report it to the supervisor.
   - For major policy violation, the applicant should inform the officer that his actions were inappropriate and proceed up the chain of command and report it to the supervisor.
   - For a law violation, the applicant must make the scene safe and protect any possible victims at the scene. Once the scene is safe, the applicant should inform the officer that his actions were inappropriate and the applicant must report it to a supervisor.

8) If you stop an officer who is driving and the officer seems intoxicated, what will you do about it?
   - Because public safety is a concern, the investigating officer should call a supervisor to the scene and investigate the case like any other case.

9) State three words that describe you. Try to select three words that create a complete composite of you as a good police officer.

• Ambitious	Assertive	Brave
• Charismatic	Cheerful	Compassionate
• Educated	Fidelity	Friendly
• Funny	Generous	Hard-working
• Honest	Honorable	Industrious
• Integrity	Law-abiding	Listener
• Logical	Loyal	Moral
• Fair	Objective	Persistent
• Punctual	Reliable	Responsible
• Smart	Strong	Thorough
• Truthful	Wise	Upstanding

10) If you are the first public safety officer who arrives at a house that is on fire and a person near the home suddenly flees as you approach, what do you do?
    - Safety is always the most important law enforcement function
    - Call out the suspect information over the police radio; let him flee
    - Try to rescue individuals in the home, if possible
    - Protect the scene; prevent individuals from entering the scene and from getting hurt

11) What is your biggest weakness? Be honest but do not give a weakness that may disqualify you.
    - Example: I do not speak Spanish. I understand its importance in law enforcement and I plan to study it when I get a chance. I have been focusing my resources on developing other skills.
    - Example: I am objectively driven and I have high expectations. Sometimes, other individuals do not feel the same way that I feel and they believe my expectations are too high.

- Stating that you do not have a weakness is unlikely and not believable
- Stating that your biggest weakness is that you work too hard or too long will be perceived as refusing to answer the question truthfully

12) What do you do to relieve stress?

I enjoy exercising, competing with friends in a variety of games, which include both physical games and games of strategy, and just going for walks.

Speeches

Police officers may be required to present public speeches. Some officers may speak to students, some to community residents, some to the media, and some to police administrators. Some officers may speak to inform, some to persuade, and some to commemorate (Lucas, 2007). The speaker is the individual who is presenting the oral message, the channel is the mechanism by which the information is transmitted, the listener is the individual who receives the message, the message is the information that is transmitted from one person to another, and the feedback is the information that is sent from the listener to the speaker. Public speaking is more formal than daily conversation. Therefore, a police officer must organize his or her thoughts in advance, tailor the message to audience, tell the information with maximum impact, and adapt the information to listener feedback. Many speeches contain two to five major points.

Research studies indicate that clear organization is important for an effective speech (Lucas, 2007). Individuals who listen to speeches demand coherence. Therefore, police officers need to employ critical thinking when making speeches. Critical thinking is the "focused, organized thinking about such things as the logical relationships among ideas, the soundness of evidence, and the difference between fact and opinion" (Lucas, p. 16). In short, an effective speech needs to have a specific purpose, a thesis (central idea), an introduction, a body (main points), and a conclusion. In addition, there should be a transition from the introduction to the body, from one main point to another main point, and from the body to the conclusion.

There are different manners in which to support the information within a speech. The different types of evidence include testimony, statistics, illustration, analogy, comparison and contrast, and explanation (BleedingEdge.net, 2012; Lucas, 2007). See Table 30 below.

Table 30
Different Types of Evidence to Support a Speech

Evidence	Description
Testimony	Using quotations or paraphrases to support information in speech
Statistics	Using numerical data and figures to support information in speech
Illustration	Using real life situations to demonstrate information in speech
Analogy	Comparing two similar cases and inferring that what is true for the first case is also true for the second case
Comparison and contrast	Comparing the similarities and differences between two cases; one case may be better than the other case
Explanation	Using facts to clarify a topic or process in a speech

Following are several examples of outlines for speeches.

Example 1. Outline for Speech - Fireworks Speech

Specific Purpose: To convince the audience that the U.S. Consumer Product Safety Commission should ban all consumer fireworks within the United States.

Thesis: The U.S. Consumer Product Safety Commission should ban all consumer fireworks within the United States.

Introduction:

TESTIMONY
    I. The Declaration, 2007: United States democratic principles and citizens' expectations
    II. Overview of my credentials.
    III. Why I have interest in consumer fireworks.

TESTIMONY
    IV. Center, 2007: Reasons for the audience to have interest in consumer fireworks.
    V. Preview of thesis and main points.

Transition: To effectively protect the public, the U.S. Consumer Product Safety Commission should ban all consumer fireworks. Main point number 1.

Body:

    I. Consumer fireworks pose a significant threat.

        A. Consumer fireworks pose a significant threat and kill and injure many people each year.

TESTIMONY
            1. Greene, 2007; Graves, 2006; Hall, 2007; HealthGrades, 2007: experts agree that consumer fireworks are weapons that kill and injure many people each year.

STATISTICS
            2. Greene, 2007; Hall, 2007: on-going danger – statistics

ILLUSTRATION
                a. Coloian, 2004: Stacy Miller in PA, nurse severely injured

ANALOGY	b.	<u>U.S., 2006</u>: Sparklers are like power outlets
ANALOGY	c.	<u>Areddy, 2007</u>: Russian roulette - recalls
EXPLANATION	3.	<u>Safra, 2002</u>: fireworks are weapons
COMPARISON/ANALOGY	a.	handguns : fireworks
ANALOGY	b.	do not swim with sharks, swim with piranhas

Transition: In addition to injuring people, fireworks also damage property.

    B. Consumer fireworks pose a significant threat and damage much property each year.

TESTIMONY	1.	<u>Hall, 2007</u>: fireworks result in much property damage.
EXPLANATION	a.	fires
ILLUSTRATION	1)	<u>Braswell, 2007</u>: wildfires
ILLUSTRATION	2)	<u>Hall, 2007</u>: structural fires
STATISTICS	b.	cost

Transition: In addition to injuring people and property, fireworks also terrorize animals.

    C. Consumer fireworks pose a significant threat and terrorize many animals each year.

EXPLANATION	1.	Consumer fireworks cause distress to animals.
TESTIMONY	a.	<u>Equine, 2000</u>: horses
TESTIMONY	b.	<u>King, 2007; Crosby, 2007; Hahn, 2007</u>: dogs, cats
ILLUSTRATION	1)	<u>Wilkes, 1997</u>: Sammy

Transition: Consumer fireworks are dangerous to person, property, and animals. Main point number 2.

    II. Current federal consumer fireworks laws and regulations are ineffective.

        A. Federal laws and regulations are ineffective.

TESTIMONY	1.	U.S., 2001; National, 2007: Current laws – U.S. Consumer Product Safety Commission, U.S. Department of Transportation
EXPLANATION	2.	Inadequacies of current law
TESTIMONY	a.	Higgins, 2006; Areddy, 2007; American, 2007: capitalism and patriotism – supply and demand
STATISTICS	b.	Hall, 2007: 95% injuries with approved fireworks
ANALOGY	c.	pass the buck to the states

    B. State and local laws are ineffective.

TESTIMONY	1.	National, 2007; American 2007; Center, 2007: states' laws are a nightmare
TESTIMONY	a.	American, 2007: Only 5 states have banned consumer fireworks
ANALOGY	1)	fireworks are like ants: they're everywhere
TESTIMONY/ ANALOGY	b.	Morris, 2006; Indiana, 2007: Indiana passes the buck
EXPLANATION	c.	general police response
TESTIMONY	1)	Downs, 2007; Clarke, 2007: low priority for police
TESTIMONY/ ANALOGY	2)	Editorial, 2007: the straw that's breaking the camel's back
TESTIMONY	2.	U.S., 2006; National, 2007: states do not follow national safety guidelines

Transition: The dangers of fireworks will not go away by themselves. Something must be done. Main point number 3.

    III. The U.S. Consumer Product Safety Commission should ban all consumer fireworks within the United States.

        A. This proposal is workable.

TESTIMONY	1.	U.S., 2001; U.S., 2004: regulating agency is in place - U.S. Consumer Product Safety Commission
EXPLANATION	a.	define all consumer fireworks as display fireworks, requiring permit
EXPLANATION	b.	enforce in third year: inform, warn, enforce
EXPLANATION	c.	penalties would fall under current Forest Service fire laws
TESTIMONY	1)	Forest, 2007: $5,000 individual or $10,000 corp. and/or 6 months in jail
EXPLANTION	2.	enforcement agency is in place – Alcohol Tobacco Firearms Explosives

    B. Consumer fireworks problems will be solved because consumer fireworks will not be available to the public.

TESTIMONY	1.	Greene, 2007: protect people
TESTIMONY	2.	Hall, 2007: protect property
TESTIMONY	3.	Hahn, 2007: protect animals

Conclusion:

    I. In conclusion, Consumer fireworks are dangerous and, in order to protect life and property, they must be banned.
    II. Restate thesis and main points.
        [Cap:] As stated earlier, U.S. citizens expect to be protected by their government and United States democratic principles demand that **all** citizens have equal protection of their rights under the law. Consumer fireworks threaten both of these ideas. Patriotism, therefore, demands that consumer fireworks be banned within the U.S. Be patriotic! Be American! Ban backyard fireworks!
    III. Invite questions from the audience.

Example 2. Outline for Subpoint Speech

This outline is based on a main subpoint that might fit in support of the following thesis: Effective laws that control the importation, possession, and use of dangerous fireworks need to be passed and enforced.

Main subpoint: Backyard do-it-yourself fireworks are dangerous and, in order to protect society, their use must be controlled.

1. Greene, 2007; Graves, 2006; Hall, 2007: experts agree that federally approved backyard fireworks are weapons that kill and injure many people each year.

    a. Greene, 2007; Graves, 2006; Hall, 2007: on-going danger – figures

        1) Coloian, 2004: Stacy Miller in PA, nurse severely injured

2. Safra, 2002: by definition, fireworks are dangerous weapons.

    a) fireworks are like handguns – both can kill and need to be controlled
    b) sharks or piranhas, giant tarantulas or black widows, polar bears or black bears, giant anacondas or rattle snakes

3. the government's job is like that of the spur-winged plover to the Nile crocodile - promoting the health and well-being of its host.

    a. Areddy, 2007: patriotism and capitalism – the use of fireworks increase
    b. society is a child in great sea of danger without a life jacket

Example 3. Outline for Persuasion Speech

Purpose: To persuade the audience to act.

I. Attention Step

   A. A young man is sitting in class. A beautiful young lady with long brown hair, brilliant green eyes, and luscious lips sits next to him. She has little white flowers at her neckline on her silky pink dress. Their eyes meet; they lock together. Her pupils dilate. She leans toward him and he is pulled to her like a magnet. Achoo! Her little white flowers are now green lily pads.

II. Need Step

   - You are congested, you feel like you're being smothered, you have sinus headaches – but do not like using nasal sprays and antibiotics
   - Bromley, 2000; Harvard, 2004: You have trouble smelling things – 10,000 different odors – health consequences
   - Bromley, 2000; Harvard, 2004: You're unable to taste foods - health consequences
   - Waldrop, 1993: You have a job and cannot afford to call in sick - Americans miss 3.5 million workdays / yr
   - Waldrop, 1993: You have children and value their education - 129 million schooldays missed / yr
   - You want fun and romance with your partner without nasal drip
   - Indoor, 1995: 100,000 dust mites per one sq yard of carpet
   - Waldrop, 1993: Twenty-two million people in the U.S. have hay fever.
   - Why suffer?
   - The answer…wash away the problem by spring cleaning your nose.

III. Satisfaction Step

- MoldenSnozle: Developed by sinus expert Robert MoldenSnozle in 1997, the MoldenSnozle is clinically proven to provide instant relief from hay fever problems by washing away contaminants within the nasal passage.
- MoldenSnozle is an all-natural saline solution nasal washing system, which uses no drugs or harmful additives.
- MoldenSnozle is a Neti Pot; it is safe, easy to use, and ergonomically shaped for a comfortable irrigating procedure.
- MoldenSnozle is not made of ceramic like competitor brands but is made with an unbreakable, antibacterial plastic, which is dishwasher safe.
- By cleansing out the nasal passages of dust, pollen, and other irritants, you will be able to breathe deeply without obstruction or burning sensation.
- You will be able to smell and taste again – potentially saving the lives of you and your family.
- You will be able to again smell the hot, oven baked cinnamon buns and smell that special arousing fragrance that your honey wears.
- You will be able to savor the taste of that scrumptious raspberry cream pie, enjoying the simple pleasures in life.
- You will be healthy and able to enjoy your work.
- Your kids will be healthy and able to get that education.
- You will be able to again enjoy that long sought after social intercourse with your partner.
- So let you and your family be hay fever free by using MoldenSnozle.

IV. Visualization Step

   A. Picture yourself taking a walk with your sweetheart out in the country during spring. You are swimming through the pollen like a fish, and you love it. Life is great. You look at your sweetheart and your eyes lock. You lean forward and your sweetheart is drawn to you like a magnet. You close your eyes. Achoo! Your face is drenched. Your sweetheart should have used MoldenSnozle.

V. Action Step

   - So hurry up and buys yours today.
   - Hay fever season is upon us and supplies are limited.
   - $12.99.
   - Available at local pharmacies.
   - So act now. Don't be left in the dust…mites.

Example 4. Outline for Courtroom Testimony Speech

Purpose: To inform the audience that a police officer's verbal and nonverbal communication in the courtroom influences the jury's decision.

Thesis: A police officer's verbal and nonverbal communications in the courtroom impact the police officer's credibility as a witness.

Introduction:

I. <u>Woods, 2007</u>: Demonstrate the need for testifying well - statistics.
II. Overview of my credentials.
III. Why I have interest in effective courtroom testimony.
IV. <u>Kingsbury, 2006; Bank, 2001</u>: Reasons for the audience to have interest in courtroom testimony.
V. Preview of thesis and main points.

Transition: To effectively serve the public, a police officer must be a credible witness in the courtroom during a jury trial.

Body:

I. A police officer's verbal communications in the courtroom impact the police officer's credibility as a witness.

 A. A police officer's written reports impact the police officer's credibility as a witness.

 1. have good content
 a. <u>Stewart, 2007</u>: if not written, cannot use
 1) no pulling rabbit out of magic hat
 b. be objective and complete – perform pre-flight helicopter check
 c. <u>Lucas, 2007</u>: be accurate and clear
 1) undefeated does not mean won all games
 d. be relevant - focus on what was seen, not on what was not seen

 2. <u>Navarro, 2004</u>: be organized, structured
 1) do not keep changing channels

3. grammar = competence
   a. who is the bigger fool, the fool or the one who follows the fool?

4. <u>Lewis, 2001</u>: weaknesses in a police officer's written report will be exposed and this impacts the police officer's credibility as a witness

B. A police officer's oral testimony impacts the police officer's credibility as a witness.

1. <u>Stewart, 2007</u>: be truthful
   a. <u>Lewis, 2001</u>: if do not know, admit it – do not weave a web of deceit
   b. <u>Being, 2001</u>: never start sentence with, "*To be honest...*"
   c. <u>Lewis, 2001</u>: if make a mistake, admit it as soon as it is realized

2. <u>Navarro, 2004; Stewart, 2007; Lewis, 2001</u>: use plain language
   a. do not use slang or police lingo - examples

3. <u>Navarro, 2004</u>: testifying is an art and the police officer is a performer
   a. picture the jury is in an amusement park
      1) <u>Boccaccini, 2002</u>: do not memorize; seems rehearsed
         a) merry-go-round
      2) <u>Navarro, 2004; Boccaccini, 2002</u>: beware of vocal pauses
         a) Ferris wheel
      3) <u>Boccaccini, 2002</u>: speak moderately fast with variations in pitch/loudness
         a) roller coaster

4. <u>Lewis, 2001</u>: weaknesses in a police officer's oral testimony will be exposed and this impacts the police officer's credibility as a witness

Transition: However, verbal communication is only part of the story. Police officers also communicate nonverbally.

II. A police officer's nonverbal communications in the courtroom also impact the police officer's credibility as a witness.

A. A police officer's appearance impacts the police officer's credibility as a witness.

　　1. Stewart, 2007; Navarro, 2004; maintain outward appearance
　　　　a. dirty yard = dirty house

B. A police officer's conduct impacts the police officer's credibility as a witness.

　　1. Navarro, 2004: project information with confidence

　　2. Boccaccini, 2002; Navarro, 2004: have a posture that shows interest
　　　　a. like boy kissing girl

　　3. Navarro, 2004; Tower, 2007; avoid negative body language
　　　　a. examples of fidgeting by demonstration
　　　　b. LaGrange, IN attempted murder trial, lost case – June 2001

Conclusion:

I. In conclusion, a police officer's effectiveness in courtroom is determined by the jury's assessment of the police officer's credibility as a witness.
II. Restate thesis and main points.
　　[Cap:] Bank, 2001: As stated earlier, United States democratic principles rely on discovering the truth through courtroom testimony. Communicate well and be credible. Be democratic! Be American!
III. Invite questions from the audience.

Impromptu Speech

Sometimes police officers are required to give impromptu speeches. The media may want to interview the officer for an ongoing event, the officer may be assigned to provide a presentation to high school students, or the officer may have to control a large scale scene with many individuals. Below is Table 31, which contains words commonly seen in law enforcement. Students are to randomly select 12 words. Once the student has selected the 12 words, the student will take a minute and will be required to tell a story that uses all 12 words.

Table 31
Words for Impromptu Story Telling

#	1	2	3	4	5	6
1	police car	helicopter	horse	off road vehicle	snow mobile	motorcycle
2	juvenile	students	residents	adult	infant	minor
3	victim	media	suspect	accused	perpetrator	individual
4	CPR	badge	identification	Radar	resistance	hot pursuit
5	baton	firearm	pepper spray	handcuffs	Taser	bean bags
6	hunch	reasonable suspicion	probable cause	preponderance of the evidence	clear & convincing evidence	beyond a reasonable doubt
7	incident report	intelligence report	case report	use of force report	probable cause affidavit	charging form
8	radio	flares	fire extinguisher	evidence kit	verbal commands	non-compliant
9	falsification	Witnesses	explosives	HazMat	radiation leak	vehicle search
10	interstate	county road	ditch	median	berm	rumble strip
11	fog line	center line	DataMaster	jail	book	law
12	witness statement	line-up	show-up	compass	canine	method of operation
13	Miranda warning	perimeter	direct traffic	stop light	spill	field sobriety tests
14	latent fingerprints	rolled fingerprints	Property Record & Receipt form	citation	warning	hot pursuit

INTERVIEWING, INTERROGATION & COMMUNICATION for LAW ENFORCEMENT

15	training	factory	registration	search scene pattern	complaint	police-community relations
16	airplane	chemicals	water	concrete	lake	speed zone
17	ice	sunny	snow	foggy	storm	hail
18	lawyer	judge	jury	police officer	maintenance workers	restaurant employee
19	crash	bank robber	flat tire	hostage	tractor	work zone
20	black eye	question	warrant	45 MPH	70 MPH	120 MPH
21	happy	sad	mad	creeping	love	married
22	sweating	hands shaking	shifty eyes	hesitant to answer	artery pulse	cried
23	blamed	motive	interrogation	lost	found	interview
24	infraction	civil matter	contract	hired	private investigator	active shooter
25	passport	driver's license	home	farm	theory	report
26	booby trap	fishing	diversionary flare	computer	policy	politician
27	mystery	end of shift	adoptive admission	double jeopardy	confession	admission
28	inspection	parole	probation	field training officer	probationary officer	target
29	scene	watch/time	observed	incline	brakes	fire
30	siren	alarm	evacuation	riot	cell	bar
31	alien	mental	social worker	child abuse	elderly abuse	homeless
32	culture	perspective	profile	quota	department	tree
33	obstacle	race	reasoning	entrapment	glasses	deer
34	power	privileged	justice	persuade	calculations	deposition
35	disposition	alibi	crime Scene	documents	file	lead
36	canvass	fake	speed	counterfeit	money	contraband
37	fair	prison	coroner	prosecutor	emergency lights	fire truck
38	ambulance	hospital	doctor	medicine	best-practice decision	collect
39	evaluated	weapon	information	hands	foot patrol	road closed
40	jurisdiction	privacy	secret	vice	detective	forensic lab
41	coffee	break	on duty	Off duty	mob	emergency
42	ring	casting	passport	bounty hunter	fool	state line
43	parking lot	plea bargain	bail	tape measure	hydroplane	guardrail
44	quarantine	metal detector	radiation detector	chance	Alco-sensor	light

45	vest	mega phone	Laser finger	lightning	bridge	water
46	magic	moon	time	letter	eye	castle
47	world	flashlight	apple	ladder	building	flower
48	lock	key	keyhole	fish	parachute	arrow
49	statement	sleep	star	magnet	dragnet	footprint
50	sting operation	food	Feds	wanted	missing	dead
51	convict	cop	indicted	nude	weds	defend
52	weds	crazy	brave	saves	sues	lost
53	civil	revealed	mayor	blames	lawyer	shoots
54	stuns	cruel	mourns	psychic	tycoon	scam
55	actor	burns	smash	strike	snubs	DNA
56	rare	tricks	blast	minor	juvenile	angel
57	romantic	bored	hits	thug	secret	crooked
58	angry	350 lb.	slay	hero	attack	bizarre
59	weeps	Rehab	child protection	Priest	stabs	movie
60	lover	steals	drugs	white collar crime	Tourist	killer
61	bite	spouse	Level 2.5	game	partner	animal
62	Sign language	odor	burn	hot	cold	body language
63	lie	polygraph	voice analysis	handwriting analysis	communication	hill
64	mountain	tax	beer	fear	integrity	dedicated
65	bike	CPR	first aid	command post	music	ordinance
66	magazine	double-lock	escape	committed	service	hunch
67	business	bell	totality of circumstances	singing	riot	gear
68	skid marks	friction	stop sticks	stop	ram	mirror
69	X-ray	knock	liability	plaintiff	status quo	error
70	clothes	travel	octopus	position	lens	shoes
71	disaster	recovery	impound	inventory	mask	excise police
72	conceal	code	profile	conservation officer	statistics	intent
73	willful	reasonable	roadblock	announcement	open field	seizure
74	map	directions	transport	waiver	file	myth
75	due process	crime control	collateral	serial	organized	promotion
76	merge	resume	protect	shy	spirit	extra
77	crown	hatchet	crab	pie	sack	jump

78	puzzle	village	elephant	pressure	heavy	drop
79	snake	whip	frown	rock	boat	box
80	pirate	photo	drink	heart	stolen	monkey
81	Public Service	traffic enforcement	gang	identity theft	blood	MUG

REFERENCES

American Pyrotechnics Association (2008). *Fireworks Related Injuries; Frequently Asked Questions About Fireworks*; *Glossary of Pyrotechnic Terms*; and *2007 State Fireworks Control Laws*. Retrieved from http://www.americanpyro.com.

Areddy, J.T. (2007, June 29). Behind the Boom in Chinese Fireworks. *Wall Street Journal,29*, 2007: B1, B3. Retrieved from http://online.wsj.com/article/SB1183063918509519 69.html

Bank, S. (2001). From mental health professional to expert witness: testifying in court. *New Directions For mental Health Services*, Fall, 57-66.

Boccaccini, M. (2002). What Do We Really Know about Witness Preparation? *Behavioral Sciences Law*, 20, 161-189.

Being an Effective Witness. (2001). A Bureau of Business Practice Newsletter: Labor Relations Bulletin, 726, 1,2,6.

BleedingEdge.net (2012). *Public Speaking Tips*. Retrieved from http://www.speaking-tips.com/Glossary.aspx#I

Braswell, G. (2007, July 5). Four Wildfires Set: Police Seek Persons Who Witnesses Saw Using Fireworks on Highway 92. *Sierra Vista Herald*. Retrieved from http://www.svherald. com/articles/2007/07/05/news/doc468c9adecc8be076576986.txt

Bromley, S. (2000). Smell and Taste Disorders: A Primary care Approach. *American Family Physician*, *61*(2), 427-436.

Center for Disease Control and Prevention (2007). *Fireworks-Related Injuries*. Retrieved from http://www.cdc.gov/ncipc/facts/fworks.htm

Clarke, C. (2007) Fireworks Complaints Slip Down List of Priorities. *York Daily Record*. 2007. Retrieved from http://www.ydr.com/doverwestyork/ci_6325328

Coloian, Margie (2004, Sept/Oct). Fireworks: A Story About Fireworks in Untrained Hands. *NFPA Journal*. Retrieved from http://www.nfpa.org/itemDetail.asp?category ID=297&itemID=28463&URL=Research%20&%20Reports/ Fact%20sheets/Seasonal%20safety/Fireworks

Crosby, Janet. Fireworks Safety and Loud Noises. 2007. *Pets and Fireworks*. Retrieved from http://vetmedicine.about.com/cs/ diseasesall/a/petsworks.htm

Denton, M. (2009). *Police oral board: The ultimate guide to a successful oral board interview*. Charleston, SC: Createspace.

Downs, M. (2007) Fireworks Complaints Flood Police Phone Lines. *Florida Today*. Retrieved from http://www.floridatoday.com

Editorial: Stay Safe From Those Rockets' Red Glare (2007, July 2). *Detroit Free Press*.

Equine Research Center (2000). Safety Around Horses: A Basic Guide for Beginning Horse People. *All About Safety Around Horses*. Retrieved from http://www.petcaretips.net/ horse_safety.html

Forest Service (2007). *Frequently Asked Questions and Answers for Stage I Fire Restrictions*. Retrieved from http://www.fs.fed. us/r4/caribou-targhee/eiifc/restrictions/faq_stage_ 1%20.pdf

Graves, Charlene, Susan Perkins, and Tracy Powell (2006, September). Fireworks-related Injuries. *Indiana Epidemiology Newsletter, 9*(9). Retrieved from http://www.in.gov/isdh/ programs/injury /pdf/FireworksInjuryReport2006.pdf

Greene, Michael (2006). Fireworks-Related Deaths, Emergency Department-Treated Injuries, and Enforcement Activities During 2006. *2006 Fireworks Annual Report*.

Hahn, J. (2007). Some Pets Petrified When It's Raining Cats and Dogs. *Office of Public Engagement*. Retrieved from http://www.cvm.uiuc.edu/petcolumns/show_article_pf.cfm?id=176

Hall, John R., Jr. (2007). Fireworks. *National Fire Protection Association*. Retrieved from http://www.nfpa.org/categoryList.asp?categoryID=297

Harvard Medical School (2004). *Taste and Smell: Your Sensitive Senses. Harvard Men's Health Watch, 8*(9), 1-4.

HealthGrades (2007). Physician's Snapshot: Dr. Charlene Graves, MD. Retrieved from http:www.healthgrades.com

Higgins, W. (2006, June 29). Will New Law Help Spark Sales? *Indianapolis Star*.

Indiana (2007). *Indiana Legislative Bills: IC 22-11-14-10.5*. Retrieved from http://www.in.gov/legislative/bills/2007/PDF/SE/SE0009.1.pdf

Indoor Allergy Alert: Contractors Should Take Charge Now (1995). *Air Conditioning Heating & Refrigeration News, 196*(14), 35.

King County Animal Services (2007). *Fear of Loud Noises*. Retrieved from http://www.kingcounty.gov/safety/AnimalService/pettips/dogtips/loudnoises.aspx

Kingsbury, K. (2006). The next crime wave. *Time, 168*(24), 70-77.

Lewis, D. (2001). *The Police Officer in the Courtroom*. Springfield, IL: Charles C Thomas.

Lucas, S.E, (2007). *The art of public speaking* (9th ed.). Boston, MA: McGraw Hill.

Morris, L. (2006, July 18). Editorial: A Welcome Local Boost: The Fury Over Fireworks is Growing, and the State is Starting to Pay Attention. *News-Sentinel (Fort Wayne, IN)*.

National Council of Fireworks (2007). *The Classification of Fireworks*. Retrieved from http://www.fireworksafety.com/home.htm

Navarro, J. (2004). Testifying in the theater of the courtroom. *FBI Law Enforcement Bulletin*, 73(9), 26-30.

Reynolds, D (1990). *The Truth, the Whole truth and Nothing But...* Springfield: Charles C Thomas.

Safra, Jacob (2002). Fireworks. *The New Encyclopedia Britannica*. 15(4).

Stewart, S. (2007). Effective courtroom performance by Indiana law enforcement. *Clark County Prosecuting Attorney for Police Officers*. Retrieved http://www.clark prosecutor.org/html/police/police2.htm

The Declaration of Independence (2011). Retrieved from http://www.ushistory.org/declaration/ document/index.htm

Tower, W. (2007). Courtroom demeanor. *Kidjacked*. Retrieved from http://kidjacked.com/defense/courtroom_demeanor.asp

U.S. Consumer Product Safety Commission (2006). CPSC Warns Consumers that Using Professional Fireworks Often Has Deadly Results. Retrieved from http://www.cpsc.gov/cpscpub/prerel/prhtm106/06197.html

U.S. Consumer Product Safety Commission (2004, June 30). *Federal Government Working to Keep Americans Safe on 4th of July*. Retrieved from http://www.cpsc.gov/cpscpub/ prerel/prhtm104/04172.html

U.S. Consumer Product safety Commission (2001). *Office of Compliance Summary of Fireworks Regulations, 16 C.F.R. Part 1500 & 1507*. Retrieved from *http://www.cpsc.gov/businfo/regsumfirework.pdf*

Waldrop, J. (1993). Spring Sneezes. *American Demographics,15*(5), 4.

Wilkes, G. (1997). *The Boom Box – Sammy in a Kennel.* Retrieved from http://www.clickandtreat.com/webart107.htm

Woods, S. (2007). By the Numbers. *Dttp: A Quarterly Journal of Government Information Practice & Perspective., 35*(1), 10-12.

CHAPTER 13. SCIENCE & TRUTH

Polygraph Tests

A polygraph test (i.e., lie detector test) is given to a suspect to ascertain if statements made by the suspect are deceptive (Frith, 2007; Harrelson, 1998; Lykken, 1998). During a polygraph test, the suspect is monitored by a polygraph machine while being interviewed and interrogated. The polygraph machine measures any changes that occur in the subject's breathing, blood pressure, heart rate, and amount of sweat. See Figure 16.

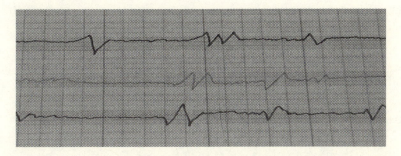

Figure 16. Polygraph test output

Polygraph machines have three main components (Frith, 2007). Each component has the separate ability to record the physiological responses of the subject while he or she is being questioned. The first part of the polygraph is the pneumograph, which records the subject's breathing rate. The second part is the galvanograph, which records electrodermal responses. The third part is the cardiograph, which records changes in the subject's blood pressure and pulse rate. The cardiograph is often considered to be more reliable in detecting deception. The typical findings of a polygraph test are 1) no deception indicated, 2) deception indicated, and 3) inconclusive.

There is debate over polygraph test results. Proponents of the polygraph test believe that a subject who is being deceptive will often exhibit involuntary physiological responses that can be scientifically recorded by the polygraph machine (Hess & Orthmann, 2010). Indeed, the correlation between positive test results and guilt is very high, which some claim is 95% accurate. Opponents of the polygraph test argue that the results are unreliable, as confirmed by the U.S. Supreme Court (del Carmen, 2014). First, the Office of Technology Assessment has indicated that correct detections range from 35 to 100%. Second, sometimes people who are simply nervous show signs of strong reaction that indicate signs of deception (Frith, 2007). Third, respiration is susceptible to voluntary control and the galvanic skin response, once triggered, is slow to recover (Jones, 2008). Fourth, individuals may be able to think of a lie after each question in order to manipulate the results. Finally, a person cannot cross examine the machine to detect any problems (Hess & Orthmann).

The polygraph test should supplement a field investigation and not be a stand-alone method of investigation. The success of the polygraph test will largely depend on the thoroughness of the investigation that happens long before the suspect ever takes the test. Having the investigator and polygraph examiner work together is the optimal way to maximize the effectiveness of the test.

In order to prevent employers from forcing employees to submit to polygraph tests, the Federal Polygraph Protection Act was passed in 1988 (American Polygraph Association, 2010). This law protects private sector employees. However, it does not protect employees of government agencies, which can include school officials, correctional facility staff, public agencies, and businesses that are under contract with the federal government.

Voice Stress Analysis

Proponents of vocal stress analysis systems (VSA) believe that they are able to detect deception by performing an analysis of the levels of stress in a subject's voice using a computer stress analysis device (Hopkins, Ratley, Benincasa, & Grieco, n.d.). See *Figure 17.* The stress is detected by examining traces made by micro-tremors in the larynx, which proponents believe are associated with stress and may be a signal that the subject is attempting to deceive (Hess

& Orthmann, 2010). However, a study by the National Institute of Justice indicates that detecting deception via voice analysis is no better than flipping a coin.

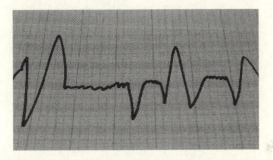

Figure 17. Electronic voice output

The National Institute of Justice's study was corroborated by Damphousse (2008), who studied over 300 arrestees. The arrestees' statements were confirmed by comparing their statements to their corresponding urine drug test results. In short, the voice stress analysis correctly identified 15% of the arrestees who told a lie. However, the voice stress analysis incorrectly labeled 8.5% of the arrestees as liars, even though they were truthful. Thus, the ability of voice stress analysis to accurately detect deception has shown to be about 50 percent.

Handwriting Analysis

There are three different types of forgery, which are traced forgery, simulated forgery, and freehand forgery (Swanson et al., 2009). First, a trace forgery is created when the perpetrator traces over the original signature. Second, a simulated forgery is created after the perpetrator learns to mimic a genuine signature. Finally, a freehand forgery is created when the perpetrator simply signs the victim's signature without making any attempt to mimic the victim's signature.

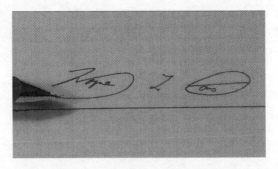

Figure 18. Handwriting analysis

Experts who examine documents claim that no two individuals write exactly the same (Frith, 2007; Saferstein, 2011). Although children may make a conscious effort to copy standard letter forms when they first learn to write, writing skills that are associated with nerve and motor responses become subconscious over time. Consequently, each person develops habits that results in unique shapes and patterns, which distinguishes that person's writings from other individual's writings. Some of the variables that distinguish one person's handwriting from another person's handwriting include slope, angularity, letter and words spacing, margins, pen movement, connections, relative dimensions of letters, and pressure. See Table 32.

Table 32
Handwriting Characteristics (Wiese & Melton, 2003)

Characteristic	Description
Flying Start	This is where and how the person starts the first letter of each word (e.g., upward stroke or downward stroke).
Retrace	During the retrace, does the person follow the original line exactly?
Loops	Does the person form rounded or narrow loops?
Upstrokes	Are letters that extend upward tall or short?
Lifts	When a letter requires a second stroke or mark (e.g., i or t), is the second stroke or mark high or low relative to the rest of the letter?

Connectors	Does the person connect letters or are there breaks between certain letters?
Flying Stop	Does the last letter stop abruptly or does it have a tail?
Spacing	Does the person space the letters out in words or are they close together?

A person's handwriting changes slightly each time the person writes (Wiese & Melton, 2003). Factors that may impact a person's handwriting include whether the person is tired, excited, hurried, nervous, etc. However, the shape of the letters and the way that they are formed are mostly consistent. Below are some characteristics that may help police officers identify forgeries.

Example of Flying Start

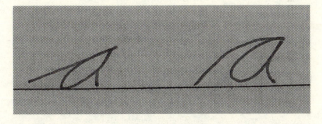

Example of exact retrace and loose retrace

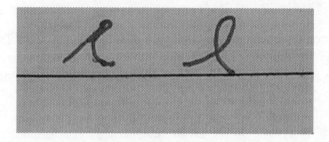

Example of narrow and wide loop

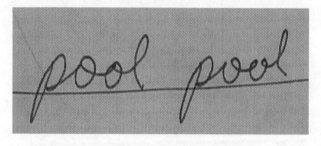

Example of closed loops and open loops

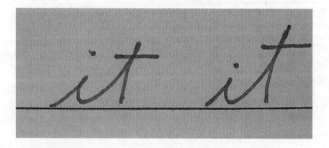

Example of short T and high T (upstrokes)

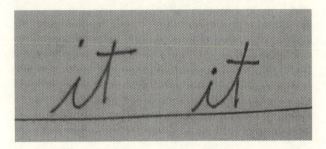

Example of high and low dot and high and low bar (lifts)

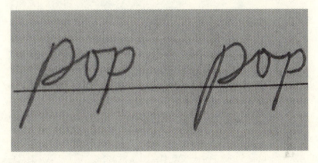

Example of level connector and dip connector following the "o"

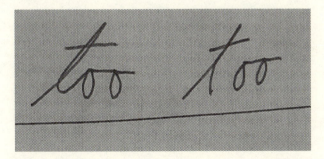

Example of connected and disconnected letters

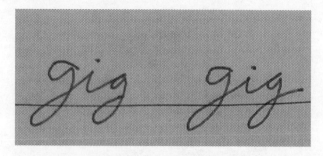

Example of quick stop and flying stop

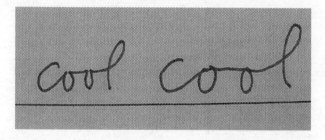

Example of letters close together and letters spaced apart

Following is a table that may be used to assess the totality of circumstances in order to determine if a suspect document is the same as the original document.

Table 33
Clues to Assess Handwriting.

	1	2	3	4	5	6	7	8
	Flying Start	Retrace	Loops	Upstrokes	Lifts	Connectors Breaks	Flying Stop	Spacing
	Upward or Downward	Yes or No	Round or Narrow	Tall or Short	High or Low	Yes: Letters or No	Quickly or Flows on	Close or Apart
K								
QD								

K = Known Source
QD = Questioned Document

Handwriting where the authenticity of the source is questionable is called a questioned document (Saferstein, 2009). Experts who examine documents obtain documents of known authorship and will compare these writings to questionable writings. Ideally, the writings of the known source should contain the same letters and words as the questionable writings. See Table 34 for some guidelines for conducting handwriting comparisons.

Table 34
Handwriting Comparison Guidelines (Swanson et al., 2009)

#	Guideline
1	The officer should provide the suspect with same type of paper and writing tool that were used in the questioned document
2	The officer should direct the suspect to use the same writing style (e.g., print or cursive) as in the questioned document
3	The officer should remove each completed page from the suspect's view
4	The officer should not provide the suspect with information on the format or grammar
5	For very short forgeries (e.g., a name), have the suspect write the information about 20 times; for longer documents, the officer should dictate the information to the suspect and have the suspect write the complete message three times
6	For reference, the officer should obtain at least 10 signatures from the victim
7	If the suspect appears to be writing strangely, the officer should have the suspect speed up, slow down, or switch hands
8	The officer should obtain non-dictated writings from the suspect from other sources (e.g., employment records)
9	The officer and the suspect should initial each page of the suspect's writing sample

    Handwriting may be used to detect truthfulness (Meyer, 2010). Research has been conducted using wireless electronic pens with pressure-sensitive tips. Participants were asked to write two paragraphs, one true and one false. The researchers measured how hard the participants pressed the pens. The findings indicated that subjects pressed harder when they lied. It has been suggested that cognitive stress causes liars to press harder. Thus, lie-writing, a lie detector that analyzes handwriting, may be better than a polygraph test because it does not depend on human interpretation.

REFERENCES

American Polygraph Association (2010). *Employee Polygraph Protection Act (EPPA)*. Retrieved from http://www.polygraph.org/section/resources/employee-polygraph-protection-act-eppa

Damphousse, K. R. (2008). *Voice stress analysis: Only 15 percent of lies about drug use detected in field test.* Retrieved from http://www.nij.gov/journals/259/Pages/voice-stress-analysis.aspx

Del Carmen, R.V. (2014). *Criminal procedures: Laws & practice* (9th ed.). Belmont, CA: Wadsworth.

Frith, A. (2007). *Forensic science.* Tulsa, OK: Usborne.

Harrelson, L. (1998). *Lietest: Deception, truth and the polygraph.* Ft. Wayne, IN: Jonas Publishing.

Hess, K.M., & Orthmann, C.H. (2010). Criminal investigation (9th ed.). Clifton Park, NY: Cengage.

Hopkins, C.S., Ratley, R.J., Benincasa, D.S., & Grieco, J.J. (n.d.). *Evaluation of voice stress analysis technology.* Retrieved from http://www.nemesysco.com/press/AFRL_REPORT2.pdf

Jones, D. (Ed.). (2008). *The CIA document of human manipulation: KUBARK counterintelligence manual* (1963). MindControlPublishing.com: Mind Control.

Lykken, D. T. (1998). *A tremor in the blood: Uses and abuses of the lie detector.* Reading, MA: Perseus Books.

Saferstein, R. (2009). *Forensic Science: From the crime scene to the crime lab.* Upper Saddle River, NJ: Prentice Hall.

Saferstein, R. (2011). *Criminalistics: An introduction to forensic science* (10th ed.). Boston, MA: Prentice Hall.

Swanson, C.R., Chamelin, N.C., Territo, L., & Taylor, R.W. (2009). *Criminal investigation* (10th ed.). Boston, MA: McGraw Hill.

Wiese, J., & Melton, H.K. (2003). *The spy's guide to security.* New York, NY: Scholastic.

CHAPTER 14. ASSESSING INFORMATION

Police officers cannot effectively serve the community if the officers do not understand the community. Therefore, police officers need to understand the information that is transmitted by community members. Police officers only need to look around to see how people communicate. There is much information all about.

Ethnography: Assessing Information in a Natural Setting

Date: Monday, November 2013
Location: Wana Cup Restaurant in Shipshewana, Indiana
Time: 11:00 am – 11:30 am

Ethnography seeks to describe a culture from the local or indigenous people's point of view (Berg, 2007). Data collection includes participant observation, participant interviewing, and artifact examination in order "to understand the cultural knowledge that group members use to make sense of the everyday experiences" (Hatch, 2002, p. 21). Thus, I entered a local restaurant to observe customers.

Sense of Vision

As I pulled up to the restaurant, I observed one car parked in front of the restaurant and 4 horse-and-buggies parked on the side of the restaurant. All of the horses were either brown or black and all of the buggies were black. The car, on the other hand, was red. All of the lights on the outside of the restaurant were gas lanterns. The entire building was gray, even the roof top. Furthermore, there was a white wooden fence in front of the building. In short, there were no extravagant colors advertising this restaurant.

Once inside the building, I observed 8 customers: 4 men and 4 women. All of customers seemed to be between 50 and 60 years of age. The customers sat at two tables, 2 men and 2 women at each table, and the men sat across from the women.

The men had some particular characteristics. First, all 4 of the men had full beards but none of them had mustaches. Second, none of them wore belts; instead, they all wore suspenders. Third, all 4 of the men wore dark blue pants, which appeared rugged, like workpants (they were not blue jeans). Fourth, all 4 of the men wore black coats, black boots, and black hats. Fifth, all 4 of the men wore eye glasses (versus contact lenses). Sixth, none of the men wore any jewelry.

The 4 women seemed to match the males whom they were with. First, all four of the women wore black coats and white bonnets. Second, all of the women wore either black or blue dresses. In other words, the colors were conservative and they were not blue jeans. Third, all 4 of the women wore black boots and black stockings. Fourth, all of these women wore eye glasses (versus contact lenses). Fifth, all of the women had black purses. Sixth, none of the women wore any jewelry.

As far as the environment, I noticed that there was a wooden sign on the wall with the Lord's Prayer on it. This seemed to be significant; indeed, the men and women closed their eyes and seemed to pray before they ate. Furthermore, I noticed that the advertisement signs above the cash register were made of cardboard, although they did have professional looking drawings on them. For example, the banana split sign had a very good drawing of a banana split on it. In addition, the colors in the building were simple. The walls had wood paneling halfway up on them. Above that, the walls were white. Finally, the unisex bathroom utilized a single cloth roller towel (i.e., a single towel that everyone uses). Thus, all of the clues indicate that the restaurant is low tech.

Finally, I noticed that there was some money (unknown amount of dollar bills) resting on a tray on top of the garbage can. No one seemed to care that it sat there. This indicates that the people probably trust one another not to take it. The waitress finally picked the money up about 10 minutes later.

Sense of Smell

Sitting next to the group, I was overwhelmed by their bodily odor. Thus, it seems as though the individuals may not bathe daily. However, this odor did not seem to bother them.

Sense of Hearing

Except for the talking among the individuals, the inside of the restaurant was quiet. There was no music playing and there were no cell phones. In addition, the entire group appeared to speak a combination of German and English. However, when a man dressed in a suit approached them, they started speaking English to him.

Summary

In short, this culture is quite different than my culture. They do not desire modern technology and do not fancy materialistic products. Indeed, they do not even drive motor vehicles. However, they do seem to have strong social bonds within their community. Furthermore, they do not seem to be concerned about what outsiders think (as evidence by the Lord's Prayer on the wall).

Artifact Data: Assessing Information in Cemeteries

Greenwood Cemetery (Lagrange, Indiana)

Much unobtrusive actuarial data can be obtained in cemeteries (Berg, 2007). Greenwood Cemetery in Lagrange, Indiana is a public cemetery with thousands of grave sites. This cemetery does not have a policy requiring that flat stones be used. Consequently, there are many different types of headstones used in this cemetery. All of the headstones face east, a Christian tradition, and there is an overall Christian theme at the site (other religious denominations are not obvious) (Graves, 2006).

Headstones from 200 years ago

Greenwood Cemetery, a municipality cemetery, contains headstones with dates ranging from persons who fought in the American Revolutionary War until the present day. Most of the headstones for military personnel are similar to one another. They are about three feet high, white, and contain a cross at the top. The headstones contain the name of the deceased, the state identifying where the person came from, the rank of the person during the war, the name of the war fought in, and the dates of birth and death. In many cases, the commanding officer's name is also included on the headstone. For example, one headstone reads as follows, "Abel Mattoon, Massachusetts, PVT, Capt. T. Williams Co, Revolutionary War, 1759-1837." Next to each of these headstones for military personnel is a metal rod, about two feet high, with a five point star on top of it with the word, "Comrade," on it.

Analysis: basically, it appears that individuals in this era want to advertise great accomplishments. By listing the commanders' names on the headstones, it appears that these historic headstones allow for confirmation of the facts. In addition, by having crosses near the top of the headstones, the headstones appear to indicate loyalty to God and country.

Headstones from 100 years ago

Another section of the cemetery contains family plots. In one example, there are six headstones for one family. The one on the farthest right is about a 10 foot high megalith, which looks like the Washington monument (Butterfield, 2003). Near the top are decorative images of diamonds. The front of this headstone reads, "In memory, father and mother." The back side states a name, the date died, and the age in years, months, and days; no actual date of birth is listed. The other five family members' headstones are to the left of the monument and are about two feet high and attached to one another via a concrete slab. For these, only names and dates are provided (e.g., Jacob Brown, 1829-1906). Of these five headstones, a male's name appears to be on both the farthest right and on the farthest left with three female names between them.

Due to their relative positions to one another, it seems as though the females are being protected by the males. Many headstones in this era seem to describe men as independent human beings, but women are depicted as attached to men.

Analysis: basically, headstones in this era describe women by their social relationships to men. Many times, a woman's headstone lists her name, wife of [man's name], and dates of birth and death. However, men's headstones do not describe their relations to women. Although most of these headstones have symbols on them, such as crosses, a hand holding the Bible, doves, and a variety of flowers (e.g., roses or Easter lilies), the text on them is brief.

Headstones from about 25 years ago

More recent headstones appear to be custom designed by making use of laser and digital technologies (Heller, 2008). Indeed, recent headstones in Greenwood Cemetery contain photographs, images, and text statements. For example, one young female who passed away in 1990 has her photograph in the center of the headstone, a fraternity emblem on the left side, an image of a swimmer on the right side, a Southwest Allen County Fire Department emblem at the bottom, and four statements from loved ones on the back. These statements include, "My darling Allison, God gave me the most precious gift in the world, it was you. You will always be with me in my heart, love always, Mom," and "To Allison, though lovers be lost, love shall not. Death shall have no dominion, Mike." In this section of the cemetery, headstones often have marriage dates on them with symbolic pictures (e.g., wedding rings interlocked or two hands holdings one another), the name of the spouse, children names, etches of recreational activities (e.g., fishing), occupations (e.g., a tractor-trailer), and they are surrounded by urns, flowers, solar lights (which represent the eternal flame), and statues of pets, such as dogs.

Analysis: basically, these headstones seem to describe family unity, social memberships, personal accomplishments, recreational activities, occupations, and pets. Furthermore, many of them contain colored photographs of the deceased, which can provide valuable physical characteristics. At the same time, crosses, angels, and doves indicate a Christian atmosphere.

Headstones from about 15 years ago

There is a baby section of headstones that date about the year 2000. On these headstones are words like, "our little angel," and "forever in our hearts." Moreover, surrounding these headstones is an abundance of angels, Easter bunnies, bears in the form of angels, toys, crosses, and flowers.

Analysis: The atmosphere seems to suggest a spiritual connotation where parents are trying to assure that their children are protected and cared for; in other words, the babies are not alone. Indeed, this area is heavily visited.

Eastbaren Cemetery (Shipshewana, Indiana)

Because there are many Amish in Lagrange County, Indiana, Eastbaren Cemetery, a private Amish cemetery with about 200 grave sites, was also visited. Every headstone in this cemetery is less than two feet high and all but four are white. The older headstones (in the 1800 era), simply state names and dates of birth and death. If marriages were involved, the spouse's name with the words "wife of" or "husband of" may be included on the headstones. More recent headstones (dated in the 1970s) may include the names of surviving family members on them (e.g., loving mother of James and Sara) along with bible verses on the back. For example, the back of one headstone reads, "Fear not little flock; for it is your father's good pleasure to give you the kingdom. Luke 12:32." Some headstones dated in the 1990s, which have both male and female names on them, may also include the marriage dates on them.

About 10% of the grave markers in this cemetery simply state a name and date. In one case, there is a wooden cross made of weathered barn siding dated 2008. On this cross is a handwritten message made with a black marker that states, "What a great sacrifice so others can live," and "we miss you."

Analysis: basically, this cemetery seeks simplicity and uniformity. There are no flowers, urns, photographs, solar lights, or statues. There are just headstones. Although some social statuses are indicated (e.g., wife of), significant others are listed (e.g., surviving family members' names), and significant events recorded (e.g., wedding dates), the atmosphere seems to focus on the afterlife and not on personal accomplishments in life. This is a sharp contrast to the Greenwood Cemetery.

The Message of Music: Assessing Information in Lyrics

Many poor individuals may use music to communicate. For example, officers need to pay attention to the music of minorities because their songs are sending messages. For example, there must be reasons why minorities sing songs about being discriminated against by police. Perhaps they have experienced such events. Even if the officers do not believe these messages, the minorities may believe them. Hence, because law enforcement involves relationships with community members, it is important for officers to listen to what the community members are saying.

Example of Assessing Information in Love Songs

The lyrics for 10 love songs, which have all been ranked number one on the billboards, have been collected and examined (About.com: Country music, n.d.; AlaskaJim.com, 2007; Songfacts, n.d.; Songlyrics.com, n.d.). Five of the songs are performed by men, and five are performed by women. The five songs performed by men include, 1) *Pretty Woman*, by Roy Orbison, 2) *Daydream Believer*, by the Monkees, 3) *El Paso*, by Marty Robbins, 4) *Running Bear*, by Johnny Preston, and 5) *Hello, I Love You*, by the Doors. The five songs performed by women include, 1) *I Will Always Love You*, by Dolly Parton, 2) *To Sir With Love*, by Lulu, 3) *Love Child*, by the Supremes, 4) *Will You Love Me Tomorrow?*, by the Shirelles, and 5) *Respect*, by Aretha Franklin. The songs performed by men will be compared to the songs performed by women by comparing themes between the lyrics. All of the song lyrics performed for each sex will be combined and an overall comparison will be made.

The unit of analysis, which "is the amount of text that is assigned a code" (Neuman, 2006, p. 327), shall be the stanza. Furthermore, because the words "I love you," may actually mean, "I am infatuated with you and want sexual intercourse even though I do not know you," the theme of each stanza shall be evaluated by using latent coding (Neuman). Indeed, latent coding may be more valid than manifest coding, which simply counts the number of times that the words appear. This means that the entire song must be read prior to any evaluations so that the overtone can be assessed. In addition, a stanza may include more than one theme. However, before a content analysis can commence, a list of variables needs to be developed (Sproull, 1995).

Variables:
1) Long term love – a long term commitment, perhaps as in marriage;
2) Infatuation – burning desire for immediate action;
3) Puppy Love –nonsexual and superficial;
4) Gain love – want other person to provide love;
5) Give love - willing to sacrifice oneself for love;
6) Believes superior to other person;
7) Believes subordinate to (i.e., worships) other person; and
8) Believes equal to other person.

Table 35
Summary of Songs Lyrics Variables

Results Variable	# of times variable appeared (Men)	# of times variable appeared (Women)
1	9	17
2	17	1
3	1	0
4	5	2
5	9	4
6	0	1
7	8	6
8	6	5

According to Table 35, the overall themes on the songs indicate that men seem to be more interested in short term love than in long term relationships as compared to women. Furthermore, men seem to want women to submit themselves in love, and they are willing to die for it. Women, on the other hand, seem to want lasting relationships. Moreover, women sometimes are willing to submit themselves to men, but they may want something in exchange (e.g., respect).

Content analysis is a useful way to assess information in everyday life. Being a police officer, it is important to analyze what is being said through both verbal and nonverbal manners. For example, if a police officer stops a pickup truck and is suspicious that there might be drugs in the vehicle, if the suspects clinch their fists (they may be preparing to fight), if they take off their hats and sunglasses (they do not want to damage them), if they start whispering to one another (they may be making a plan of attack), if they try to keep certain parts of their bodies shielded (they may be trying to conceal weapons), if they start looking around (they may be looking for witnesses, weapons, or escape routes), and if they try to position the officer between them, this may indicate a theme that violence is about to occur. Indeed, being able to recognize themes may save an officer's life.

Value of Information

The value of information is relevant. What is considered important information to some individuals may be considered less important to other individuals. Police officers need to understand that certain individuals will seek out particular information. Police officers will be more effective if they understand what information certain people value.

Read the following paragraph and highlight important information.

A man entered a home. There were surveillance cameras all about the home. Inside the home, there was a strong odor of mold in the air. There was a big flat-screen TV and a laptop in the living room. In the kitchen was a backed-up sink and the pipe was leaking. Near the sink were a woman's diamond ring and a gold watch. There was a desk in a study in which there was a wad of cash; there was also a safe in one of the closets. In one of the bedrooms was the sound of someone snoring; there was also some water dripping from the bedroom's ceiling. A car then pulled into the driveway.

Now, read the following paragraph and highlight important information from a thief's point of view. Assume the man who entered the home was the thief.

A man entered a home. There were surveillance cameras all about the home. Inside the home, there was a strong odor of mold in the air. There was a big flat-screen TV and a laptop in the living room. In the kitchen was a backed-up sink and the pipe was leaking. Near the sink were a woman's diamond ring and a gold watch. There was a desk in a study in which there was a wad of cash; there was also a safe in one of the closets. In one of the bedrooms was the sound of someone snoring; there was also some water dripping from the bedroom's ceiling. A car then pulled into the driveway.

Now, read the following paragraph and highlight important information from a potential home buyer's point of view. Assume the man who entered the home was the potential home buyer.

A man entered a home. There were surveillance cameras all about the home. Inside the home, there was a strong odor of mold in the air. There was a big flat-screen TV and a laptop in the living room. In the kitchen was a backed-up sink and the pipe was leaking. Near the sink were a woman's diamond ring and a gold watch. There was a desk in a study in which there was a wad of cash; there was also a safe in one of the closets. In one of the bedrooms was the sound of someone snoring; there was also some water dripping from the bedroom's ceiling. A car then pulled into the driveway.

Summary

A thief and potential home buyer will value the same information differently. What is important to the thief may not be important to the potential home buyer. Likewise, what is important to the potential home buyer may not be important to the thief.

REFERENCES

About.com: Country music (n.d.). *Dolly Parton – Jolene*. Retrieved from http://countrymusic.about.com/od/cdreviewsmz/fr/Jolene.htm

AlaskaJim.com (2007). Top songs of the 1960's. Retrieved from http://www.alaskajim.com/polls/2002topsongs1960s_results.htm

Berg, B. (2007). *Qualitative research methods for the social sciences* (6th ed.). Boston, MA: Pearson Education, Inc.

Butterfield, A. (2003). Monuments and memorials. *New Republic, 228*(4), 27-32.

Graves 'will be allowed to face east' (2006 September 26). *Europe Intelligence Wire*. Retrieved from http://www.accessmylibrary.com/ coms2/summary_0286-18589065_ITM

Hatch, J. (2002). *Doing qualitative research in education settings*. Albany, NY: State University of New York Press.

Heller, S. (2008). Death, be not staid. *Print, 62*(4), 90-95.

puraNeuman, W. (2006). *Social research methods: Qualitative and quantitative approaches* (6th ed.). Boston, MA: Pearson Education, Inc.

Songfacts (n.d.). *To sir with love*. Retrieved from http://www.songfacts.com/detail.php?id=2780

Songlyrics.com (n.d.). Retrieved from http://www.songlyrics.com/

Sproull, N. (1995). *Handbook of research methods: A guide for practitioners and students in the social sciences* (2nd ed.). Lanham, MD: The Scarecrow Press, Inc.

CHAPTER 15. MEDIA

Police officers need to understand the media. The media are in the business of selling information (Purpura, 2007). Thus, their business is directly related to what the customers demand. Because many people demand exciting stories, the media provide them with what they want. Often times this includes exaggerated violence.

Mass Media & Police

The police and the media have a common goal, which is to serve the public. The relationship between the police and the media is a symbiotic (Miller, Hess, & Orthmann, 2011). For example, the police and the media may work together to put out a crime alert or to advertise unsafe neighborhood practices. However, because the media are guided by the 1st Amendment (public's right to know) and the police by the 4th Amendment (right to privacy), there may be conflict between the agencies (del Carmen, 2014).

There are several consequences when police have poor media relations (Whisenand, 2011). For example, the police may lose their professional reputation and public support if they have poor media relations. The police are accountable to the public and the media are the community watchdogs. Thus, when a crisis event occurs, the police must have a trained officer readily available to communicate with the media. Subsequently, the police need to monitor the messages that the media deliver to the public because the police departments are hypersensitive to criticism and will take defensive countermeasures. For example, the department may take away a valuable tool used by officers because one officer was portrayed by the media as using the tool improperly. Finally, police should use the media as a conduit to obtain third-party support. The public often wants to help the police in crisis situations and the media can assist.

If the police are required to lie to the media, then the police should offer an explanation or apology at the appropriate time (Miller et al., 2011). For example, public safety may require the police to be less than truthful. However, once the threat has passed, then the police should clear things up.

Developing a partnership with the media is essential for effective police-community relations (Miller et al., 2011). The media are powerful and they can influence local residents, which may lead to their support. On the other hand, the media can also influence residents to not support the local police.

Police departments may learn how to use the media for their personal agendas. Bureaucratic police departments have a vested interest in justifying their existence via statistics (Kappeler & Potter, 2005). Advertising high crime rates will give the public the perception that the police are needed. In other words, it is good police business when the media create myths that crime rates are high, especially when the crime rates are not actually high. If the media continue to repeat the information, it soon becomes a truism.

Mass Media and the Public

Mass communication is a formal system of conveying much information to large groups of people in a short amount of time (Kappeler & Potter, 2005). Consequently, the media can spread fear over a great distance very quickly. By advertising particular crimes, the media may create an epidemic where none really exists (Kappeler & Potter, 2005). Media frenzies spread quickly, which give false impressions and magnitudes of criminal events. Once a theme has been established, similar stories are accepted as newsworthy. In addition, stories that do not match the theme may be modified so that they do match the theme. Thus, the misperception of a crime wave may continue to grow out of control.

A small number of people control most of the information (Kappeler & Potter, 2005). Although about 80% of all crime does not attract an audience, the media select the crime problems that they want to publicize, which are often the most gruesome criminal acts that are uncovered. The choice of crime coverage is driven by the competitive market and by the demand of the consumer.

The media have been known not to report the news accurately (Kappeler & Potter, 2005). For example, distorted coverage has exaggerated the degree that African Americans have been portrayed as criminals and Caucasians as victims. Furthermore, media stories have ignored the real social causes of crime and have created the perception that particular crimes are social problems. In short, media coverage gives the perception that the only way to control crime is by hiring more police officers, by passing more laws, by building more prisons, and by handing down longer sentences.

In addition, television media use graphics to get attention (Kappeler & Potter, 2005). Because television media are under time constraints, they are unable to provide the context that gives the information true meaning. Thus, the viewers only hear part of the story and they generate truth based on limited intelligence. Because some repugnant crimes do occur, partial truths that exaggerate such crimes only make the problem seem worse.

Mass Media: The Elite Controlling Minorities

The media have been used by individuals in power to control minorities. For example, hemp, which is collected from the cannabis plant, makes a higher quality paper at a lower cost than does wood pulp (Gahlinger, 2004). However, because William Hearst, a huge newspaper publisher, owned millions of acres of woodland, he lobbied to outlaw marijuana. During the 1920s, Hearst linked the marijuana use in New Orleans to murder, rape, poverty, and disease (Yaroschuk, 2000). This served two purposes: to make money by selling newspapers and to persuade lawmakers in congress to pass laws outlawing the growing of hemp. Although this did not result in the passage of federal laws outlawing the cultivation of hemp, Louisiana jumped on the opportunity to restrict the use of marijuana, hoping that it would be a means to control the black population.

Prior to the Great Depression of 1929, Mexicans in the southwest were considered a welcomed labor force (Gahlinger, 2004; Yaroschuk, 2000). However, once the Great Depression began, that Mexican labor force was no longer needed. In order to reduce the number of Mexican citizens working within the United States, the San Antonio Gazette published newspaper articles that stigmatized the Mexicans, stating that they commonly used marijuana, which turned them into frenzied and dangerous criminals. The media's goal was to force the Mexicans back to Mexico.

Many people distrust the government and formal news media. For example, in 1936, the film *Reefer Madness* was used as a scare tactic to describe the dangers of smoking marijuana (Roleff, 2005; Spurling, 1993). However, because the film overly exaggerated the effects of marijuana use, the formal media lost their credibility; their credibility is still questioned today. Consequently, marijuana advocates now transmit their own information using other types of media, such as bumper stickers, tee shirts, music, magazines, and the internet.

Freedom of Information Act

The Freedom of Information Act makes the records of government agencies accessible to the public (Miller et al., 2011). The act supports the idea that the people have a right to know. However, police may withhold certain information that involves national security, an active case, or the privacy rights of an individual.

REFERENCES

Del Carmen, R.V. (2014). *Criminal procedures: Laws & practice* (9th ed.). Belmont, CA: Wadsworth.

Gahlinger, P. (2004). Illegal Drugs: A complete guide to their history, chemistry, use, and abuse. New York: Plume.

Kappeler, V.E., & Potter, G.W. (2005). *The mythology of crime and criminal justice* (4th ed.). Long Grove, IL: Waveland.

Miller, L.S., Hess, K.M., & Orthmann, C.H. (2011). *Community policing: Partnerships for problem solving* (6th ed.). Clifton Park, NY: Delmar Cengage.

Purpura, P. (2007). *Terrorism and homeland security: An introduction with applications.* Boston, MA: Butterworth-Heinemann. Tabachnick, B.G., & Fidell, L.S. (2007). *Using multivariate statistics* (5th ed.). Boston, MA: Pearson Education, Inc.

Roleff, T. (2005). Drug Abuse: Opposing viewpoints. Detroit: Thomson Gale.

Spurling, A. (Producer). (1993). *Altered states: A history of drug use in America.* [Motion Picture]. Films Media Group.

Whisenand, P.M. (2011). *Supervising police personnel: The fifteen responsibilities* (7th ed.). Upper Saddle River, NJ: Prentice Hall.

Yaroschuk, T. (Producer & Writer). (2000). Hooked: Illegal drugs and how they got that way (Vol. 1) [Motion Picture]. The History Channel: A&E.

CHAPTER 16. POLICE & TECHNOLOGY

Cyberspace & Electronic Information

Cyberspace and electronic information are essential parts of American culture (Purpura, 2007). Businesses, governments, the economy, and society all depend on information technology. Spyware, malware, phishing, spam, viruses, worms, and identify theft are all part of the electronic communication system. Indeed, criminals engage in cyberterrorism by exploiting and attacking cyberspace as a method to achieve their goals. Furthermore, because identity theft is a major problem today, many Americans are personally at risk of being attacked. Consequently, personal credits may be ruined and much financial damage may be realized. Because computers are all around, cyberterrorism is a risk.

Police officers need to enhance their job performance by using modern technology. Because a central mission of the police community is to continuously improve public service, attention must be given to all available resources. When officers attempt a job, best practice dictates that officers make use of all available resources, if practical. Otherwise, the officers' performance will be less than optimal and this will be a disservice to the public. Therefore, administrators must support the implementation of technology in order to help officers best serve local residents. Indeed, society is becoming more sophisticated as technology continues to improve. In order to be successful in today's community, officers must learn to effectively use the tools that are currently available.

Incorporating technology in law enforcement is beneficial to officers. By using electronic bulletin boards, newsletters, and emails, for example, officers will be able to share information with one another in order to improve the learning process. Indeed, officers will be able to guide one another to continually improve the way that they work.

Technology and Public Service

Law and order depends largely on local residents. Thus, police departments must utilize the public as a resource. This means the police must engage community members in crime preventative strategies. This can only happen if the police work with community members.

Police officers need to combine technology with project-based activities to draw local residents into the subject matter. This will encourage cooperation and it will foster the residents' ability to internalize new concepts. Indeed, residents are eager to work with computers and they are more receptive to information when it is presented via technology. Furthermore, technology-based activities will allow the residents to have some control over projects and this will allow them to learn through trial and error. Thus, using technology to perform project-based activities will create a more active and engaging environment, it will foster the local residents' ability to think critically and to solve problems, and it will help local residents to better communicate with the global community.

Best Practices

Technology allows for different learning styles. According to Howard Gardner, a leading psychologist, people learn through seven different intellectual capacities (Ryan & Cooper, 2007). These distinct intelligences are a) linguistic, b) logical-mathematical, c) bodily-kinesthetic, d) musical, e) spatial, f) intrapersonal, and g) interpersonal. By employing differential instruction, officers can use technology in a way that matches the way that different individuals learn. Thus, technology can help local residents learn according to their own unique abilities.

Linguistic learners learn best through language (Ryan & Cooper, 2007). Thus, officers can utilize computers to teach concepts through writing and editing. For example, officers can teach local residents to express abstract concepts by using poems and word processing documents.

Logical-mathematical learners learn best through tangible and inquiry-based projects (Ryan & Cooper, 2007). Officers can use computer games to teach critical thinking skills and drill-and-practice programs to teach essential knowledge. In addition, database programs can be used to illustrate quantitative information.

Bodily-kinesthetic learners learn best through movement (Ryan & Cooper, 2007). Computers are effective tools for bodily-kinesthetic learners because when using a computer, local residents must actively use the keyboard, joystick, mouse, disk burner, and other devices. In addition, officers can use presentation software to simulate real-life scenarios. In these cases, the local residents will interact with the computer, make important decisions, and act out their choices.

Musical learners learn best by listening and by creating rhythms and patterns (Ryan & Cooper, 2007). Computers are effective tools for musical learners because many computer programs are readily available that play music. Furthermore, local residents can develop critical thinking skills by breaking down and rebuilding melodies.

Spatial learners learn best through visual experiences (Ryan & Cooper, 2007). Computers are effective tools for spatial learners because residents can learn through graphic programs, such as computer-aided designs and paint programs. These programs allow local residents to visualize concepts. Furthermore, local residents can express themselves with the use of presentation software.

Intrapersonal learners are self-motivated and learn best through meta-cognitive processes (Ryan & Cooper, 2007). Because local residents have different learning abilities, computers allow residents to learn at their own pace. Furthermore, computers can provide residents with additional instruction and training in areas where they need help. Because intrapersonal learners are not sure how to share their ideas beyond their own community, they can be encouraged to use blogs, which will allow them to express themselves in an ordered manner and to a larger community.

Interpersonal learners learn best through interactions with other people (Ryan & Cooper, 2007). For these residents, computers encourage cooperative learning by allowing individuals to work together. For example, an interpersonal learner can use online survey tools to generate data for one another. This will enhance the creative and communication skills of the residents.

Barriers to Technology

There are several barriers to implementing technology in the field. Some of the major barriers may include a lack of adequate training, a lack of hardware, a lack of software, and a lack of input concerning choice of software. Although there is a great amount of technological information available, overwhelming officers with this information is an ineffective way to promote the use of technology in the field. Instead, administrators need to focus on sound educational principles and to create the conditions, as well as the motivation and competencies, so that officers are able to implement technology in the field. In short, learning is a team effort and administrators must provide officers with the necessary support so that they can achieve their goals. As in football, without proper training, equipment, and direction, it is unreasonable to expect success.

Overcoming Barriers

There are several ways to overcome the barriers that impede the use of technology in the field. First, because officers will respond to technology that is directed at helping them achieve their goals, training should be curriculum rich and should focus on properly applying technology. Second, administrators need to provide professional development plans and mentors to ensure that adequate support is provided. Finally, before officers will be able to effectively use available technology, they must know that tools exist. Hence, officers must be exposed to the existence of available resources via training and mentoring.

Factors for Success

There are several factors that will help technology succeed in the field. First, a detailed plan that provides a clear vision of the goals and steps necessary for the effective implementation and management of the technology will need to be developed. This will include funding, which may be obtained from the government, and the installation of the technology. Second, officers will need to know how to integrate the technology into the field, and this will require on-going training. Third, administrators will need to support the process by providing funding and other support, such as by restructuring the officers' schedules. Finally, administrators will need to reflect on the process so that any corrective adjustments can be made. Indeed, a system without feedback is unstable.

REFERENCES

Purpura, P. (2007). *Terrorism and homeland security: An introduction with applications.* Boston, MA: Butterworth-Heinemann. Tabachnick, B.G., & Fidell, L.S. (2007). *Using multivariate statistics* (5th ed.). Boston, MA: Pearson Education, Inc.

Ryan, K., and Cooper, J. (2007). *Those who can, teach* (11th ed.). Boston, MA: Houghton Mifflin Company.

CHAPTER 17. INDIVIDUALS WITH DISABILITIES

General Practices for Interviewing People with Disabilities

When a police officer interviews a person with has a disability, it is important to talk directly to the individual without appearing to be uncomfortable (Indiana Protection, 2008). If the person appears to be confused and agitated, it might be wise to discontinue the use of sirens and emergency lights, if possible. An officer should identify herself and explain the reason why she is there. Use a steady, calm voice. Ask simple, direct questions. Be prepared to repeat any of the questions, if necessary.

If the person has a caregiver, seek to gain the caretaker's assistance to help ensure that the person with the disability understands the requests (Indiana Protection, 2008). It is important not to jump to conclusions when working with someone with a disability. For example, a person who has a physical disability may be mistaken for someone who is under the influence of alcohol. Agitation due to the inability to understand, or from being understood, could be misinterpreted for aggressive, challenging behavior. It is important to look and ask for any identification and medical alert bracelets, which could provide emergency contact information. Do not assume a person with a physical disability has an intellectual disability.

Before assisting a person with a disability, the officer should first found out, in a direct manner, the way in which the person can be assisted (Indiana Protection, 2008). This is important because each disability can be different. Do not assume that a person needs help solely on the fact that the person has a disability.

Interviewing People with Intellectual Disabilities

Individuals with intellectual disabilities may not be able to understand the importance of the police officer's role in a particular situation (Indiana Protection, 2008). They may not understand the seriousness of their actions and they may appear to be nonsensical in how they discuss the situation. They may not understand what they have agreed to in the interview, and they may say anything in order to gain the approval of the officer involved in the interview.

Individuals who have intellectual disabilities may be unsure of what they remember and they may give confusing answers (Indiana Protection, 2008). It is important to allow enough time for them to think through what they are being asked. The officer may have to use illustrations or to point to objects to ensure that the individuals are able to follow the questions. In order to maintain rapport and cooperation, it is crucial to avoid using "baby talk" when talking with a person who has an intellectual disability. Use simple, direct sentences, speak at a moderate pace, and ask one question at a time.

Interviewing Individuals with Autism Disorders

Autism is a disorder in which social and communication skills are impaired (Indiana Protection, 2008). The ability of the person to communicate is often limited; the person may demonstrate no verbal ability. Instead, the person may rely on gestures or repeated phrases. The person may make limited eye contact and could interpret any colloquial phrases in a literal manner. Individuals with autism may show signs of distress or erratic behavior for no observable reason and they can be very sensitive to touch and excess lighting. Individuals with autism may not comprehend the consequences of their actions or understand their legal rights. They may have trouble remembering details of situations and may not understand the questions being asked of them.

In order to best assist individuals with autism, the officer should speak clearly and slowly and should ask direct and simple questions (Indiana Protection, 2008). In some cases, it may be best to remove them from situations in which there is a high level of visual and auditory stimulation. In addition, unless it is dangerous behavior, the officer should not stop them from performing repetitive motions. If the officer does, this may escalate their erratic behaviors.

Interviewing Individuals with Mental Illness

If an individual begins to act strange and show odd behaviors, it is best to ask the person if he or she has any mental health issues (Indiana Protection, 2008). Ask the question in the most respectful manner possible, but be prepared for the person to avoid giving an answer or denying any problem. The stigma of mental illness is quite severe in U.S. culture and most people will want to avoid that particular label.

If the person acknowledges having a mental illness, it is important to not overwhelm the person with questions (Indiana Protection, 2008). Keeping questions clear and short may produce optimal results. Give the person ample physical space in order to keep him or her from feeling cornered or trapped.

Interviewing Individuals with Visual Impairment

When dealing with individuals who are experiencing visual impairment, it is best for officers to announce their presence first before entering the area (Indiana Protection, 2008). If another person enters the room, the officers should tell the person with the visual impairment who has entered the room and the reason for the arrival. Avoid speaking louder to the person (they are not hearing impaired). Any written information will need to be orally communicated to the visually impaired person.

If assistance is offered to a visually impaired person, the officer should avoid grabbing the person by the arm to guide him (Indiana Protection, 2008). The officer should ask the person to describe the assistance needed. The officer should allow the person to hold her arm for guidance and should let the person know if they are approaching areas such as stairs, narrow hallways and other challenging areas. When guiding the person to a place to sit, the officer should place the person's hand on the back of the chair.

Interviewing Individuals with Hearing Impairments

Interviewing individuals with hearing impairments can create a series of challenges, particularly when a sign language interpreter is not available (Indiana Protection, 2008). Some people with hearing impairments are not deaf; they may simply be hard of hearing. A hearing aid is not a sign that the person can fully hear and understand what is being said. Some individuals can read lips.

If someone is deaf, written communications can be very useful, as long as the officer and person with the hearing problem understand the same language (Indiana Protection, 2008). When an officer interviews a person with a hearing problem, the officer should face the person directly and should speak in a clear voice with a normal tone. Do not shout at the person. Attempt to reduce any noise in the background that could inhibit communications. Utilize writing, if possible. Write clearly and give the person enough time to read and process the questions.

A person with hearing problems may appear to be extremely confused or disoriented; this should not automatically be taken as aggressive and oppositional behavior (Indiana Protection, 2008). If a person with a severe hearing impairment is the focus of an investigation, it is important to remember that only a certified sign language interpreter should be utilized when the Miranda warning is given.

Following is a summary of how police officers should respond to individuals with disabilities (Indiana Protection and Advocacy Services, 2008). Individuals with disabilities may be suspects, victims, or witnesses. Some disabilities are easily recognizable while other disabilities are not easily recognizable. Most people with disabilities react the same way to law enforcement situations as does the general public. Some will need special accommodations specific to their disabilities.

Police Officers Encountering Individuals With Disabilities

- General tips for all people with disabilities
- Intellectual Disabilities
- Autism/Autism Spectrum Disorder
- Epilepsy
- Cerebral palsy
- Mobile Impairments
- Mental Illness
- Visual Impairment/Blind
- Hearing Impairment/Deaf
- People with Service Animals
- Other Disabilities/conditions
- Helpful Resources

General Tips

- Refer to the individual before the disability.
    For example:
    Correct: I am speaking to a person who is blind.
    Incorrect: I am speaking to a blind person.
- Check for hearing aid; see if it is working.
- Ask simply questions; wait for a response.
- Give one direction at a time; too many directions may confuse the person.
- Provide simple choices; some individuals may only respond to the last choice.
- Explain written documents in easy to understand terms (this includes the Miranda warning).
- Before seeking assistance from a caregiver, the officer should find out from the person the help that is needed.
- Every person and every disability is unique.
- Respect the individuals' independence as much as possible; allow them to move on their own, if possible.
- Ask the individuals if they need help before help is provided.
- If possible, gather all of a person's medications before the person is moved from a location.
- Collect needed communication devices (speech synthesizers, alphabet board, head pointer, etc.).
- Department should provide contact information for support personnel who can assist with a variety of disabilities.

Interpreting Behavior

- Be cautious about interpreting behaviors because different conditions may exhibit similar characteristics. For example, a person with cerebral palsy may appear to be intoxicated.
- Non-compliant behavior may be due to a lack of understanding or due to fear.
- Some individuals may require extra time to process what is happening and to respond.
- Person may have an ID bracelet, emergency medical card, or a medical alert bracelet.
- Officer should seek assistance from the person's caregiver, who may understand the person's needs and method of communicating.

INTERVIEWING, INTERROGATION & COMMUNICATION for LAW ENFORCEMENT

Police Response	
If the individual	**Police officer should**
Does not seem to understand	Reword question using different and easier words; use direct and concrete phrases; if no improvement, check for hearing loss.
Seems preoccupied	Get the attention of person before ask questions.
Cannot seem to concentrate	Be brief and repeat directions.
Agitated or over-stimulated	Be calm, remove distractions, and give firm and clear directions.
Is displaying poor judgment	Not expect to engage in rational conversation.
Is having trouble with reality	Be simple, direct, and truthful.
Is disoriented/confused	Check for hearing loss; If no hearing loss, redirect thoughts to current situation. Give one direction at a time and use direct and clear phrases.
Is fearful	Reassure the person that he or she is safe.
Seems to be changing emotions	Remain calm and ignore change in emotions.

Intellectual Disabilities

- Individuals with intellectual disabilities strongly object to the term "mental retardation"
- Officers should call it "intellectual disability"
- Individuals may not understand the seriousness of their actions
- Individuals may not understand their Constitutional rights
- They may easily be persuaded by others
- They may eagerly confess in order to please officer
- Allow extra time for person to process information and to respond.
- Treat the person with dignity and respect (do not use baby talk).
- Use short sentences and simple words.
- Point at pictures and objects to illustrate words.
- Make eye contact with the person; use the person's name often.
- Look for an identification card, which may provide contact information.
- Give one direction or ask one question at a time.
- Ask the person to repeat the direction/question in his or her own words to assess the person's understanding.
- Tell the person how long the encounter is expected to last and when things will return to normal (if known).
- Using a watch to indicate time may be meaningless to the person. Tie time to common everyday events, such as breakfast or lunch.
- Clearly indicate when the person may contact other people (family members, case managers, etc.).

Autism/Autism Spectrum Disorder

- Communication and social skills impaired
- May not be initially obvious
- Individual may be non-verbal or have limited verbal skills
- Individual may have difficulty expressing needs
- Individual may gesture or point instead of speaking
- Individual may repeat phrases instead of communicating conventionally
- Individual may appear deaf; may not respond to verbal cues
- Individual may make little, if any, eye contact
- Individual may interpret language in literal manner
    For example: if asked if they want to waive their Miranda warning, they may wave their hand
- Officers should avoid using words that have multiple meanings
- In a criminal justice scenario, person may not understand consequence of his or her actions
- Individual may have hard time remembering facts and details
- Individual may not understand what he is agreeing to
- Individual may not provide credible responses
- Individual with autism do feel pain
- Individual may display extreme distress for no apparent reason
- Individual may show no fear of danger
- Individual may exhibit inappropriate giggling
- Individual may engage in self-stimulating behavior (body rocking, repeating phrases, etc.)
- Individual may be extremely sensitive to sound, light, or touch

Interacting with Person Autism/Autism Spectrum Disorder

- Speak slowly and clearly
- Use simple language; rephrase as necessary
- Explain what is going to happen before it happens, at every step
- People with autism have difficulty with change; they prefer the routine
- Person may have trouble concentrating in highly-stimulating area
- Officer may have to lead person to quiet area
- Approach individuals from front because they startle easily
- Do not shout or touch person; talk in calm voice
- Do not encroach upon individual's personal space
- Allow repetitive movements (biting self, body rocking, flickering an object) unless it is a safety concerns to self or others; intervention can escalate behaviors

Individuals with Epilepsy

- Episodic medical condition in which individuals have no control; seizure activity in brain
- Seizure may cause person to act strangely; may cause disturbance
- May affect speech, consciousness, and movement
- Person may not be able to respond or interact normally during seizure or for quite a while afterward
- Person may be confused and disoriented and may not be able to understand officer

Seizure Symptoms

- Spitting
- Running
- Biting
- Shouting/Screaming
- Flailing movements
- Abusive language

Partial Seizure Symptoms

- Eyes flutter
- Blank stare
- Acts dazed

Interacting with Person who has Epilepsy

- Check for medical identification bracelet
- Note length of seizure; seizure more than 5 minutes could be a medical emergency
- If seizure > 5 minutes, have person transported to hospital
- If it is known that the person has epilepsy, assume observed behaviors are seizure-related
- Some individuals have a Vagus Nerve Stimulator (VNS) to help control seizures; it is an implant just under the skin in the upper chest
- Person may have Patient Emergency Medical Card and Cyberonics Magnet; follow instructions on card
- Do not forcibly restrain person during seizure or just after seizure
- Restraints may injure the person
- Person may perceive such actions as an attack
- Person may try to protect self by forcibly resisting
- If person has seizure while in custody, provide medical attention
- If person has convulsive seizure, place person on side to prevent choking
- Do not place anything in person's mouth (to hold tongue down)
- Hog-tying, placing a person face down, or using a choke hold on a person who is having a seizure or who has just had a seizure can obstruct breathing and cause death
- Failure to provide medication in a timely manner to a person with epilepsy could produce fatal rebound seizures

Person with Cerebral Palsy

- Disorder caused by damage to brain
- Affects ability to control movements and posture
- May vary from mild to extreme
- Mild cerebral palsy impacts balance and may make the person appear to be intoxicated or under the influence of drugs
- Severe cerebral palsy will alter major motor activities

Cerebral Palsy

- Sometimes associated with other problems, such as epilepsy, hearing problems, vision problems, or intellectual problems
- Do not assume person with cerebral palsy has intellectual disability
- Do not assume the person is intoxicated
- If have difficulty understanding the person's speech, slow down and ask one question at a time
- Give person time to respond; ask person to repeat, if necessary
- If person is using communication board or other communication device, allow the person time to communicate
- If person has a mobility or intellectual problem, deal with those issues too

Interacting with Individuals with Mobility Impairment

- Do not make assumptions about mobility limitations
- Communicate with person about ability to move about
- Two individuals may be using mobility devices for different reasons (one may use them to alleviate pain while moving about and one may need them to move about)
- If conversation will take several minutes, sit down and speak with the individual at eye level
- If the officer needs to move the individual out of the wheelchair, the officer should ask the individual about the most effective way to accomplish this task
- Placing individual in police car may not be safe
- Consider using a van suitable for transporting individuals in wheelchair
- Individuals who use wheelchairs are trained to move about
- Officer should offer assistance but should provide only what the individuals request
- If individual is placed into paddy wagon, officer should ensure individual knows how to hold onto the railing when handcuffed
- Officer should not assume that an individual who has a mobility impairment has an intellectual impairment
- Officer should speak to individual normally
- Only move the individual when required, and inform the individual what needs to be done
- Use care when removing individuals from their mobility devices because it may cause harm

Interacting with Individuals with Mental Illness

- Individual with a mental illness may become confused
- Individual may exhibit bizarre behavior
- Officer should ask person about mental health issues
- Individual may refuse to discuss personal health concerns
- Officer should use simple, clear, and brief language
- Officer should address one item at a time
- If individual becomes agitated, move to a quiet area
- Officer should speak calmly and should give individual plenty of space
- Officer should keep focused on the purpose of the assignment
- If remove individuals from site, let them bring along their prescription medications

Interacting with Individuals with Visual Impairments/Blind

- Some individuals are legally blind but still have some sight; others are totally sightless
- Officer should speak out and announce presence before entering area
- Officer should announce when people enter and leave the area
- Officer should announce if bystanders are around
- Visual impairment does not equate to hearing impairment; thus, speak normally and do not avoid words like "see" and "look"
- Do not touch the person unless assistance is needed
- Officer may need to let individual grasp arm for guidance
- Individual may walk slightly behind the officer to gauge the officer's reactions to obstacles
- Officer should announce doors, steps, etc.
- When about to sit down, officer should place individual's hand on back of chair
- Officer will have to read written information

Interacting with Individuals with Hearing Impairments/Deaf

- There are varying degrees of hearing impairment; some are totally deaf
- Hearing aids may increase volume, which includes background noise, and may not necessarily enhance clarity
- Individuals may not understand what is being said
- Officer may have to communicate by written means; some may not understand English
- Some individuals may read lips, others may require a sign language interpreter
- When entering a room, officer should toggle lights to get individual's attention
- Officer should get individual's attention before speaking
- Officer should face individual when speaking and should not obstruct mouth
- Officer should reduce background noise and speak slowly and normally
- If interpreter is present, officer should make eye contact with individual and not interpreter
- Officer may be able to write down information
- One officer should communicate at a time
- Officer may use hand gestures as visual cues
- Individual may appear confused as a result of miscommunication
- Miranda warning should be provided by a certified sign language interpreter

Individuals with Service Animals

- There are many different kinds of animals that are used to assist individuals with disabilities
- Service animal = dog or other common domestic animal specifically trained to assist person with a disability
- Animals may help with psychiatric, cognitive, and mental disabilities
- Service animals ≠ wild animals, farm animals, rabbits, reptiles, ferrets, rodents, amphibians
- Service animals provide services that include guiding individuals who are visually impaired, alerting individuals who are hearing impaired, pulling wheel chairs, fetching items, warning individuals when they are about to have a seizure, retrieving the phone or medications, assisting individuals with navigation
- Animals that provide comfort, emotional support, therapeutic benefits, and emotional support are companion animals and not service animals
- Service animals should be moved with the owner
- The owner must have control over the service animal
- The service animal can be removed if it is a threat
- Seek the owner's permission before touching the animal or speaking to the animal
- Use the leash, if required to move the animal
- An individual who employs a service animal is not required to show an officer proof that a service animal is required
- Officer may ask about the service that the animal provides to the individual
- If have doubt about the legitimacy of the service animal, investigate with a supervisor later

Individuals with Communication Impairments

- Individuals may stutter or may have had a stroke
- Officer should slow down and ask one question at a time
- Individuals may use an electronic communication board
- Officer should provide the individual enough time to use the board and to answer the questions

Individuals with Traumatic Brain Injury

- Individuals with traumatic brain injury may perceive information differently than the officer
- Individual may be argumentative or belligerent
- Officer needs to keep the individual focused on the issue at hand
- Officer should slow down, ask one question at a time, and allow enough time for response

Individuals with Tourette's Syndrome

- Individual may display frequent and repetitive movements of face, arms, and limbs
- Individual may have vocal tics
- Individual may involuntarily swear

Behavioral Disturbance

- Individual who displays a medical or psychiatric problem and is a safety concern should be evaluated by medical personnel

Reference

Indiana Protection and Advocacy Services (2008). *TIPS for law enforcement and corrections personnel: Encounters involving people with disabilities.* Indianapolis, IN.

CHAPTER 18. SPECIAL SITUATIONS

Hostage Negotiations

Negotiating with individuals who have taken innocent bystanders hostage as a bargaining tool requires specialized communication training. According to Wallace and Roberson (2013), hostage negotiation is one of the most highly publicized procedures in which law enforcement engage. The process of negotiating with a criminal or mentally unstable person in a hostage situation can be the supreme test of a law enforcement officer's communication skills.

Hostage situations may be placed into five different categories: criminal, ideological, domestic, frustration-driven, and thought-disordered (Harmening, 2014). The good news for the law enforcement officer is the techniques for each scenario will be the same (Fuselier and Noesner, 1990). A solid understanding of hostage negotiation procedures is crucial for all law enforcement professionals as they may be involved with such scenarios during their tenure in public service.

Table 36
Types of Hostage-taker (Harmening, 2014)

Type of Hostage-taker	Description
Criminal	Purposeful if hostage-taker uses hostages as a means to a criminal act. Defensive if hostage-taker did not intend to take hostages but did so as events developed (may use them as a bargaining chip).

Ideological	Passive if hostage-taker does not intend to harm hostages but plans to live on in order to protest cause in future (e.g., animal activities). Often ends peacefully. Violent if hostage-taker is willing to kill hostages to make a political, social, or religious statement.
Domestic	Custody - when parent takes child in violation of court order. Relationship - when, after a breakup, a person holds spouse or significant other at gunpoint for revenge. Defensive – when a person attacks approaching police and barricades self in home with family members (there is no intent to harm family members).
Frustration-driven	Final Statement – when a hostage-taker believes he is out of options and plans to kill the hostages, self, or both to make frustrations heard via dramatic event. Passive – when a person is frustrated with a personal situation and takes hostages to remedy a personal problem. Often ends peacefully.
Thought-disordered	Paranoid – when a hostage-taker is mentally ill and suffers from delusional beliefs. Hostage-taker believes he is in danger and may believe hostages are involved (may harm hostages); may use hostages as a bargaining chip to get out of imagined danger. Mission-oriented – when delusional hostage-taker takes hostages because some imaginary force directed him to do so.

The ability to totally control the hostage situation is usually very limited. However, the officer needs to take as much control as possible because lives may depend on the officer's actions. The officer who is on the scene will need to do his or her best to contain the situation until someone who is specifically trained in hostage negotiations is able to take charge. Until that time, the officer will need to utilize exceptional communication skills to engage the suspect in dialogue.

Steps for controlling the situation

1. Secure a perimeter and contain the situation (Harmening, 2014). Cut off all potential escape routes. Do not let any unauthorized persons enter the scene. Once negotiations have started, do not let bystanders or the media disrupt the negotiations.
2. Establish a communication link (Harmening, 2014). Engage the hostage-takers immediately to distract them from responding violently when additional police arrive at the scene. Make contact by any available means. Telephones and cell phones may be used, a throw phone may be used, or, as a last resort, a bullhorn may be used.
3. Establish a rapport with the hostage-takers (Harmening, 2014). The negotiator should convey honesty, credibility, and a sense of confidence that the situation can be resolved peacefully. The negotiator's voice should remain calm and the negotiator should allow the hostage-takers to vent. The negotiator should keep the discussion focused on the hostage-takers and not on the hostages, should downplay the event, and should complement the hostage-takers for any positive actions taken.
4. Never give the hostage-takers anything without getting something back in return (Harmening, 2014). Get concessions without agitating the hostage-takers. Hostage-takers expect a give and take relationship. Never solicit a demand, never give more than agreed to, and avoid saying "no" to a demand. Every time the hostage-takers give concessions, the negotiator increases his power over the situation.

If possible, the negotiator should strive to offer the hostage-takers a win-win solution such that both parties feel they are getting what they desire (Fuselier & Noesner, 1990). However, the reality of each situation is different and there is no guarantee that such a solution is available. Often, negotiators will work toward moving the hostage-takers from pursuing demands that are not realistic to objectives that are more obtainable. If hostage-takers desire to surrender, the negotiator will need to communicate the process for surrender directly to the hostage-takers to ensure a smooth resolution to the situation.

Table 37
Signs of Hostage-taker Negotiations (Harmening, 2014)

Signs of Success	Signs of Danger
When hostage-takers talk about personal needs and concerns	When the hostage-takers deny suicidal thoughts (not being honest)
When the hostage-takers talk for extended periods of time	When the hostage-takers refuse to establish rapport
If no hostage has been harmed, that may indicate there is no intention to harm hostages	When the hostage-takers insist on face-to-face negotiations (violent intentions)
When the hostage-takers refer to hostages by their first names	When the hostage-takers set a deadline for their own deaths
When the hostage-takers let a deadline pass without consequence	When the hostage-takers start discussing the final disposition of their property (i.e., their will)
When the hostage-takers release a hostage	When the hostage-takers refuse to negotiate
When the hostage-takers routinely exchange material goods for hostages	When the hostage-takers insist that a particular person be brought to the scene (gain audience for own deaths)
When the hostage-takers shift from offensive threats to defensive threats	When the hostage-takers isolate or dehumanize the hostages (hostages are viewed as objects)
When the hostage-takers reduce their expectations	When the hostage-takers tie weapons to their hands (no intentions on giving up weapons)

When the hostage-takers decrease their threatening behavior	When the hostage-takers make outrageous demands, continually change their demands, or make ambiguous demands (stalling for time; enjoying attention or building up courage for final stand)

Death Notifications

Sometimes law enforcement officers may have to inform family members of the death of their loved one. This can be one of the most devastating moments of any family member's life. This moment can be made worse if it is not conducted in a sensitive, professional manner. When giving a death notification, it is important to have as much information about the specifics of the death as possible. Death notifications should be made in person and not over the telephone. When arriving to give notification, officers should ask to enter the home of the family by stating they have information about the family member that they would rather discuss inside the home. After entering the home, officers will need to make sure the appropriate family members are available. Once this has been determined, the officers will need to tell the family members in a clear, straight, forward, and sensitive manner that their relative has died.

It is not uncommon for family members to sob, faint, become angry, or become despondent. The officers will need to focus on helping the family members with their needs. The officers should provide the family members with all available information. This is one of the toughest parts of law enforcement work, but it is a necessary duty.

Interviewing Sex Abused Child

The only witness to a child sexual assault may be the young child who was abused. It is possible that the whole investigation will ride on the child's ability to recall what happened. It is crucial to obtain good solid facts from the child in order to confirm warranted suspicions and to avoid misleading accusations.

An interview protocol devised by the Eunice Kennedy Shriver National Institute of Child and Health Development (NICHD) has shown promise in working with children in these kinds of cases (Harris, 2010). This interview procedure is broken into three sections: introduction, rapport building, and free recall. The interview will begin with the officer discussing what will be covered in the interview. The officer will then proceed to talk with the child about topics that are not related to the abuse. This will create a more relaxed interaction between the child and officer and will create a deeper level of rapport between the two.

In the latter part of the interview, the officer will discuss with the child any recollection that the child may have pertaining to the incident and will encourage the child to talk in as much detail as possible about the incident. The officer's goal is to get the child to talk without much prodding by only asking open-ended questions. This procedure may pull out more information from the child than by asking closed-ended questions.

Cyberspace Crime: Internet Dangers

Although there are Internet safety laws to protect children, such as the Children's Online Privacy Protection Act, which is designed to keep anyone from obtaining a child's personal information, these laws may not be that effective because Internet predators may not voluntarily follow these laws (Dowshen, 2008). Furthermore, because no one knows the number of chat room predators who are actually out there, children may be commonly targeted. Indeed, there are pedophiles on the Internet who aggressively seek to exploit children.

The Internet can expose users to many different people and different cultures (U.S. Department of Justice, n.d.). Furthermore, some people use the Internet to target children for sexual exploitation. Although some predators immediately engage in sexually explicit conversation with children, other predators seduce their targets by providing them attention, kindness, affection, and gifts and they slowly introduce sexual content. Because adolescents are at the age where they are moving away from the control of their parents and are becoming curious about their sexuality, they are prime targets for sexual predators on the Internet.

There are several ways that parents can protect their children from Internet predators, which include observing the warning signs and taking appropriate actions (U.S. Department of Justice, n.d.). The warning signs that indicate a child may be in the process of being seduced by on-line predator include the following: 1) the child spends a large amount of time on-line, especially at night; 2) there is pornography on the child's computer; 3) the child receives telephone calls from strangers (sometimes they are long distance); 4) the child receives gifts in the mail from strangers; 5) the child turns off the computer when a parent walks into the room; 6) the child becomes withdrawn from the family; and 7) the child uses another person's on-line account. In order to minimize the chances that children will be exploited by on-line predators, there are several things that parents can do. First, parents need to openly communicate with their children and explain the potential dangers that exist on-line. Second, parents can spend time with their children on-line and have their children demonstrate their favorite on-line activities. Third, parents need to keep computers in common areas so that they can monitor their children's communications. Fourth, parents can utilize parental controls and blocking software to create barricades that prevent their children from accessing highly suspect areas. Fifth, parents should randomly check their children's e-mail information to see if predators are in the process of attacking their children (however, the U.S. postal service may also be used). Sixth, parents need to teach their children how to use the many legitimate and appropriate Web sites that are available on-line. Seventh, parents should investigate the computer safeguards that are on other computers that their children may commonly use, which include the computers at school, the computers at the local library, and computers at friends' homes. Eighth, the parents must realize that if their children are targeted by predators, their children are the victims and are not responsible for being attacked. Ninth, parents need to instruct their children never to meet face-to-face with people who they have only met on-line, that they should never upload photographs of themselves or provide any personal information, that they should never respond to bulletin board postings that are sexually suggestive, and that Internet information is often times deceitful. Finally, in order to find out more about Internet safety, parents can investigate the many different Web sites that are available (Inhope - Internet hotline providers, 2008).

Sex Offender Registries

There is evidence that sex offender registries, which provide local law enforcement with information on the whereabouts of sexual predators, and community notification, which notifies community residents of the home addresses of the predators, reduce the frequency of sex offenses, but only involving local victims (Prescott & Rockoff, 2008). However, there is little evidence that these measures reduce sexual crimes against strangers. The problem with the registry system is that it requires lawbreakers to comply with the law and to register with authorities (Graham, 2006). Many times the information provided by the offenders is less than accurate. Because many offenders believe that the burden of registering is too much, they simply take their chances of perhaps being caught and perhaps being prosecuted. Therefore, the state registry system needs to include the physical verification of all the information provided by the sexual offenders. Without doing this, sex offender programs may not be very effective and may not be an adequate warning system for parents. However, because the Internet crosses great distances, and because true identities can be hidden, the registering of sexual offenders in local communities may still be inconsequential in preventing Internet crimes.

Local Law Enforcement

In 2008, the Office of Community Oriented Policing Services provided $9.9 million in grant monies to state and local governments to help combat child sexual predators (U.S.

Department of Justice, 2008). However, local law enforcement is designed to keep peace in the local community here and now. Internet crimes cross many jurisdictions, the perpetrators have anonymity, and such problems can consume a lot of resources to solve (if they can be solved). Local law enforcement departments, whose officers may be evaluated by quotas, do not have the right structure to handle Internet crimes. The federal government, on the other hand, can cross state lines and can spend more resources to focus on these specific problems. Thus, federal law enforcement agencies, such as the Federal Bureau of Investigation, can do a much better job at investigating domestic Internet crimes.

Crimes Against Children (Hess & Orthmann, 2010)

Crimes Against Children

- Maltreatment (neglect & abuse)
- Sexual exploitation (pornography & prostitution)
- Trafficking & abduction

Common Types of Maltreatment

- Neglect (most common to be fatal)
- Physical Abuse
- Emotional Abuse
- Sexual Abuse

Children as Victims

- 25% of violent crime victims are juveniles; most are female
- > 1/3 of juvenile victims of violent crime are < 12 years old
- ~ 2/3 of violent crimes involving juveniles occur within the home
- Most statutory rapes involve adult men and girls under 14 years of age
- African American youths are twice as likely (%) to be murdered than Caucasian youths

Child Abuse

- Biggest single cause of death of young children
- Can result in serious permanent physical, mental, and emotional damage
- May lead to future criminal behavior

Causes of Child Abuse

- Poverty
- Violence between parents

Three Components of Child Abuse Law

- Criminal definitions and penalties
- Mandate to report suspected cases
- Civil process for removing abused children from home

Child Protective Services

- Acts on behalf of children
- Requires professionals who come into contact with children to report abuse

Challenges in Investigating Child Abuse

- Need to protect child
- Possibility of parental involvement
- Need to collaborate with other agencies
- Difficulty of interviewing children
- Credibility of children

Protect Child

If the possibility of present danger to child exists, child must be removed into protective custody

Interviewing Child

- Consider age of child
- Ability of child to describe what happened
- Potential for retaliation by suspect
- In most child abuse cases, children tell the truth to the best of their ability
- Most reports of child abuse are made by a 3rd party, such as a teacher, doctor, or siblings

Interviewing Child

- Essential to establish a comfortable rapport
- Use of anatomical dolls

Evidence of Abuse

- Surroundings
- Home conditions
- Clothing
- Bruises
- Medical reports
- Behaviors

Child Abuse

- Often by people they know
- Most perpetrators are women who are younger than 40 years old
- Sexual abuse in family is most common sexual abuse problem, but often not reported

Sudden Infant Death Syndrome

- Most frequently determined cause of sudden unexplained infant death (3000-4000/yr)
- Police officer must observe infant's position (often times moved)
- Police officer must observe crib and surrounding area
- Police officer must observe presence of objects in crib
- Police officer must observe dangerous items in room
- Police officer must observe medications given to infant
- Police officer must observe temperature of room
- Police officer must observe air quality

Pedophiles Reactions to being Discovered

- Complete denial
- Minimizing the act
- Justifying the act
- Blaming the victim
- Claim to be sick

Children as Witnesses in Court

- Courtroom testimony may not be best way to elicit information from children
- Some courts have attempted to help children testify in court (e.g., by removing the accused from the courtroom)
- Some courts allow child interviews to be videotaped to avoid multiple interviews
- Being challenged under 6th Amendment to confront witnesses

Preventing Crimes Against Children

- Educate children about potential dangers
- Keep open communications
- Guidebook, Personal Safety for Children (http://www.missingkids.com)
- Digital technology (fingerprints, personal information) can be dispatched within minutes

Domestic Violence (Hess & Orthmann, 2010)

Domestic Violence

- Physical, sexual, economic, and emotional abuse, alone or in combination, often by an intimate partner to establish and maintain power over the other partner
- 3 phases: Honeymoon, tension-building, acute battering episode

Police Response

- Many departments have mandatory arrest policy for domestic abuse if 2 conditions exist: a statement by the victim and some sort of physical evidence (e.g., a bruise)
- Arrest with PC even without signed complaint by victim
- Research suggests that arresting the suspect may be a deterrent
- Other research suggests that arresting the suspect may intensify the problem
- Victims may be afraid to call police
- Some couples like to argue and fight
- Separate victim, witnesses, and suspects as soon as practical before interviewing them
- Use persuasion during interrogation
- Third degree – physical force is illegal
- Deception allowed – morals and ethical systems determine good behavior

Restraining Orders

- Court ordered
- Enforceable nationwide
- Usually takes several weeks to obtain
- Can obtain emergency restraining order within 24 hours

Elderly Abuse (Hess & Orthmann, 2010)

Elderly Abuse

- Physical and emotional abuse, financial exploitation, and general neglect of the elderly.
- Current level of elderly abuse is unknown

Signs of Physical Elderly Abuse

- Injury incompatible with given explanation
- Burns
- Cuts, pinch marks, scratches
- Bruises
- Dehydration
- Sunken eyes
- Soiled clothing
- Hidden injuries
- Frequent use of emergency room

Doctors Ask

- Has anyone at home hurt you?
- Has anyone scolded or threatened you?
- Have you ever signed documents that you do not understand?
- Are you often alone?
- Are you afraid of anyone at home?
- Has anyone touched you without your consent?
- Has anyone made you do things that you did not want to do?

Signs of Financial Abuse

- Recent acquaintance expresses interest in finances
- A relative that has no visible means of support is overtly interested in elder's financial affairs
- A relative expresses concern over spending elder's money for medical care
- Utility and other bills not being paid
- The elder's placement is not consistent with estate
- Relative isolates elder, and provides excuses
- Relative gives implausible explanations for finances
- Bank information sent to relative and unavailable to elder

Signs of Financial Abuse

- Relative attends bank with elder and refuses to let elder talk for self
- Elder confused about missing money
- Suspicious signatures on elder's checks
- Elder signed blank checks
- Unusual amount of bank activity
- A will, or power of attorney, is drafted but elder does not understand it

Abuse at Care Taking Facility

- Physical condition/quality of care, untreated injuries, undocumented injuries
- Characteristics of facility (odors, urine)
- Inconsistencies (medical records, statements)
- Staff behaviors (follow investigator too closely, lack of knowledge about client)

Criminal Investigations for Various Crimes

Reports

- Reports are a permanent written record of the facts for further investigation and for prosecuting the case
- Start taking notes as soon as possible and continue throughput the investigation
- Record all information that helps answer Who? What? Where? When? How? Why?

Proving Elements of Assault

- Establish intent to cause injury
- Record severity of injury - photograph
- Determine if weapon was used
- Collect clothing and weapons of victim and suspect
- Look for bloodstains, fibers, etc.

Traffic Stops (Miller, Schultz, & Hunt, 2011)

Officer –Violator Contact

- Explain in polite but confident manner the reason for the traffic stop
- During routine traffic stops only, have driver remain seated in vehicle
- Never stand between the vehicles
- After completing citation, present it to offender
- May have offender sign it, promising to appear (not an admission of guilt)
- During final period of contact, remain polite and control the conversation
- Do not enter into debate or argument with the driver
- Tell driver that he is free to leave and to drive safely

Summary of Traffic Stop

- Do stop your car out of traffic lane, behind violator's car
- Do record license plate before approaching the car (write it inside vehicle & call it to post)
- Do decide what you are going to do and say
- Do make direct and active statement regarding alleged violation
- Do compare information on DL and establish identity
- Do write a citation/warning as rapidly as possible, observing vehicle and occupants
- Do explain citation and how to handle it
- Do retain DL until citation is completed and signed
- Let driver know when he is free to leave
- Do not consider the traffic violation as a personal affront
- Do not argue with, berate, or threaten the violator
- Do not expose yourself to personal hazards – be alert
- Do not open the conversation in a sarcastic or derogatory manner
- Do not accept anything the violator offers you except the documents requested
- Do not detain the violator any longer than is absolutely necessary to do your job
- Do not follow the violator's vehicle immediately after termination of enforcement action (unless driver commits another violation when leaving scene)
- Do not quote fines (if quote is wrong, officer will get complaint)

Felony Stop (Miller, Schultz, & Hunt, 2011)

Felony Stop - Removing Vehicle Occupants

1) Driver
2) Front-seat passengers
3) Rear-seat passengers

Felony Stop

- Assume all suspects are experts in weapons, hand fighting, and have a criminal record
- Once the suspect's vehicle is stopped, immediately exit police car and draw weapon
- Take cover behind the police car's open door
- Always leave passenger side unlocked prior to stop for access by support officers
- Depending on situation, backup officer may use shotgun as primary weapon
- Give commands in loud and clear voice
- May use public address system
- Order driver to shut off engine and to place palms flat against windshield
- Order front-seat passengers to place palms flat against windshield
- Order rear-seat passengers to place hands on top of heads and in plain view

Police Officer's Directions to Driver

- Driver, use left hand only, carefully remove ignition keys
- Driver, with left hand, drop keys out of window
- Driver, place both hands out of open window
- Driver, open driver's side door from outside
- Driver, exit vehicle, raise hands, face away from me, take several steps to the left
- Driver, raise your arms as high as you can (if shirt is tucked in, have driver grip back shirt neck and lift up to expose waist)
- Have suspect turn slowly around while in a standing position so officers can view all sides of the driver's waist and body for possible weapons
- Driver, walk backwards toward me (guide suspect to proper location)
- Place suspect in kneeling or prone position close to the police car or order suspect to walk backwards to a designated team of arresting officers
- Handcuff/secure driver
- Repeat process for passengers (modify process as necessary)
- After all known occupants are secured, order any other passengers out of vehicle (they may be hiding) ; do not approach vehicle yet
- If no one responds, with weapons drawn, approach vehicle and secure it

Front-seat Passengers

- Order passengers to slide across the seat and exit via the driver's door with hands up and in plain sight
- Give orders similar to driver

Rear-seat Passengers
2 Door Vehicles

- Order passengers, one at a time, to crawl over the back seat and exit the driver's side door
- Give orders similar to driver

Rear-seat Passengers
4 Door Vehicles

- Order rear seat passenger to open left rear door from outside with left hand
- Exit vehicle from left side
- Any other passengers should slide out and exit from same door with hands always in plain view above their head
- Give orders similar to driver

DUI Investigative Notes

(Intended solely for practicing Field Sobriety Tests; there is no claim to the significance or validity of the tests. However, there must be some reference level to determine if a suspect has passed or failed each test.)

Field Sobriety Directions

Walk-and-turn

Have the suspect place his left foot on the line and his right foot in front of his left (heel to toe).

Have the suspect stand in this position, demonstrate and explain the test before he begins.

Take nine steps

Stay on line

Count the steps out loud

Watch your feet

Once you start, do not stop

Keep hands at side

During turn, swivel on left foot and take small steps with right foot to turn around

After the turn, take 9 steps and return to the starting point in the same fashion.

Do you understand? Begin.

One-leg stand

Have the suspect stand with his heels together and his arms at his side.

Have the suspect stand in this position, demonstrate and explain the test before he begins.

Lift your foot (either foot) 6" off of the ground

Keep your leg straight in front of you

Watch your foot

Keep your arms at you side

Count out loud up to 30

Count 1001, 1002, 1003, 1004,....

Do you understand? Begin.

Horizontal Nystagmus

Face toward me and do not turn your head; only move your eyes

Follow my finger with your eyes

[Move finger from side to side; move finger so that eyes can be assessed at 45 degrees and at maximum deviation; record eye movements]

Finger Count

Count from 1 to 4, touching the tip of your thumb to the tip of your fingers

Count from pinky to index finger, then index finger to pinky

Count 1, 2, 3, 4, 4, 3, 2, 1

Do you understand? Begin.

Backward Count

Example: Tell the suspect to count backward from 33 to 14.

Alphabet:

Ask the suspect to indicate his level of education.

Ask suspect if he knows the alphabet.

Ask suspect to recite alphabet (but not to sing it).

Alco-sensor test

Place the breath tube on the instrument.

Press read button to indicate that no measurement is currently on the instrument.

Press set button to set instrument.

Place tube in suspect's mouth.

Place hand behind tube to detect breath.

Tell suspect to blow into breath tube.

Tell suspect you want a steady breath and for him to blow until you tell him to stop.

After several seconds, press the read button to take a reading.

Determine reading (a reading will automatically come up or can press read button).

Toggle set and read buttons and swing instrument to clear out current readings.

Horizontal Nystagmus

Horizontal Nystagmus   Test Results   ◊ Passed   ◊ Failed

If suspect exhibited 4 or more clues, then it is a failed test.

6 total clues of impairment - 3 for each eye

1. Lack of Smooth Pursuit
2. Distinct Nystagmus at Maximum Deviation
3. Onset of Nystagmus Prior to 45 degrees (includes Nystagmus while eyes at rest)

Horizontal Nystagmus Test (check box only if characteristic observed)   Left   Right
◊   Lack of Smooth Pursuit   ____   ____
◊   Distinct Nystagmus at Maximum Deviation   ____   ____
◊   Onset of Nystagmus Prior to 45 degrees (includes while   ____   ____
    eyes at rest)

Tests to detect head injuries (if check yes, then the test is suspect)

Eyes have Equal Tracking   ◊ Yes   ◊ No   ◊ Does not apply
Eyes have Equal Size Pupils   ◊ Yes   ◊ No   ◊ Does not apply

Walk-and-Turn

Walk-and-Turn Test Results ◊ **Passed** ◊ **Failed**

If suspect exhibited 2 or more clues, then it is a failed test.

8 clues of impairment

1. Cannot maintain balance during Instructions stage
2. Starts too soon
3. Stops while walking
4. Misses heel-to-toe ½ inch or more between steps
5. Steps off of the line
6. Raises arms 6" or more
7. Turns improperly
8. Takes wrong number of steps

		R9	L8	R7	L6	R5	L4	R3	L2	R1	←
L	R	L1	R2	L3	R4	L5	R6	L7	R8	L9	→

Walk-and-Turn

INSTRUCTIONS STAGE

| Keeps balance | ◊ Yes | ◊ No |
| Starts too soon | ◊ Yes | ◊ No |

WALKING STAGE	**First Nine Steps**	**Second Nine Steps**
Stops Walking	_____	_____
Misses Heel-to-toe	_____	_____
Steps off of line	_____	_____
Raises Arms > 6"	_____	_____
Actual Number of Steps Taken	_____	_____

Improper turn (describe) _____

Cannot perform Test (Explain) _____

Other: _____

One Leg Stand

One Leg Stand   Test Results   ◊ Passed   ◊ Failed

If suspect exhibited 2 or more clues, then it is a failed test.

4 clues of impairment

1. Sways while balancing
2. Raises arms more than 6"
3. Hops
4. Puts foot down

Puts foot down 3 times is a failed test. Foot stood on _____ L _____ R

Check (if yes)	Performance
	Sways while balancing
	Raises arms more than 6"
	Hops
	Puts foot down

Puts foot down 3 times (failed test)   ◊ Yes   ◊ No

Type of footwear _____

Cannot perform test (explain) _____

_____

Other _____

_____

Backward Count

Backward Count   Test Results   ◊ Passed   ◊ Failed

If suspect exhibited 2 or more clues, then it is a failed test.

3 clues of impairment

- ◊ Hesitation
- ◊ Incomplete (Left out numbers) _____
- ◊ Continued past number and counted to _____
- ◊ Other _____

Asked participant to count from _____ to _____.

Alphabet A-Z

Alphabet (A-Z)　Test Results　◊ Passed　◊ Failed

If suspect exhibited 2 or more clues, then it is a failed test.

4 clues of impairment

- ◊ Left out letters: _____
- ◊ Hesitated
- ◊ Incomplete
- ◊ Sang Alphabet
- ◊ Other (describe) _____

Finger Count

Finger Count   Test Results   ◊ Passed   ◊ Failed

If suspect exhibited 2 or more clues, then it is a failed test.

4 clues of impairment

- ◊ Hesitation
- ◊ Misses tip of thumb to tip of finger
- ◊ Does not count 1-2-3-4-4-3-2-1
- ◊ Count not in alignment with appropriate finger
- ◊ Other _____

IMPLIED CONSENT WARNING

I have probable cause to believe that you have operated a vehicle while intoxicated. I must now offer to you the opportunity to submit to a chemical test, and inform you that your refusal to submit to a chemical test will result in the suspension of your driving privileges for _____ months.

Will you now take a chemical test?

Some departments arrest at this point. After all, there is probable cause. Other departments arrest after the DataMaster test. In the latter case, the additional evidence gained by the DataMaster test is considered part of the totality of circumstance (a refusal will result in an arrest because there is probable cause).

DataMaster Evidence Ticket

Below is information that is recorded on a DataMaster evidence ticket.

State of _____

Instrument # _____

Date: _____

Subject name _____

DOB _____

SSN _____

Operator's name _____

Department _____

Breath Analysis

Calibration/Self Tests _____ passed _____ failed

Subject's sample _____ passed _____ failed _____ refused BrAC % _____

Start Observation Time _____ Time of DataMaster Test _____

Operator's name _____ Signature _____ Badge # _____

Affidavit for Probable Cause: Driving While Intoxicated

State of _____ in the _____ Court in the County of _____

State of _____

    vs.

_____

_____

I, _____, a law enforcer with the _____ Department, swear that on the ___ day of _____ 20___, at about ___ ☐am ☐ pm (Name) _____, the accused, a (race) _____, (sex) ☐ male ☐ female, (date of birth) _____, was observed at (location) _____ in _____ County, _____ (State) operating a motor vehicle (description) _____. The accused, having ☐ ___ (State) driver's license ☐ social security number ☐ other identification number (list number) _____ operated a motor vehicle under the following circumstances:

Preliminary Observations

☐ I observed the accused operate the motor vehicle in my presence.
☐ _____ observed the accused operate a motor vehicle.
☐ I had reason to believe that the accused operated a motor vehicle because

_____

☐ The accused committed the following traffic violations: _____
☐ On private property, the accused's driving was erratic and unusual because

_____

Reason for the Traffic Investigation

☐ The accused committed the following traffic violations: _____
☐ The accused was already stopped when I approached.
☐ Other: _____

Crash?

Was there a crash involved? ☐ no ☐ yes   Number of vehicles involved in crash _____
☐ I witnessed the accused's crash.
☐ _____ witnessed the crash and identified the accused as a driver involved in the crash.
☐ The accused admitted to being the driver involved in the crash.
☐ The result of the crash was ☐ property damage _____ ☐ personal injury (name) _____

Field Observations

I had probable cause to believe that the accused was intoxicated because I observed (check all that apply):

☐ odor of alcoholic beverage	☐ alcohol beverage containers in view	☐ admitted consuming alcohol
☐ blood shot eyes	☐ improperly left vehicle in gear	☐ leaned against vehicle
☐ slurred Speech	☐ failed to shut off vehicle at crash scene	☐ soiled/disorderly clothing
☐ poor manual dexterity	☐ was involved in crash	☐ could not open door
☐ poor balance	☐ could not exit vehicle on own	☐ fell asleep at scene
☐ belligerent attitude	☐ staggered from vehicle	☐ excessive giggling

Field Sobriety Tests (check all of the tests that were administered and the corresponding results)

- ☐ Horizontal Nystagmus ☐ Passed ☐ Failed
- ☐ Walk-and-turn ☐ Passed ☐ Failed
- ☐ One-leg stand ☐ Passed ☐ Failed
- ☐ Finger count ☐ Passed ☐ Failed
- ☐ Backward count ☐ Passed ☐ Failed _____ (list range & describe response)
- ☐ Alphabet ☐ Passed ☐ Failed _____ (describe response)
- ☐ Rhomberg balance ☐ Passed ☐ Failed
- ☐ Finger-to-nose ☐ Passed ☐ Failed
- ☐ Other ☐ Passed ☐ Failed _____ (describe test)
- ☐ Alco-sensor 0. _____ grams of alcohol ☐ Passed ☐ Failed per 210 liters of breath.

Chemical Test

- ☐ I informed the accused of the state implied consent law & the accused ☐ submitted to ☐ refused the chemical test.
- ☐ The accused was unable to take the chemical test because ☐ injured ☐ unconscious ☐ too intoxicated
- ☐ _____, a certified chemical test operator, performed a chemical DataMaster test on the accused at (location) _____. The alcohol concentration was equivalent to 0._____ gram of alcohol per 210 liters of breath.
- ☐ I was informed by _____ that a blood test was conducted on accused at _____ ☐ am ☐ pm and that the result was an alcohol concentration equivalent 0._____ gram of alcohol per 100 milliliters of blood.
- ☐ I was informed by _____ that a ☐ blood ☐ urine ☐ other test was conducted on accused at _____ ☐ am ☐ pm at (location) _____ and that the result was positive for the controlled substance _____.

I swear or affirm that under penalty of perjury that the foregoing facts are true.

_____   _____   _____
Signature of Affiant   Date   Print name and Department

Previous Convictions

I, _____, have examined the accused driving/criminal record and have determined that the accused has a prior Operating While Intoxicated conviction on (date) _____ from _____ Court in _____ County, _____ (State) having cause number _____.

I swear or affirm that under penalty of perjury that the foregoing facts are true.

_____   _____
        Signature of Affiant   Date

Receipt for Driver's License (confiscated by police)

_____ Police Department   ORI # _____
Charges _____
Date of arrest _____ time _____ ☐ am ☐ pm
Driver's license number _____ License state _____
Name _____ DOB _____
Current address _____
Sex _____ Weight _____ Height _____ Eyes _____ Hair _____
The above motorist ☐ refused the alcohol test ☐ failed the alcohol test 0.____%.
County _____

_____ _____ _____ _____
Date   Department   Signature of Officer   Badge #

DAVIS, LESLIE, DAVIS

CHARGING FORM FOR DRIVING WHILE INTOXICATED

State of _____ IN THE _____ COURT
County of _____ CAUSE NO. _____

State of _____
vs.
_____
DOB: _____
SSN: _____

INFORMATION FOR (OFFENSE TITLE): _____
CODE _____ **CLASS** _____ ☐ **MISDEMEANOR** ☐ **FELONY**
COMES NOW, _____ (name of officer), who being duly sworn upon oath, says that on or about : (date of offense) _____, 20___, at (location of offense) _____, in _____ County, _____ (State), one (defendant) _____ of (Defendant's address) _____ did then and there RECKLESSLY, KNOWINGLY, or INTENTIONALLY: (describe elements of the crime)

_____
_____
_____
_____

All of which is contrary to the form of the statute in such cases made and provided, and against the peace and dignity of the State of _____.

I swear or affirm under penalty of perjury that the foregoing representations are true.

Date _____ Arresting officer's name (printed) _____
Arresting Officer's Signature & Badge # _____
Witness List: _____
Approved by (Prosecutor) _____

CONSENT TO SEARCH

_____ Police Department

LOCATION _____
DATE _____ TIME _____ OFFICER _____

YOUR RIGHTS: YOU HAVE THE FOLLOWING CONSTITUTIONAL RIGHTS.

YOU HAVE THE RIGHT TO REQUIRE THAT A SEARCH WARRANT BE OBTAINED BEFORE ANY SEARCH OF YOUR PROPERTY.

YOU HAVE THE RIGHT TO REFUSE TO CONSENT TO A WARRANTLESS SEARCH.

YOU HAVE THE RIGHT TO TALK TO A LAWYER BEFORE GIVING CONSENT TO SUCH SEARCH.

IF YOU CANNOT AFFORD A LAWYER, ONE WILL BE APPOINTED TO YOU.

IF YOU ARE A JUVENILE, YOU HAVE THE RIGHT TO TALK WITH YOUR PARENT OR GUARDIAN BEFORE ANY CONSENT TO SUCH A SEARCH.

WAIVER AND CONSENT

BOTH WAIVERS AND CONSENTS MUST BE SIGNED IF JUVENILE.

I HAVE READ THE STATEMENT OF MY RIGHTS AND UNDERSTAND WHAT MY RIGHTS ARE. I DO NOT WANT A LAWYER AT THIS TIME. I CONSENT TO A WARRANTLESS SEARCH BY OFFICERS OF THE POLICE DEPARTMENT OF THE FOLLOWING DESCRIBED PROPERTY LOCATED AT _____.
I AUTHORIZE THESE OFFICERS TO SEIZE ANY ARTICLE OF PROPERTY WHICH THEY CONSIDER EVIDENCE. I UNDERSTAND AND KNOW WHAT I AM DOING. NO PROMISES OR THREATS HAVE

BEEN MADE TO ME AND NO PRESSURE OR COERION OF ANY KIND HAS BEEN USED AGAINST ME.

_____ _____ _____
Name (printed)   Name (signed)   Date

AS PARENT OR LEGAL GUARDIAN OF _____, I HAVE READ THE JUVENILE'S RIGHTS AND MY RIGHTS SET OUT ABOVE AND I UNDERSTAND THEM. NEITHER THE JUVENILE NOT I WANT A LAWYER AT THIS TIME. THE JUVENILE AND I CONSENT TO THE WARRANTLESS SEARCH OF OUR PROPERTY BY OFFICERS OF THE POLICE DEPARTMENT. I AUTHORIZE THE OFFICERS TO SEARCH THE FOLLOWING DESCRIBED PROPERTY LOCATED AT
_____.

I FURTHER AUTHORIZE THE OFFICERS TO SEIZE ANY ARTICLE OF PROPERTY WHICH THEY CONSIDER EVIDENCE. I UNDERSTAND AND KNOW WHAT I AM DOING. NO PROMISES OR THREATS HAVE BEEN MADE TO ME AND NO PRESSURE OR COERION OF ANY KIND HAS BEEN USED AGAINST ME.

_____ _____ _____
Name (printed)   Name (signed)   Date

WITNESSES: _____ _____
DATE _____ TIME _____

INTERVIEWING, INTERROGATION & COMMUNICATION for LAW ENFORCEMENT

AFFIDAVIT FOR SEARCH WARRANT

State of _____ IN THE _____ COURT
County of _____ CAUSE NO. _____

State of _____
VS.

_____

COMES NOW, _____ (name of law enforcer), who being duly sworn upon oath, swears that he/she has good reason to believe that in the _____ described as _____, currently located at _____, seized in _____ County, _____ (State) there is now in or about said _____, being concealed certain property, namely: _____.

Furthermore, the property:

_____ Was obtained unlawfully.
_____ Is possessed unlawfully.
_____ Is used or possessed with intent to be used as the means of committing another crime.
_____ Is concealed to prevent a crime from being discovered.
_____ Tends to show that a particular person committed a crime.

See record of proceedings for the facts and information tending to establish probable cause for the issuance of a search warrant.

This affidavit is made for the purpose of obtaining a search warrant from _____ Court, _____ County, _____ (State) to examine _____ to search for the aforementioned evidence.

_____ Subscribed and sworn to be true before me this ___day of ___, 20___
(Affiant)

_____   _____
       Judge   Court

SEARCH WARRANT

State of _____   IN THE _____ COURT
County of _____   CAUSE NO. _____

State of _____
VS.
_____

To: Any Constable, Police Officer, Sheriff or Conservator of the Peace:

GREETINGS:

WHEREAS, there has presented before me testimony of _____, a sworn law enforcement officer, for the purpose of establishing probable cause for the issuance of a Search Warrant. The Court, after hearing the testimony, now finds that probable cause exists for the issuance of said Search Warrant of the **location** described as follows:

_____

YOU ARE, THEREFORE, commanded in the name of the State of _____ with the necessary and proper assistance in the day time or night time to enter into the location aforementioned and there diligently search for **goods and chattels** described as

_____

And that you are to bring the same or any part thereof found on such search forthwith before the Court and to be processed according to law.

GIVEN under my hand this _____ day of _____, 20___.

_____   _____COUNTY _____ COURT
     JUDGE

REFERENCES

Dowshen, S. (2008). Internet safety. *Kids Health for Parents.* Retrieved from http://kidshealth.org/parent/positive/family/net_safety.html

Fuselier, G.D. & Noesner, G.W. (1990). Confronting the terrorist hostage taker. *Law Enforcement Bulletin, 59*(7), 6-11.

Graham, C. (2006, June 19). Virginia beefs up sex-offender registry: Are enhancements enough to make registry an effective tool? *Augusta Free Press.* Retrieved from http://augustafreepress.com/index.php?s=enhancements+ enough+registry+effective+tool

Harmening, W.M. (2014). *Crisis intervention: The criminal justice response to chaos, mayhem, and disorder.* Boston, MA: Pearson.

Harris, S. (2010). *Toward a better way to interview child victims of sexual abuse.* Retrieved from http://www.nij.gov/journals/267/Pages/child-victim-interview.aspx

Hess, K.M, & Orthmann, C.H. (2010). *Criminal investigation* (9th ed.). Clifton Park, NY: Delmar Cengage.

Inhope - Internet hotline providers (2008). *DMOZ: Open directory project.* Retrieved from http://www.dmoz.org/Computers/Internet/Child_Safety/

Miller, M.R., Schultz, D.O., & Hunt, D.D. (2011). *Police patrol.* Mason, OH: Cengage.

Prescott, J., and Rockoff, J. (2008). Are sex offender registries effective? *Sentencing Law and Policy.* Retrieved from http://sentencing.typepad.com/sentencing_law_and_policy/ 2008/03/are-sex-offende.html

U.S. Department of Justice (2008). *Fact sheet: Supporting state and local law enforcement accomplishments 2001-2008*. Retrieved from http://www.usdoj.gov/opa/pr/2008/November/08-opa-993.html

U.S. Department of Justice, Federal Bureau of Investigation (n.d.). *A parent's guide to Internet safety*. Retrieved from http://www.fbi.gov/ publications/pguide/pguidee.htm

Wallace, H. & Roberson, C. (2013). *Written and Interpersonal Communication: Methods for Law Enforcement*. (5th Ed). Boston, MA: Pearson.

APPENDIX A. CRIME SCENE SEARCH PATTERNS

Techniques for Searching the Crime Scene

The purpose of a crime scene search is to locate physical evidence, which may be used to help solve a crime (Swanson, et al., 2009). Evidence may help determine a) if a crime was committed, b) the motive, c) the method of operation, d) the suspect, and e) those individuals who are not suspects. Police officers commonly search crime scenes. It is important to search the crime scene correctly and thoroughly because any evidence found at the scene may make or break a case. Not only may evidence indicate a person's guilt, it may also indicate a person's innocence. However, before crime scene evidence can be used in court, it must first be discovered by police officers in the field. Eight different crime scene searches techniques will be discussed. The particular crime scene search pattern that an officer should use will depend on several variables, which include available resources, the surrounding environment, and how the crime scene and evidence present themselves. See Table 38.

Table 38
Crime Scene Search Patterns (Saferstein, 2009)

Crime Scene Search Pattern	Pros	Cons
Line	Can find small items in known area	May take many officers and resources; should have well established boundaries
Strip	May be employed by one officer	Not as detailed as grid search, thus may overlook evidence; should have well established boundaries

Grid	Two sequential strip searches perpendicular to one another; very detailed search; search same area twice in different directions	May take much time and resources; should have well established boundaries
Lane	Concurrent strip search by two officers; their paths never cross; two sets of eyes are better than one	Needs two officers; not as detailed as grid search, thus may overlook evidence
Circle	May be employed with no visibility and without the capability of maintaining position (e.g., underwater in current)	Not very practical at many crime scenes
Spiral	May be employed by one officer; allows overview of crime scene while minimizing crime scene contamination	May not be a perfect spiral, thus may miss evidence
Quadrant or Zone	Good for large area; can use a different search technique appropriate to each zone	May take many officers and resources
Ray or Wheel	Good for large area; if known starting point, can search in all directions; can find items when have no idea of which direction to look	As searchers spread out, the distance between the individual searchers increases and evidence may be overlooked

Line Search Pattern

The line search involves one or more officers who start on a line and proceed in the same direction. This technique is effective if the officers want to cover a large area in a particular direction or if they want to cover a small area in great detail. If the search area is not chosen correctly, evidence may be missed (Saferstein, 2009).

Strip Search Pattern

The strip search technique involves an officer that weaves back and forth through the crime scene. The officer starts at the boundary on one side of the crime scene and moves toward the other side. Once near the other side, the officer does a "U" turn and continues back toward the original side. The officer continues this pattern as he or she moves across the crime scene. This search pattern allows a police department to cover a reasonable amount of area with limited manpower and time. This technique is effective if the crime scene has clear boundaries (Saferstein, 2009). If the boundaries are not clearly defined, then valuable evidence may be overlooked.

Grid Search Pattern

The grid search technique involves two or more officers that perform overlapping strip searches, which form a grid (Saferstein, 2009). A grid search pattern is basically two strip search patterns that are perpendicular to each other. Although this technique is thorough, it consumes more time and human resources than does a single strip search. This technique is good if the crime scene has clear boundaries. If the boundaries are not clearly defined, then valuable evidence may be overlooked.

Lane Search Pattern

The lane search pattern involves two officers that weave back and forth through the crime scene but who do not cross each other's path. The officers start at the boundary on one side of the crime scene and move toward the other side (Saferstein, 2009). Once near the other side, the officers do a "U" turn and continue back toward the original side. The officers continue this pattern as they move across the crime scene. This technique is good if the crime scene has clear boundaries. If the boundaries are not clearly defined, then valuable evidence may be overlooked.

Circle Search Pattern

The circle search technique involves an officer searching the scene via concentric circles. The officer will have a rope with knots tied in it about every 5 feet (arm span of the officer) and the officer will tie the rope to a stake. The officer will set the stake at a fixed point. The officer will start from the knot closest to the stake and will search a circular area around the stake. Once cleared, the officer will move outward toward the next knot and continue the process. This technique is very good when searching areas that have no visibility and where the officer cannot verify or maintain his or her exact position. For example, an officer who is scuba driving in dark waters with strong currents may effectively use this technique. The officer will feel for evidence in the black and unstable environment. However, the fixed point must be near the evidence or the evidence will not be discovered using this search pattern.

Spiral Search Pattern

The spiral search pattern is usually performed outdoors and involves only one officer (Saferstein, 2009; Swanson et al., 2009). The inward spiral is useful because an officer will move from an area with little evidence toward an area that is more heavily concentrated with evidence. The outward spiral pattern may be useful if an officer happens to come upon the main piece of evidence before the officer realizes that he or she is in a crime scene. In general, either spiral technique is effective in locating footprints leading from the crime scene. However, because the spiral search pattern may not be a true spiral, important evidence may be missed.

Quadrant or Zone Search Pattern

The quadrant or zone search technique involves breaking down a large crime scene into smaller and more manageable sections. The proper search pattern employed in each section will be independent of the other sections.

Ray or Wheel Search Pattern

The ray or wheel search technique will be used when the officers have a known starting point but do not know in which direction the evidence will be found. Officers proceed in every direction and may cover a large area (e.g., a technique used by warships to look for enemy ships at sea). This technique may be good if a child is lost in the woods and the searching officers only know where the child started. However, this search pattern fails to cover much area between the rays (i.e., searching officers).

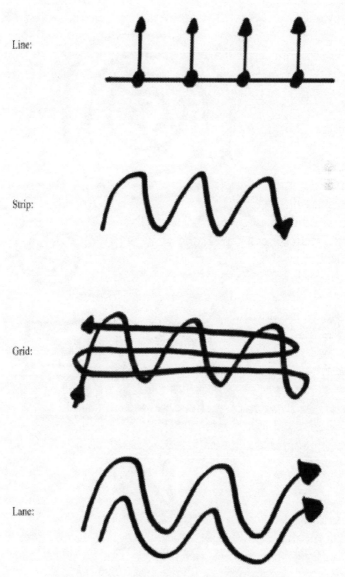

Figure 19. Crime scene search patterns.

Figure 19 (continued). Crime scene search patterns.

Line Search Pattern (if more than one officer, the lines may be conducted concurrently). Follow the sequence for the search pattern.

1 → . . . .

2 → . . . .

3 → . . . .

4 → . . . .

5 → . . . .

6 → . . . .

7 → . . . .

8 → . . . .

Strip Search Pattern (seeking an item that is 4 spaces wide and that is not diagonal). Follow the sequence for the search pattern.

```
   .    .    .    1    .    .    .    2    .    .
   
   .    .    4    .    .    .    3    .    .    .
   
   .    5    .    .    .    6    .    .    .    7.
   
  10    .    .    .    9    .    .    .    8    .
   
   .    .    .   11    .    .    .   12    .    .
   
   .    .   14    .    .    .   13    .    .    .
   
   .    .    .    .    .    .    .    .    .    .
   
   .    .    .    .    .    .    .    .    .    .
```

Quadrant Search Pattern. Follow the sequence for the search pattern.

```
1     .     .     .     .     .     .     .     .     11

.     2     .     .     .     .     .     12    .

.     .     3     .     .     .     13    .     .

.     .     .     4     .     .     14    .     .

.     .     .     .     5     15    .     .     .     .

.     .     .     .     16    6     .     .     .     .

.     .     .     17    .     .     7     .     .     .

.     .     18    .     .     .     .     8     .     .

.     19    .     .     .     .     .     .     9     .

20    .     .     .     .     .     .     .     .     10
```

Perform an outward spiral search pattern.

REFERENCES

Saferstein, R. (2009). *Forensic science: From the crime scene to the crime lab.* Upper Saddle River, NJ: Pearson Prentice Hall.

Swanson, C.R., Chamelin, N.C., Territo, L., & Taylor, R.W. (2009). *Criminal investigation* (10th ed.). Boston, MA: McGraw Hill.

APPENDIX B. CRIME SCENE INVESTIGATIONS

Crime scenes can be hazardous for police officers in a variety of ways (Swanson, Chamelin, Territo, & Taylor, 2009). First, officers may be stung by bees, bitten by ticks carrying lyme disease, bitten by mosquitoes carrying West Nile Virus, and bitten by dogs. Second, officers may be exposed to poisonous plants, such as poison ivy and poison oak. Third, police officers may breathe in deadly fumes, dust, or other contaminants. Fourth, contaminants may be absorbed through the skin. Finally, perpetrators may set up booby traps. Health consequences that may be experienced by police officers include blindness, breathing problems, and death.

Police officers search crime scenes to locate and collect evidence, which may be used to eliminate innocent individuals and may be used to identify perpetrators (Swanson et al., 2009). In addition, the evidence may be used to determine the perpetrator's method of operation, which could be used as a trademark to distinguish a particular perpetrator's work. However, the first priority for an officer at a crime scene is safety (which includes personal safety) and medical attention must be provided to all persons who need it. Consequently, police officers need to develop a crime scene entry log and the officer must record all individuals who enter and leave the crime scene.

It is possible for medical personnel to respond to the scene and to leave the scene before the police officers arrive. In this case, the responding police officers should interview anyone at the scene to find out what happened. Furthermore, an officer will have to go to the hospital and interview all medical personnel who worked the scene. This is important because the medical personnel may have changed the crime scene (e.g., may have moved something).

The first officer arriving at the crime scene is charged with preserving and protecting the area (Saferstein, 2009). The lead investigator is charged with developing the most effective strategy for systematically searching and documenting the entire crime scene. The investigating officer should perform an initial walk through to determine the perpetrator's path of entry and exit. The investigating officer may follow the path established by medical personnel, if they responded to the scene, to avoid any additional disturbance of the crime scene. If no path has been established by medical personnel, the officer should follow an indirect path toward the center of the crime scene. Following the perpetrator's path may cause the officer to destroy important evidence by accident.

During the initial walk through, the investigating officer should develop an overall plan to mark and photograph the evidence. The goal is to mark and photograph the evidence without damaging any of it. Thus, the investigating officer must have an organized plan of action. The lead investigator is responsible for both determining the crime scene search pattern and determining what evidence will be marked for photographing.

The entire crime scene will need to be photographed. This means that the entire scene will be photographed from four corners. After that, each piece of evidence will be photographed at mid-range and close-up, with and without a measuring device. In other words, each piece of evidence will be photographed at least four separate times.

After it is photographed, the crime scene will also be sketched. The officer should take measurements and may draw a rough sketch in the field. Once back at the police post, the officer may use a computer program to create a more professional-looking crime scene drawing.

After the scene has been sketched, the evidence will then be collected. The officer must bag the evidence and record certain information on a property record and receipt form. The information required on the evidence bag includes the case number, property record and receipt number, suspect's name, officer's name, officer's identification number, a description of the evidence, the date, and the name of the officer's police department.

Crime Scene Supplies

Police officers must be prepared to encounter a crime scene whenever they are working. Above all else, police officers must practice safe techniques. This means that police officers must use the right equipment and tools and employ proper police practices (e.g., using latex gloves). See Table 39 for a short list of some basic crime scene supplies.

Table 39
Basic Crime Scene Supplies (Swanson et al., 2009)

Basic Crime Scene Supplies
Crime scene barrier tape
Stakes/poles
Evidence markers
Spray paints/chalk
Privacy screen/blanket
Magnifying glass
Magnetic compass/global positioning system
Area map
Rain-repellent tarps
Small mirror
Metal detector
Ladders
Rope
Video recorder/audio recorder/camera
Disinfectant wipes
Gloves/booties
Biohazard bags
Evidence containers/tape/markers
Casting materials
Fingerprint powders
Crime Scene Entry Log Sheet
Photography Log Sheet

Crime Scene Entry Log Sheet

ALL PERSONS ENTERING THE CRIME SCENE MUST SIGN THIS SHEET

AGENCY: _____ Case #: _____
SCENE LOCATION: _____

Note: Officers assigned to maintain scene security must also log in and out on this sheet and should state their reason as "Log Officers."

Name & Title	Signature	Agency	In Date/Time	Out Date/Time	Reason for Entering Scene
			/	/	
			/	/	
			/	/	
			/	/	
			/	/	
			/	/	

Page _____ of _____

Photography Log Sheet

pg _____ of _____

AGENCY: _____ Case #: _____
SCENE LOCATION: _____

Photo #	Evidence Marker #	Description of Evidence Photographed

Name & Title   Badge #   Signature   Agency

Communicating with Nature

Clues from crime may come from nature (Frith, 2007). For example, entomologists are experts who study insects to find clues that may reveal when and where a person died. When samples are collected from insects, the growth stage of the insect may indicate the length of time of death, and the type of insect may indicate time of day of death (e.g., some insects are only active at certain times of the day).

Leaves, soil, seeds, dust, fungus, and pollen may attach themselves to people in the area (Frith, 2007). If a certain type of pollen, for example, only exist in a particular area, and if the same pollen is discovered on a suspect, then that may indicate that the suspect was in the area. Crime scene investigators may search for pollen in a corpse's nose to determine if the victim was in the same area as the suspect. Such information has led to convictions in court.

Although fires, if hot enough, may reduce nearly everything to soot and ash, fires will eventually go out and will allow for the examination of evidence (Frith, 2007). As a general rule, fires travel up and out, creating a V shape of soot and burned areas. The bottom of the V indicates the origin of the fire. Thus, fire scene investigators may work back through the trail of burned-out debris to locate the origin of the fire. It is not uncommon for arsonists to want to destroy something near the origin of the fire.

Once a fire starts, it will keep burning as long as it has enough fuel and oxygen (Frith, 2007). If a suspect wants to start a fire quickly, he or she may use an accelerant, such as gasoline or alcohol. If there is a heavily burned trail on the floor, this may indicate a spilled accelerant. Crime scene investigators will look for evidence of accelerants to determine whether the fire was intentionally set. Police may use canines to detect accelerants.

Forgeries and Fakes

All articles can be faked. Users of fraudulent documents include terrorists, fugitives, drug traffickers, and illegal immigrants. A counterfeit document is a copy or imitation of an authentic document without legal authority with the intent to pass off the document as genuine. An altered document is a genuine document that has been modified in one or more of its elements without destroying the identity of the original document. Art and antique forgery, although criminal, can be quite profitable in a capitalistic society (Dickens, 2008). Therefore, police officers need to be aware of what to look for when investigating articles for fakes.

Table 40
Ways to Identify Fakes, Forgeries, and Counterfeits
(Dickens, 2008; U.S. Department of the Treasury, n.d.)

	Clues	Description
1	Odor	Antique paintings should smell old; the odor of succinic acid indicates an inappropriate amber varnish
2	Discounted price	To attract bargain hunters, forgers often price forgeries at about half of the actual painting's worth.
3	Catalog description	The catalog and label description may not match the description on the receipt; terms in the catalog may be used to mislead the buyer (e.g., *in the style of*)
4	Pattern of wear	Wear should be uneven and consistent with everyday use (e.g., a chair's feet may be uneven)
5	Signs of aging	Items may be artificially aged and advertised as high quality; a chair, for example, may be examined with a magnifying glass to exam low quality stress cracks at holes; used and worn items should not be rough – therefore, look underneath items (e.g., chairs) for smoothness; if painted, look in nooks and crannies for cover-ups.

6	Overpainting	Forgers may paint over an old painting. Shine a bright light through the painting to see if images from a prior painting show through.
7	Labels	Frayed edges on the item's label suggests that the labels are not original or that the item is fake; tea is used to age labels
8	Printed transfers	Colored items that are produced on a copy machine will reveal tiny dots of color
9	Fixings	Look at the nails, screws, and hooks to see if they are old.
10	Opaquing marks	Missing details, such as part of a line or box missing, as if covered up before it was photo copied
11	Trash marks	Small remnants of original data that the forger failed to remove from the original document and are still visible on the document
12	Security thread	A thin thread or ribbon running through the bank note
13	Microprinting	Print appears as a line to the naked eye but can be read under magnification; difficult to photocopy
14	Watermark	Varying paper density that appears darker or lighter when held up to a light source; does not copy on color copiers
15	Color-shifting inks	Color of ink changes when image viewed at different angles
16	Fine-Line Printing Patterns	Appears normal to naked eye but is difficult for current technology to copy

Crime Scene Investigation

Criminal investigations are an important part of police work. People's lives may depend on the consequences of an investigation. In order to effectively determine the method of operation for the crime, and who are responsible for the crime, police officers must properly investigate a variety of crime scenes. Above all else, safety at the crime scene is most important. After all safety issues have been resolved, and all injured individuals have been handled, evidence needs to be collected. Failure to properly collect evidence may result in disciplinary action.

Grassy Area - Abandoned Vehicle Search

1. Call for backup
2. Interview everyone already at scene. If there is a person at the crime scene before the officer arrives, the officer will need to interview the potential witness. If the victims are gone, the officer will need to find out where they went. If paramedics took victims to the hospital, send an officer to the hospital to interview paramedics and victims. Find out exactly what they did at the scene. The victims may provide additional information.
3. With backup, approach abandoned vehicle in a direct manner; check for victim/suspect
4. Set perimeter
5. Create crime scene log
6. Use latex gloves
7. Photographer will photograph entire scene from outside perimeter
8. Lead investigator decides crime scene search pattern
9. Lead investigator determines evidence and marks evidence
10. Photographer photographs all evidence with & without marker (medium range & close up)
11. Backup officer sketches scene
12. Single officer should collect all evidence (chain of custody)

After photographs and sketch, if there is a body inside the vehicle, the body will need to be leaned forward to see if there is any evidence behind the body. The body will be returned to its original position. Evidence needs to be recorded before anything changes and the scene is disturbed.

Search Crime Scene Outside – No Victims/Suspects at Scene

1. Call for backup.
2. Interview everyone already at scene. If there is a person at the crime scene before the officer arrives, the officer will need to interview the potential witness. If the victims are gone, the officer will need to find out where they went. If paramedics took victims to the hospital, send an officer to the hospital to interview paramedics and victims. Find out exactly what they did at the scene. The victims may provide additional information.
3. Set perimeter
4. Create crime scene log
5. Use latex gloves
6. Photographer will photograph entire scene from outside perimeter
7. Lead investigator decides crime scene search pattern
8. Lead investigator determines evidence and marks evidence
9. Photographer photographs all evidence with & without marker (medium range & close up)
10. Backup officer sketches scene
11. Single officer should collect all evidence (chain of custody)

After photographs and sketch, if there is a body at the scene, the body will need to be rolled halfway over to see if there is any evidence under the body. The body will be returned to its original position. Evidence needs to be recorded before anything changes and the scene is disturbed.

Crime Scene Search – Inside Room – No Suspects/Victims at Scene

1. Call for backup.
2. Interview everyone already at scene. If there is a person at the crime scene before the officer arrives, the officer will need to interview the potential witness. If the victims are gone, the officer will need to find out where they went. If paramedics took victims to the hospital, send an officer to the hospital to interview paramedics and victims. Find out exactly what they did at the scene. The victims may provide additional information.
3. Set perimeter
4. Create crime scene log
5. Use latex gloves
6. Lead investigator will walk through area without disturbing evidence, and observe items of evidence (head toward 4 corners of room)
7. Photographer will photograph overview of scene from all 4 corners of room
8. Lead investigator decides on crime scene search pattern
9. Lead investigator determines evidence and will mark evidence
10. Photographer will photograph all evidence with & without marker (medium range & close up)
11. Officer sketches scene
12. Single officer should collect all evidence (chain of custody)

After photographs and sketch, if there is a body at the scene, the body will need to be rolled halfway over to see if there is any evidence under the body. The body will be returned to its original position. Evidence needs to be recorded before anything changes and the scene is disturbed.

Vehicle Search – Traffic Stop

1. Use leather gloves
2. Decide on search pattern (front seat then back seat, driver side then passenger side, etc.)
3. Be consistent in search pattern from car to car
4. Search driver side front seat first, start from top and work downward
5. Search passenger side front seat, start from top and work downward
6. Search driver side back seat, start from top and work downward
7. Search passenger side back seat, start from top and work downward
8. Search trunk

Common places to find contraband: Ashtrays, glove box, center console, under seats, visor, door tray, back pouch of front seat.

Search of Person

1. Use leather gloves
2. Same sex searches (to minimize liability)
3. Double-lock handcuff suspect
4. Start at top and work downward (head to feet)
5. Decide on search pattern (front then back, left side then right side, etc.)
6. Be consistent from person to person
7. Grab and twist areas across torso
8. Safely pull pockets out (do not reach into pockets)
9. Remove belt – inspect belt
10. Sit suspect down and remove shoes
11. Inspect socks and inside of shoes

Common places to find contraband: waistline, pockets, shoes, hair, groin area, bra.

Collecting Blood Evidence

Dry Blood

1) Put on latex gloves
2) Use distilled water to moisten cotton swab
3) Rub or tap cotton swab onto blood covered surface (do not cover entire swab in blood)
4) Let blood on swab air dry
5) Place swab into box or paper bag
6) Mark evidence bag/box
7) Place biohazard sticker on evidence bag/box
8) Place latex gloves in biohazard container

Wet Blood

1) Put on latex gloves
2) Rub or tap cotton swab onto blood covered surface (do not cover entire swab in blood)
3) Let blood on swab air dry
4) Place swab into box or paper bag
5) Mark evidence bag/box
6) Place biohazard sticker on evidence bag/box
7) Place latex gloves in biohazard container

Castings - Overview

Footprint casting

Put latex gloves on
Set metal ring around footprint
Use tweezers to remove grass/debris from inside footprint
Spray hardening material into footprint
Mix casting material so that it is not lumpy
Pour casting material next to print and let it initially run into print
After casting layer is inside print, pour rest of casting inside print
Let set until dry

Forensic casting – chisel mark

Put latex gloves on
Obtain correct amount of casting (e.g., Mikrosil) and hardening material
Properly mix the casting and hardening materials
Use tool (e.g., flat stick) to spread casting material over chisel mark
Let dry
Peel dried casting off of mark

REFERENCES

Dickens, E. (2008). *Fakes & forgeries.* Sywell, United Kingdom: Igloo.

Frith, A. (2007). *Forensic science.* Tulsa, OK: Usborne.

Saferstein, R. (2009). *Forensic science: From the crime scene to the crime lab.* Upper Saddle River, NJ: Pearson Prentice Hall.

Swanson, C.R., Chamelin, N.C., Territo, L., & Taylor, R.W. (2009). *Criminal investigation* (10th ed.). Boston, MA: McGraw Hill.

U.S. Department of the Treasury, Bureau of Engraving and Printing (n.d.). *Security Features.* Retrieved from http://www.moneyfactory.gov/anticounterfeiting/securityfeatures.html

Printed in the United States
By Bookmasters